# The Big Fat Blue Book

## of answers to everyday problems

**2476 simple tricks, trade secrets and little known shortcuts to more money better health and life satisfaction**

# The Big Fat Blue Book

If you have any queries, please contact Customer Services at: Personal and Finance Confidential, 7th Floor, Sea Containers House, 20 Upper Ground, London SE1 9JD. You may also call 020 7633 3636 or send a fax to 020 7633 3740.

Printed in Great Britain by The Cromwell Press, Trowbridge, Wiltshire.

ISBN 1 8999 64 89 4

# Contents

## Property

How to build a fortune through
property and retire wealthy . . . . . . . . . . . . . . . . . . . . . . . . 1

## Your Health

Here's what doctors do to feel better,
live longer and enjoy the best of health . . . . . . . . . . . . . . 21

## Your Wealth & Retirement

Discover the little-known techniques
to slash your tax and build your fortune
while others miss out. . . . . . . . . . . . . . . . . . . . . . . . . . . . 71

## Your Personal Safety

Beat the thieves! 107 tips for keeping
your home, your family and your wallet safe! . . . . . . . . . . 95

## Trade Secrets

How to get FREE holidays, FREE travel...
even FREE money right now! . . . . . . . . . . . . . . . . . . . . . 113

## Sex & Beauty

Look great, feel beautiful, and enjoy the
best sex of your life with these sizzling tips . . . . . . . . . . . 139

## Betting Insider

The bets the bookies fear!
Discover the only ways to make
real money... including the bet that never loses! . . . . . . . 171

## Easy Money

**Simple ways to make anything up to
£5,000 a month in your spare time** . . . . . . . . . . . . . . . . . . 195

## Your Nearest & Dearest

**Guarantee your family's future wealth, health and
happiness with these canny tips** . . . . . . . . . . . . . . . . . . . . 229

## Trade Secrets

**Make your home and garden beautiful
by using vinegar, Bovril and bubblewrap..?
Dozens of amazing secrets revealed inside** . . . . . . . . . . . . 249

## Better Business

**Discover the proven ways to get your
business up, running and making BIG money** . . . . . . . . 279

## Your Career

**Short, sharp tips to get you a raise,
get you promoted and make you indispensable
to your boss** . . . . . . . . . . . . . . . . . . . . . . . . . . . . . . . . . . . 297

# FOREWORD

## Improve your life – simply and quickly – with the selected wisdom of 548 experts and 7 years' research...

People often say today we live in the 'information age'. Email, magazines, television, the internet, radio, newspapers, books...never before have we had so much opinion and data thrown at us each and every day.

But how much of this information actually proves useful? Don't you sometimes wish you could filter out the junk...cut through the hype and spin...and simply enjoy straightforward, proven and accurate advice instead?

## Better sex...more money...pay less tax...confidence and success...

This book is designed to help you achieve just that. It is the result of a unique publishing project launched in Britain seven years ago. Every month since then, Personal & Finance Confidential has uncovered the very latest news from the leading experts in health, investment, careers and business advice. It only shares with its readers the most valuable and effective information.

Now, in these pages, you have the combined wisdom of everyone involved with this unique and exciting project. You will not find the wealth of useful information contained here anywhere else. It has taken 548 accredited professionals and experts seven years to uncover, verify and publish these details. And some of this information has proved very difficult to gather...

- You will save money, time, heartache and hassle by knowing how the experts go about tackling life's hurdles and obstacles.
- You will discover straightforward tips you can use – today – to simplify everyday tasks and free up more time for the things you enjoy.
- This book is packed with information that big business, the investment industry, drug companies, even the government would rather you didn't know!
- The little-known investment, business and careers secrets revealed in

this book could help you start your own profit-making venture…add thousands to your annual income…and boost your personal wealth to provide for a secure and luxurious retirement.

Plus, this book shares with you the best tips and ideas sent in by our readers themselves. They have shared some truly startling findings with our dedicated team of researchers over the years. After testing them thoroughly, we have been only too happy to publish the best – because there's no substitute for hard-won experience…especially when it's someone else's!

# PROPERTY
## How to build a fortune through property and retire wealthy

# 101 tips and techniques to find you the perfect mortgage... cut the cost of buying a house by £10,950 or more... and double the value of your property investments

Since the stock market began tumbling at the start of 2000, the average British house has soared 68% in value. Residential property now accounts for over half the nation's total wealth. And with 4 million extra homes needed to meet new demand by 2025, this boom is set to continue.

But how do you set about joining the thousands of seemingly ordinary people who have quietly turned this opportunity into cash profits? How do you avoid getting ripped off by estate agents and solicitors' fees? What are the sure-fire signs of an upcoming property "hotspot"...and how do you avoid moneypits in need of serious repair and rebuilding?

The 101 simple facts, insights and techniques revealed here come exclusively from proven property investors and developers. These tips have already been tried and tested, saving you time, money and heartache whenever and wherever you buy or sell. You could even build yourself a regular rental income – plus clear capital gains – from your own string of property investments!

## Hot property! 101 tips and techniques to save you £10,950 or more... find you the perfect mortgage... and double the value of your investment

## This proven formula predicts the future of the UK property market

Is the property market going to crash? The key indicators to watch are easily available in the national press, on TV and on the internet.

# 1. Mortgage vs. Income

The amount of money you have to spend on housing is vital. As long as people can afford their mortgages, property prices are usually stable. If people can't afford new mortgages, then houses don't get bought and sold. In 2003, the standard new mortgage payment equated to 15% of earnings. Over the long term, this rate is normally 22% of earnings and has been higher. So 15% is a very safe proportion.

# 2. Prices vs. Income

In mid-2003, the average national salary was around £21,000 a year. The average house price was about £102,000. That's a ratio of 4.85 (just divide the house price by the salary). Work out the ratio for your local area. The lower this ratio, the stronger house prices are. Back in 1989, just before the last crash, it reached 5 nationally. But in London, it was nearer 8. Between 1985 and 2002, this ratio fluctuated between 2.9 and 5. Right now, we are at the higher end of the comfort range.

# 3. Interest Rates

During the last property crash interest rates were 15% and higher. Today, the newspapers tell us interest rates are very low and can only go higher. But what about today's low inflation? Interest rates minus inflation gives you the Real Rate of Interest. Historically, today's rate is about average. Check the Financial Times for predictions and reports on long-term interest rate movements.

# 4. Demand

It is a simple economic fact that, when demand is high and supply is low, prices will be strong. Current demand for certain types of housing is very high, whilst supply remains low, particularly in the south. Contact your local housing office for your regional housing demand and supply figures (see your Yellow Pages).

# 5. Employment

In the last property crash, unemployment was high at over 3 million. Today, the government reckons unemployment to be just around 1 million.

But watch the recruitment industry's figures. Plenty of people are out of work but not claiming the dole. This makes them invisible to the government's figures.

## Further resources:

Council of Mortgage Lenders: www.cml.org.uk
Office of National Statistics: www.statistics.gov
Estate agents' windows and local newspapers
Financial Times: www.ft.com
Your local housing office (see Yellow Pages)

## What your solicitor doesn't want you to know...
## How to buy a house 40 days faster and save £1,030

The cosy world of property conveyancing has kept many solicitors well fed for years. But are they getting the job done? Conveyancing (the legal transfer on property ownership) takes 62 days on average. That's 62 days of possibly losing the house you want to buy.

But online conveyancing specialists, Easymove, can get you to completion in just over three weeks. Using trained consultants working in a network of estate agents and supported by a major legal firm, they have speeded up the process of buying a property. Plus, they will not charge if the deal falls through. Potentially, this could save you £1,030, the average cost of a sale that does not successfully complete. Visit www.go-easymove.co.uk for more details.

## This secret file can stop you getting a mortgage

A secret file exists on every adult in the UK, detailing their past loans. Held by so-called credit reference agencies, any late, failed or defaulted loans will be on your record. But it might also contain serious errors and mistakes. These can stop you getting a mortgage, even though they're nothing to do with you!
It may come as a shock but, even if you've paid every bill on time and are on first-name terms with your bank manager, you may still be classed a bad credit risk. Submit a "statement of correction" to clean your record up. Contact either:
www.equifax.co.uk
Tel: 0845 600 1772 or

www.experian.co.uk
Tel: 0870 241 4297.

## Save £300 on the cost of your next home with this DIY survey

Many housebuyers waste money each year on professional surveyor's fees. How? Because the surveyor simply uncovers glaring problems even a novice could spot. The buyer decides against going ahead with the purchase, but still has to pay the surveyor upwards of £300 for his time.

If you're visiting several different properties with a view to buying, save money on wasted surveyor's fees. Here are the Top Five Warning Signs you should look for.

● A sagging roof
● Long visible cracks in external walls
● Rotten woodwork
● Smell and visible signs of damp, especially in the basement or attic
● Concrete backyard? Check it isn't higher than the damp course in the walls.

Take note! These problems shouldn't necessarily put you off buying if other features of the property outweigh them. Just be aware of how much it could cost you to put things right.

## What your surveyor won't tell you about woodworm, dry rot and this £650 rip-off

Recently published UK statistics suggest every year more than 30,000 homes may be treated for woodworm and dry rot unnecessarily. At an average treatment cost of £650, this amounts to a staggering £19.5 million – scammed from British homeowners – annually.

Plus, the number of homes being sprayed now totals 6,000 per week. Given that there are only about 20 million homes in the country – a lot of which are nearly new – this means many homes have been treated more than once, unnecessarily.

Here's what you should know about beating this scandal and saving yourself money.

**1. Go** with an independent surveyor. You pay a one-off fee, and you will be told whether or not the work really needs to be carried out. A lot of the time damp and timber salesmen are working on commission with sales targets to meet. Watch out.

**2. Challenge** that "rising damp" claim. Rising damp is nowhere near as common as we are led to believe. Houses built since 1877 have damp-proof courses built in.

**3. Check** your drains aren't blocked or your roof isn't leaking instead.

**4. How well** ventilated is the house? Any damp may simply need curing with a simple dehumidifier.

**5. Do you** have high ground levels? This could cause penetrating damp but not rising damp.

**6. Always** bring in an independent expert and use your common sense.

**7. Check** your timbers really do need work. It is not unusual for 'experts' to recommend eradicating insects that actually do no harm.

**8. Ask about** recent treatments. The chemicals used in treatment can defeat woodworm for many years to come. So when buying a house, ask the vendor if they've paid for treatment recently.

**9. Always** get at least three quotations.

**10. You may** notice that the surveyor won't even get his/her hands dirty. If they specify a problem, ask questions and get them to explain their conclusions to you. Make sure they record their findings.

**11. Always** look at your property before and with your surveyor. If in doubt have the timbers or damp checked independently.

## This little-known regulation could cost you £10,000 when you sell your home

It wasn't reported in the press. It was hardly announced by the government. But as of April 1, 2002, all replacement windows must be fitted with a special energy-efficient glass, called Pilkington K. This new regulation puts the onus on the homeowner to do things right. If you don't, it could cost you dear when you come to sell your home.

Any replacement windows fitted after April 1, 2002 must comply with the regulations. Otherwise, you will be liable for the cost of replacing the glass with Pilkington K when you come to sell your home. With double-glazing for the average home now costing around £10,000, it's scandalous that some suppliers fail to inform their customers of the new law.

What's more, you can wait between 6 and 10 weeks to have double-glazing fitted. Can you wait that long when selling your home?

When the time comes to sell your property, your purchaser's solicitors will ask for evidence that any replacement glazing installed after April 2002 complies with the new Building Regulations. You will be able to prove compliance in two ways:

- **a certificate** showing that the work has been done by an installer who is registered under the FENSA Scheme (visit www.fensa.org.uk for details).
- **a certificate** from the local authority saying that the installation has approval under the Building Regulations.

If you are considering replacement glazing, make sure the companies giving you quotes are fully compliant with FENSA and that you will be getting the new kind of glass.

## How to cut 17.5% off the cost of building your own home

Anyone building a new house within the UK, with planning permission in their own name, is entitled to a VAT refund on the building materials. The tax office advises all 'do-it-yourself' homebuilders to contact them in the early stages of the development. Customs & Excise have a guide for house builders "VAT refunds for do-it-yourself builders and converters" (Notice 719). It offers advice on how and when a claim for a VAT refund should be made. To find out more, go to www.hmce.gov.uk.

## Top estate agent's secret for quick sales at top prices

The key to selling your house fast, for the best price, is to remove all trace of your life before potential buyers come to view it. They need to visualise their own furniture and belongings in the house.
- Ban your kids and pets from the living room until you've sold.
- Avoid having the TV as the focal spot in your living room.

- Highlight a fireplace or French windows instead.
- Repaint walls in neutral colours if necessary. Consider changing the carpet or flooring to make it feel clean and modern.
- Hide fans, humidifiers or free-standing heaters. They send out a negative message to buyers and suggest there are problems with the house.

## Invest in ugly homes and make a killing in the property market

Old-fashioned or unusual decoration… properties that have been stuck on the market for some time… vacant possession, where no one is renting or living in a property at the moment… all these factors can be used to get a discount on the purchase price, and boost your profits when you come to sell.

But be careful. You want cosmetic distress only. Think ugly, not derelict!

## How to spot an up-and-coming area

Potential for capital growth can be recognised through property evidence of:
- Government intervention.
- Regional development schemes.
- Close to high-price area.
- New developments in road and rail access.
- Leisure or educational developments.
- Grant-housing or employment subsidies.

## Warning! The two worst ways to add value to your house

If you're looking to add value to your property for re-selling, do not bother with swimming pools or double-glazing. They add nothing to the value, because most people don't find them attractive.

The four most effective ways of adding value to a property are:
1. Building a garage.
2. Updating the kitchen and/or bathroom.
3. Loft conversions.
4. Additional rooms (like conservatories or utility rooms).

# Eight tips to buy property at auction for knock-down prices

Buying at auction may enable you to pick up a property that's significantly undervalued. Here's all you need to know:

**1. Get to know** your local auction, how it works and who the 'movers and shakers' are.

**2. Get the catalogue** in advance and start planning!

**3. Visit and view** each property you are interested in.

**4. Decide how much** you can afford. Be prepared to stop bidding at that price.

**5. Get the legal pack** from the auctioneer.

**6. Get your finance** ready. Don't forget that insurance is your responsibility immediately your bid is accepted.

**7. Get a survey.**

**8. Understand how** to register, bid and buy.

During and after the event, make sure you record and analyse everything. This will give you lots of information about the area, the auction and the auctioneer – which you can use next time!

# This property insider's secret cuts 50% off price

Property reversions enable you to buy property, usually from an older person or couple who want to realise some cash from their home, at anything up to 50% off the market value.

Agreements vary but generally the arrangement is that you buy the property for a substantial discount. Plus, the existing owner is allowed to live in it either at a minimal rent or entirely rent-free. The property becomes yours when they move on.

Reputable organisations that arrange reversions also ensure dependants are fully in agreement, and all parties are completely informed and in agreement. To find out further details visit www.ageconcern.co.uk/ageconcern/media/factsheet_12.pdf.

## The No.1 question to ask for big property discounts

Whenever you're viewing a property, ask yourself this crucial question: "What is the owner's motivation for selling?"

Divorce, redundancy, and other changes in personal circumstances sometimes dictate a property must be sold quickly or below value. If you can figure out why the buyer is selling, you can better judge how much of a discount to aim for below the asking price.

Also consider properties that are being sold privately by the owner, as often discounts are available. Look for these at: www.propertybroker.com.

## The four big fat lies about 'buy-to-let' investment today

Right now, analysts are predicting a collapse in the buy-to-let market. They cite rising house prices, a shortage of tenants and high initial costs. But professional property investors and full-time landlords are still buying flats and houses to let out.

What do they know that the rest of us don't?

**Myth 1:** "The housing market is about to crash"

**What the experts say:** Nearly 14% of British adults now live alone, double the number 20 years ago. Since 1980, England's population has grown by 2.3 million. Average life expectancy has almost doubled since 1900. The government predicts we need 4 million new homes by 2025. And yet the newspapers think we're headed for a crash!

**Myth 2:** "There aren't enough tenants"

**What the experts say:** There will always be young professionals moving around in their first or second job. They earn above average salaries, but would rather rent than buy straight away. Plus, lots of educated Europeans are posted to the UK by their company every year. They are going to live here long term, and just need somewhere to live for a couple of years.

**Myth 3:** "It's too expensive to get into the buy-to-let market now"

**What the experts say:** Interest rates are at an historic 50-year low. You can still get some very good deals from banks and building societies. They will lend up to 85% of the value of the property you're buying, which means you only need to put down a small amount of your money in order to be exposed to any price rises in the market. And a fixed rate mortgage will give you the security of knowing exactly what costs you need to cover on the mortgage.

**Myth 4:** "Yields on rental properties are falling"

**What the experts say:** A lot of people don't do their sums properly and don't allow for periods when the property will be unoccupied. Anyone in difficulty will soon start to sell up and abandon the idea of being a landlord – reducing supply in the market and improving the position of those who remain.

## Landlords! Save money but earn the same monthly rent "part-furnished"

Contrary to what you might think, there is no difference in the rental income between furnished or unfurnished properties. Part furnished is a great option – you supply curtains, carpets, a fridge, cooker and washing machine. This costs you less, because you don't have to worry about the regulations for let furnishings, and your tenant is more likely to take better care of the property as a whole if they have their own things around them. Also tenants think that their rent is cheaper if it's unfurnished – so periods of vacancy will be shorter too.

## Buy-to-let landlords! Are you making these 7 classic mistakes?

### 1. Don't buy a house or flat that you would like to live in
You're not the person who will be renting it! Consult estate agents in the area on what makes a good rental property instead.

### 2. Don't spend more than £250,000 on a property
Young professionals won't be able to afford the rent that you will need to charge to cover the mortgage, no matter where you buy.

### 3. Think rationally about the deal

Buying in a purpose-built block of flats being promoted by a property development company is probably not a good idea. It's likely that all of the units will come onto the rental market at the same time, which will drive down the rent you can hope to achieve.

### 4. Don't expect capital gains to bale you out

Hoping you will make money from a rise in the value of your buy-to-let investment goes against the very reason you want to get in – income in the form of monthly rental payments. You need to be sure that the rental income will more than cover your mortgage payments. Any capital appreciation in the value of the property should simply be an added bonus.

### 5. Decide what sort of tenant you want

Foreign professionals and public sector workers make good, reliable tenants. This will affect the type of property you buy, so you'll need to do your homework on commuter links, desirability and facilities.

### 6. Allow for hidden costs

Make sure you've allotted at least two to three months when the property is empty into your calculations, and that you allow for repairs and maintenance to the property in your budget. Do your sums properly and review them at regular intervals.

### 7. Don't forget to make use of tax allowances

These include being able to offset expenses and some mortgage interest against tax.

## How to become a buy-to-let landlord for next-to-nothing

By forming an investment club to deal in property, you won't need to have much money upfront to get into the lucrative rental market. Buying properties through investment clubs is popular in the US, and now it is catching on here. Simply make sure the solicitor responsible for progressing the sale understands you want to form a legal partnership, and contact ProShare for more advice.

## How to secure the best-value buy-to-let mortgage

Only 11% of homes in the UK are rented, which is low compared to the rest of Europe. So demand is high and likely to grow as numbers of single parent families and older single people continue to increase.

And today, nearly 100 mortgage providers have buy-to-let schemes. Some lenders are happy to loan you 100% based on the potential rental income alone, so they have no interest in your own income from your job. Visit www.arla.co.uk/btl/lenders.htm for details of the best deals.

## Proven secret for doubling your income from property investments

Invest in smaller properties, and the return on your money will be much greater. The average annual rental from a one-bedroom flat as a percentage of the property value is 12.5%. But with a four-bedroom house it is only 6.3%.

So if you spend £100,000 on two one-bedroom flats, your annual income on average will be £12,500, whereas the same £100,000 spent on just one bigger house will generate only £6,300 in a year from rent. Even in the South East it is still possible to get one-bedroom units for about £60,000. A 100% mortgage at 6% on such a property would mean monthly mortgage payments of approximately £360. The rents generated by one-bedroom properties in the South East are around £550 per month.

Collect your local property pages and speak to agents about letting and buying. And if the figures don't work where you are, go further afield.

## What to do if your mortgage lender demands you use a letting agent

Some lenders will insist you use an agent to manage your property. They may also stipulate that the agent be registered with the Association of Residential Letting Agents. You can find one easily by looking at www.arla.co.uk or calling 01494 431680. Agency fees range from about 10% to 15% of the rental income but then the agent will assume responsibility for:

- introducing and vetting prospective tenants
- preparing the tenancy agreements
- advising on inventories, changes to utility accounts and Council Tax
- collecting rent and paying the balances to your account.

## Landlords! How to find the perfect tenants

Get references from your tenants from four sources for maximum security:
- their previous landlord
- their employer
- their bank
- a credit reference from www.equifax.co.uk or www.experian.co.uk.

Then take a deposit of one and a half times the monthly rental. For example, on £400 monthly rent this would be a £600 deposit. This will help cover late rent or other upfront expenses you need to be aware of, such as annual gas checks (cost £50), smoke alarms on buildings built after 1993 and repairs to heating and the structure of the building.

## Enjoy great returns from property without buying any!

Even if you don't have the capital to buy another place, or the leverage to get a reasonable loan, you can still get a piece of the property pie. There are specific property unit trusts available and you can obtain details of these from www.aput.co.uk/funds.list/index.html.

A unit trust investment will allow you to invest a relatively small amount in a pool of properties, and many people will feel safer with this route. The returns can be good. Last year the FTSE real estate index rose by 28.8%, and, for example, the TR Henderson property trust showed a 35.9% return over the past 12 months – pretty impressive when compared to interest rates or the FTSE 100.

## The 7 hidden pitfalls to avoid when buying a home in France

Follow a few rules and you can find and buy a French property to fulfil all your needs. Just beware these 7 hidden pitfalls.

**1. NEVER** buy just from looking at a photograph. There are those who have!

**2. DON'T** let anyone talk you into buying a property that does not fit the majority of the various factors you need according to your likes and dislikes. For example, permanent and holiday homes have different needs.
- Are you retired or looking for work?

- How will your children be educated?
- Will you need medical support nearby?
- How is the property orientated?
- What is the direction of the prevailing wind?

**3. MAKE SURE** anyone offering to sell you a property is properly registered in France. Otherwise your purchase will not be legal. Always ask to see their 'Carte Professionelle' to identify them as a registered estate agent.

**4. WATCH OUT** for rights of way, ownership of access and previous grazing rights when buying property from farmers. Surveyors do not exist in France, but some French-based British surveyors can be found through the same sources as agents. They can help uncover this kind of future headache. To undertake a detailed search, go to the local town hall (mairie) and ask to examine the land registry plans (cadastre) checking when it was last updated.

**5. MAKE FRIENDS** with the local townhall. Most of them welcome people who will contribute to the locality and the commune's taxes. But some have been known to cause problems later on.

**6. DON'T** be tempted to agree to pay part of the purchase price in cash "dessous la table" – literally, under the table. Trying to reduce sales tax in this way will rebound on you.

**7. BEWARE** the French love affair with paperwork. Small business owners, for instance, have reported having to leave their French retreats due to hassle from huge amounts of ever-changing paper work, and the high levels and varieties of tax.

## Urgent! This kind of property will soar in value over the next 3-5 years

To enjoy maximum capital gains from your next property purchase, look to add value by renovating and refurbishing a house in an up-and-coming area. Over 3 to 5 years, newly popular areas have been proven to double your money and more.

Alternatively, keep an eye on trends in the market, by studying prices and For Sale signs in your local area. For example, houses have risen in price more rapidly than two-bedroom flats over the last couple of years in Greater London.

## Estate agents' secrets

## These three tricks guarantee top-price when you sell your home

### 1. Don't let estate agents' fees stop you selling

Using an estate agent who's willing to negotiate on fees can prove a false economy. They tend to be the cheaper, lower-spend estate agents, probably with a shop window well away from the busy High Street where you need to have your home advertised.

### 2. Invite 4 estate agents to tea… and watch them fight!

To get a discounted deal with a good estate agent, invite the top four in your local area round to view your home… and then ask them who will give you a discount on their fee. Caution! This will only work if a) you have a really nice place, and b) you aren't being too greedy with the asking price. A saving of 0.25% from a top agent should be regarded as good haggling.

### 3. Get your kitchen & bathroom to sell your house

- Redecorating these two rooms will more than pay for itself.
- Paint all walls white or a similar light shade.
- Clean windows and pull curtains right back to maximise natural light.
- Remove all clutter.
- Also remember to repaint your front door and tidy your garden. First impressions count.

## Why cleaning your teeth could stop you selling your house

If you're trying to sell your house, potential buyers will not linger long in a bathroom full of your personal effects. And this will make it harder for them to decide to buy. Tidy away all your personal items before each viewing. For a finishing touch, invest in a new shower curtain and some co-ordinated towels.

## The perfect property for retirement fund investors

Many smart investors today view the stock market as far too risky for all their retirement fund. Instead, they're using property to build a larger, more secure nest egg for the future.

If you want to join them, with the minimum of hassle, then you want long-term capital growth in your investment's value. And the best combination of building features for achieving this is:

- a modern interior with all mod cons.
- in a pretty period building
- but never remove any period features.

Modern-style buildings are more likely to go in and out of fashion, especially purpose-built flats. Georgian and early Victorian properties are set to continue as Britain's favourite style of home long into the future.

## Buy a stake in bricks'n'mortar for just pennies on the pound

There are nearly a hundred different property companies listed on the London Stock Exchange. You can buy shares for a few pounds (plus the buying costs). Look in the FT financial pages for the companies listed under Real Estate.

## Why you should always assume an estate agent is lying to you

Not all estate agents are deliberately misleading. But keep an eye out. If you ask how long a property has been on the market, don't believe the timescale. Chances are, the property has been on the market much longer than they say.

## Why cheeky homebuyers get what they want

If you're looking to buy a new home, don't be afraid to make a low offer. The estate agent is working for the vendor. So he will be trying to get the highest possible bid out of you, despite knowing a lower bid would be acceptable.

So ignore the agent, and come up with an offer that reflects the state of the market.

- Compare the property with other similar houses.
- Assess the likely competition from other potential buyers.
- Never be afraid to make a low offer.

But be aware – if the market is really hot don't make a stupidly low offer. The agent could think you were a time-waster and write you out of the equation.

## Put in an offer on a house? How to make sure you're not gazumped

If you live in a sellers' market right now, and you have just made an offer on a new home, use these tips to ensure you don't get gazumped by greedy investors and unfair estate agents.

- Get a written agreement from the vendor stipulating 28 days to exchange of contracts.
- Keep checking the property remains off the market, by visiting the appropriate websites.
- Get your mortgage broker and solicitor moving at break-neck speed.
- Keep the estate agent up to date at all times.

In a buyers' market, you hold the aces of course. If you're not convinced the agent is being straight tell him you'll pull out if you find it's still being marketed. Plus, you will be making random checks.

## Five insider secrets for viewing hot property before anyone else

Estate agents always favour those buyers able to buy quickly. They hate window shoppers. So to have your estate agent on the phone, inviting you to view their best new properties first, you need:
- to be in the middle of selling your home, or
- at least have it under offer
- to have your new mortgage arranged in principle, or
- offer to meet the estate agent's recommended mortgage broker.
- Most importantly, be proactive. Phone the agent regularly, and try to become friends with them.

# YOUR HEALTH

## Here's what doctors do to feel better, live longer and enjoy the best of health

# 213 little-known secrets to help you live longer…in better health

Ever-growing patient lists, red tape, shrinking budgets, violent patients, staffing problems…Is it any wonder British doctors now spare only 6 minutes on average for each patient they see?

But you don't have to put up with being brushed off or ignored next time you visit your GP. There are simple, proven techniques – approved by forward-thinking health practitioners – you can use to make sure your doctor listens to what you say. Plus, there are hundreds of little-known ways you can boost your health yourself today, and protect yourself against common illnesses and disease long into the future.

Forget about crazy diets or exercise programmes. Good health can be as simple as knowing which delicious foods will help you fend off colds and flu, fight against heart disease, ease the pain of arthritis, and cut your risk of cancer.

## Is your body warning you of ill health? The 4 telltale signs you must look out for

**Twitching eyelids:** This sign, or twitching of a small muscle anywhere in the body, is a hallmark of magnesium deficiency and occurs due to magnesium's role in muscle relaxation. Magnesium deficiency is one of the more common mineral deficiencies, possibly because it's so readily depleted by stress, alcohol and coffee. Other obvious signs of low magnesium include leg cramps, insomnia and depression. Low levels also increase our susceptibility to conditions like cardiovascular disease, high blood pressure and kidney stones.

**FACT:** Wheat loses 90% of its magnesium during the milling process, so it can be difficult for a typical diet to provide adequate amounts. Good sources of magnesium are whole wheat, tofu, kelp, nuts and brown rice.

**Cracks in the corners of your mouth:** Officially called angular cheilosis, this sign, together with mouth ulcers, and most infections of the mouth or tongue, is telltale of a vitamin B deficiency. This is due to their role in cell turnover – the mouth is susceptible as it's an area regularly scalded and abraded. In fact, the mouth can be the first indicator of low B in the body. Other body signs may be dermatitis, fatigue (Bs have a critical role in energy production) and poor stress response.

**FACT:** The B group is primarily found in whole grains, vegetables, legumes, nuts, seeds and organ meats. White bread, white pasta and white rice are deficient in these vitamins. Stress, alcohol and coffee account for massive depletion of all B vitamins due to their water-soluble nature.

**Bleeding gums:** Vitamin C has a vital role in manufacturing connective tissue, so it's crucial for wound healing, healthy gums and blood vessels. It's also crucial for immunity. The classic vitamin C deficiency disease, scurvy, can occur when levels are low enough, but even marginal deficiency can present itself with bleeding gums, mostly seen when brushing teeth, or biting into hard fruit. Vitamin C deficiency signs often occur in clusters, so you may experience easy bruising at the same time, which similarly occurs due to increased fragility of blood vessels.

**FACT:** The key is to eat freshly prepared fruit and vegetables. The richest sources are peppers, guava, broccoli, Brussels sprouts, berries and citrus fruits. Tobacco and stress rapidly deplete the nutrient.

**Goose bump skin:** Skin that feels or looks like 'goose bumps', especially on the upper arm, indicates vitamin A deficiency. This condition, known as follicular hyperkeratosis, is basically a blockage of the hair follicles. Beyond skin, vitamin A has important roles in maintaining eye health and vision, respiratory health and immunity.

**FACT:** It's important to consume good levels of dark green, yellow and orange vegetables. It's also critical to maintain your zinc and vitamin C status, as these nutrients play a crucial role in converting the form of vitamin A you get from vegetables and fruit into the functional form for your body.

## A healthy tongue looks rosy red. What colour is yours?

A pale tongue can warn you are suffering anaemia, and need more iron in your diet. Liver from organically raised animals is the best source. But remember to avoid liver during pregnancy. Its high levels of vitamin A can harm unborn babies.

## What to do if cracked lips never heal

If you have persistent cracks at the corners of your mouth, and no amount of moisturiser gets rid of them, look to your diet. It is highly likely you are lacking riboflavin, vitamin B2 and other B vitamins. Take a B-complex supplement to eradicate the problem, available from your pharmacy.

## Do you have white spots on your fingernails?

White spots on your fingernails almost always point to a zinc deficiency in your body. The problem is, zinc is not found in large quantities in many foods. Oysters, pumpkin seeds and pulses can prove expensive. So supplement with zinc capsules from your local pharmacy instead. Another sign of zinc deficiency is a desire for more sugar and salt than usual.

## What are your fingernails trying to tell you?

- Thick, tough and possibly yellow nails can indicate cardiovascular or lymphatic problems.
- Brittle nails can mean lack of calcium.
- A concave nail, curving inwards, can indicate nutritional deficiencies.
- A convex nail, curving outwards, can show respiratory disorders.
- Are there any lines on your nails? Horizontal they indicate stress, or crash dieting. Rheumatoid arthritis can be linked to vertical and pronounced lines.

## Do you bruise easily? Nature is warning you of serious trouble ahead

Easy bruising does not mean you are a weakling. It points to a nutritional deficiency that can lead to uncontrolled internal bleeding – a very dangerous condition. Supplement your diet with 5-10mg of vitamin K each day and boost your intake of natural flavonoids by adding red, blue and purple fruits to your diet.

## Computer users! Beware the strain of working 8-hour days

Eye strain, soreness, visual fatigue and headaches can all result from a computer screen set at an uncomfortable height or angle. You can avoid these 21st century work-related hazards simply by adjusting the position of your screen.

● When sitting comfortably and looking at the screen, your eyes should 'land' at the top of it. If they don't, you're likely to experience eye-related difficulties later on.
● You may find it easier to re-position your chair, rather than the computer.

Arrange the screen at 90 degrees to your desk, to minimise reflections from ceiling lights and/or high windows.

Take regular breaks. Fatigue and stress aren't helped by the bright light given off by computer screens. Spend at least 5 minutes every hour doing non-computer work. This will rest your eyes.

## How stretching your ankles could ease chronic back pain

Shortened Achilles tendons can cause chronic back pain. They prevent you from walking well, putting stress on your spine. Here's how to relax and strengthen your tendons, reducing the risk to your back.

● Stand 60-90cm away from a wall, facing it.
● Lean towards the wall, putting palms flat against it with both feet on the ground.
● Move one foot half the distance to the wall.
● Keep your other leg straight at the knee, with your heel flat on the floor.
● Now, bend the forward knee and both arms slowly and rhythmically. The back heel must be kept on the floor and the tail tucked in at all times.
● Continue for 20 seconds. Relax. Change legs and repeat ten times.

## How to avoid backache by sitting properly at your desk

Keep your feet firmly on the floor when working. Dangling legs affect your circulation, create bad posture and lead to backache.

# How to avoid computer-related hand and wrist injuries

Do this simple exercise every morning before work. Hold your arms out straight in front of you. Lift up your hands at 90 degrees, and spread your fingers. Hold for five seconds, lower, and relax. Then clench your fists, and lower your wrists at 90 degrees. Hold for five seconds, straighten, and relax. Repeat ten times, and repeat at lunchtime, just before starting work for the afternoon.

# How leaning on a wall beats back strain and injury

This great daily exercise only takes a few minutes. It helps re-align the muscles in your back, to help undo the strains of everyday life.

- Stand with your back against a wall, with your feet 14-20cm (5-8 inches) away from the skirting board.
- Now try to flatten the small of your back against the wall, by pulling in your stomach muscles. Do not bend your knees.
- Hold this position for five seconds, then relax and repeat five times.
- Keep breathing regularly and evenly throughout.

# Is your office lighting making you ill?

White fluorescent lighting tubes, used in most offices, schools and hospitals in the UK, were first implicated in health scares back in the 1970s. The electromagnetic fields around fluorescent tubes can be 4 to 6 times above the accepted exposure levels for an office when sitting down, and up to 32 times when you stand up.

Fluorescent lighting was not meant to come into such general use. It was a temporary, emergency feature that was only ever intended to keep factories working 24 hours a day during the second world war. This form of lighting is banned in German hospitals and clinics. As far back as 1982, it was the subject of a study at Sydney University, Australia into skin cancers. And school children are at risk from it too. One study observed fluorescent lights causing nervous fatigue, irritability, lapses of attention and hyperactive behaviour. Another study, carried out by eight dentists, even found a very significant increase in the number of cavities and tooth decay in those children working under standard fluorescent lighting.

But complaints of headaches, eye problems, electrical sensitivity and other health complaints in the workplace have all been eliminated when these flourescent tubes are replaced with full spectrum lighting. This mimics the effect of natural sunlight. A well-known London investment bank now using FSL reports low staff illness and turnover, plus higher productivity.

While FSL is more expensive than fluorescent lighting, it actually lasts twice as long. So if you wish to approach your boss with a proposal to switch to FSL in the office, make sure you balance the health benefits against the cost. Less absenteeism and increased productivity will make FSL more cost-effective in the long run. Contact your local lighting stockist for further details.

## Could you be suffering from the UK's No. 1 disability and not know it?

Arthritis is the single biggest cause of disability in the UK, affecting over eight million people. There are over 200 different kinds of arthritis, but the majority of sufferers are affected by either osteoarthritis or rheumatoid arthritis.

- Osteoarthritis is the most common form of arthritis and can affect any joint in your body.
- Rheumatoid arthritis is often more severe. It's a chronic autoimmune disease meaning antibodies are formed to attack your body's own cells. The synovial membrane, which protects and lubricates joints, becomes inflamed and causes pain and swelling.

You should see a doctor if you suffer from joint pain, discomfort, stiffness or fatigue – all common symptoms of arthritis. The condition can manifest itself in other degrees of physical impairment, such as loss of strength or grip. There are different types of arthritic pain – sharp and stabbing, persistent or a dull ache.

## Reduce the pain of arthritis in just 12 weeks by eating a delicious Mediterranean diet

Research undertaken by Dr Athena Linos of the University of Athens Medical School compared a group of 145 rheumatoid arthritis sufferers with 188 people without the disease. Results showed that those with a high intake of cooked vegetables and olive oil were 75% less likely to develop rheumatoid arthritis than those who included very little in their diets.

Previous research has suggested that people with the highest life long consumption of olive oil had a 2.5 times lower risk of developing rheumatoid arthritis than those with the lowest intakes.

## Avoid these foods to cut your risk of developing arthritis

Once arthritic joint damage has occurred, it cannot be reversed. It's vital you take preventative steps to help protect your joints and ward off arthritis:

- Avoid animal fats and refined foods to help your joints stay healthy.
- Avoid saturated fats, chemical additives, yeast, caffeine, citrus, salt, dairy products, soft drinks, white flour, aubergine, red peppers, tomatoes and potatoes. These foods can play a part in increasing inflammation.

## How the sting of a bee can improve arthritic mobility by 66%

Recently scientists have discovered the health-giving properties of bee venom in the management of arthritis. This has led to the formulation of two products under the brand name Nectar Ease.

Melittin, a polypeptide, makes up 50% of the dry weight of bee venom and is one of the most potent anti-inflammatory agents known. A clinical trial conducted at the University of Auckland School of Medicine, involving 20 patients with arthritis, found that 66% of the group experienced a reduction in pain levels and greater mobility when treated with Nectar Ease.

A second trial (of 97 sufferers) monitored by rheumatologist Dr Alan Doube, proved just as successful in easing the level of pain and mobility in those with osteoarthritis and rheumatism. Take one capsule a day, increasing to three-four a day as required (check with your doctor as bee venom does contain allergy-inducing compounds) in divided doses. You can buy this from any health food store.

## How ginger can help ease the pain of arthritis

Researchers at the University of Miami School of Medicine have found that ginger extract can ease pain and relieve stiffness in arthritis sufferers. A study was carried out involving 250 patients with painful arthritis of the knee. For six weeks some of the patients were given dummy pills, while others were given ginger extract tablets.

At the end of the study the levels of stiffness, restricted movement and pain were improved in two-thirds of those taking the ginger. This is a cheap yet effective aid that can help sufferers.

## Why decaf coffee is actually bad for you

New research from the US reveals that women drinking more than four cups of decaf coffee a day have twice the normal risk of rheumatoid arthritis. The Iowa's Women's Health Study also reports that women drinking regular coffee show no increased risk – and those drinking three cups of tea or more actually reduce their risk by sixty per cent.

## Ease the pain of arthritis with salt and mud

Some spa treatments are excellent at treating conditions such as arthritis and rheumatism. And in France, spa treatments are so much an everyday part of medicine that every citizen is eligible for a week's treatment at a spa each year if medically necessary.

The French coast is dotted with health resorts that offer thalassotherapy. Thalassotherapy means treatment using seawater and seaweed in baths or pools. It soothes your body using water jets or body wraps. Try the Previthal centre near Mont St. Michel, where you can enjoy a thalassotherapy weekend for around £100, including unlimited access to the baths and rest spaces and four treatments a day. Visit www.previthal.com for details.

## Ease arthritis pain with Britain's favourite food

Curry powder contains turmeric, a yellow spice that works like aspirin to reduce inflammation in your body. And thanks to a substance found in turmeric, curcumin, it is now recognized as a powerful remedy for treating all forms of arthritis – including osteoarthritis, rheumatoid arthritis, painful joints and even gout. You will enjoy all these benefits simply by eating a good Indian curry – Britain's favourite take-away meal.

# Is this vitamin rip-off damaging your health?

Don't get conned into paying more for your health supplements than you need to. Many "mega-dose" pills contain far more than you need. Some high doses could even prove dangerous

Don't take more than 200mg of vitamin C, for instance. The body's cells can't absorb more than about 100mg per day, and the concentration of vitamin C in the blood begins to level off at 200mg per day. The US Recommended Dietary Allowance (RDA) of vitamin C is 90mg a day for men and 75mg for women. Smokers should get an additional 35mg a day.

These amounts are significantly lower than the dose in many multivitamins. Taking more than 200mg per day is a waste of money.

# The truth about health-food supplements

British consumers are paying through the nose for second-rate health supplements. For instance, omega oil – crucial to the health of your heart and brain – can vary wildly in quality.

But if you were to try and get your omega 3 intake just from your diet, you would find it difficult to eat as much fresh fish as required. Supplementation really is necessary.

Don't be tempted to take fish liver oils to get your essential fatty acids either. You would give yourself liver damage if you took enough tablets! Instead opt for high quality products such as Omega-Brite, Pro Omega, or Trader Darwin's Hi-Potency Omega-3 EPA for the best concentrations of omega 3.

# Are you addicted to over-the-counter medicines?

Watch out for the warning signs of over-the-counter addiction. Solpadeine, Syndol, Feminax, Co-Codamol, Nurofen Plus, Do-Do tablets, Sudafed decongestant, Nytol, Codeine Linctus, Galcodine Linctus and Collis Brown mixture are the most dangerous.

If you find yourself taking more than the daily dose for more than one week, stop immediately. Go to your doctor to have your illness treated properly. And you are in very serious danger if you find yourself taking painkillers to avoid possible symptoms.

Buying a second bottle and continuing to take the tablets even after you are better is a sure sign of addiction. Seek medical help straight away.

## Why won't your doctor listen to what you tell him?

A recent study revealed most doctors listen to their patients for an average of just 18 seconds before interrupting. If they don't interrupt, doctors worry patients will drone on and on. But this is your health at stake!

Uninterrupted patients talk for an average of only two and a half minutes – the time needed to cover important information and get your message across. Beware. Doctors interrupt with lots of direct questions requiring either 'yes' or 'no' answers. This makes for short, effective information gathering.

But this brusque approach can make you feel as if you're being interrogated or, even worse, words are being put in your mouth. So ask your doctor to take a little time listening to you when you sit down to describe what's wrong. Be polite, but firm.

## How to work with your doctor to treat your illness fast

Many patients fail to receive the treatment they need from their GPs because of a lack of communication and understanding. Follow these steps to help your doctor understand your symptoms better, so he can tackle your illness faster and more effectively.

### 1. Keep a record of your symptoms

If your doctor requests information and you cannot come up with it, you feel inadequate and defensive – and you worry that it might affect the quality of the treatment you receive. So before your appointment, make written notes of any relevant facts, and take them in with you.

### 2. Adopt a positive approach

The first few minutes spent with your doctor are tremendously important. They set the pace for the consultation. Be positive that this time, something good will come from your appointment.

### 3. Get your story across

Refer to your written notes of the important points you want to get across. This eliminates the common cry of "Oh no, I forgot to mention…" after you've left the surgery.

### 4. Use your own words

If you don't stop him, your GP can easily slip into 'doctor speak'. "Where was that stomach ache – near your umbilicus?". No one outside the profession knows what this means. It makes you feel stupid and unimportant. Don't stand for it. Politely say "It would make me feel better to tell you what it's really like in my own words."

### 5. Ask questions – lots of questions

- What are you most embarrassed to ask?
- What didn't you understand from your last consultation?
- Do you know what to do if you forget to take your medicine?

## Worrying new health problem? End uncertainty and get an accurate diagnosis fast

To help your doctor get a quick understanding of any new health problems you may suffer, keep a diary of your symptoms for one month

- Every day, write down your symptoms and what you were doing before they started.
- Keep a note of food, drinks, and your emotional state.
- Then describe the physical symptoms you had.
- Once you've finished your month's record, look for patterns in your notes. This will help your doctor identify any possible causes or triggers.

## What your doctor doesn't know about high blood pressure and bananas…

Bananas are rich in potassium. Potassium helps your body lose sodium, the harmful substance in salt that increases blood pressure. Little-known US studies show that eating two bananas a day can reduce your blood pressure by 10% in just one week.

## Scandal! Overworked doctors brainwashed into prescribing the wrong drugs

Recent research has found that 83% of Britain's doctors rely on pharmaceutical companies and their sales teams for information about new medications. Only 17% look elsewhere. And those greedy drug companies have almost a complete monopoly on medical research. Plus, they offer GPs gifts and perks as an extra incentive for them to prescribe their drugs.

## Why won't your doctor reveal how your drugs could harm you?

Up to 80% of the information your doctor needs to make a diagnosis comes from you. It's important that no matter how scared you are, how intimidating your doctor is or how embarrassing the problem is – the key is to be specific.

**1. Bring your medicines and supplements to your doctor.** At least once a year inform your doctor about everything you're taking – including prescriptions, supplements, over-the-counter medicines, herbs etc.

**2. Ask about your medicine.** What is it for exactly? Why have you prescribed this particular drug? What are the side effects? Is this safe to take with other medication? How long do I take it for and at what quantity? Do I take it with food? Can I drink alcohol with this?

**3. If you're offered a drug that you haven't heard of, ask how long it's been used to treat your condition.** Has it been marketed under any other name, or for any other condition? Ask what the success rate is. All doctors have a Data Sheet Compendium listing the drug's profile and they can refer to this. If you want further information, ask to look in the doctors' bible, the MMS. This book will list any interactions and side effects.

## Do you understand your prescription?

When you pick up your prescription, check it. You could easily be given the wrong dose or strength. Ask your pharmacist to clarify everything before you leave the chemist.

# The truth about Britain's greedy drug companies

Natural substances cannot be patented. This is why natural and herbal supplements are not tested under laboratory conditions, like chemical drugs. The big  pharmaceutical companies don't want to waste money proving or disproving the effectiveness of treatments they can't make money from.

So natural remedies remain controversial, because no one will accept the evidence for their power. But up to 5,000 GPs in the UK now have access to the EMIS drug database, which has recently added more than 3,000 homeopathic preparations to its file. The Society of Homeopaths will be able to provide you with a list of practitioners with access to this information. Tel: 01604 621 400 or visit www.homeopathy-soh.org.

# Are you being prescribed old drugs with new names?

Your prescribed medicine could be just an old drug disguised in a different package. Drug companies spend many years and many millions of pounds creating new drugs. But as soon as a new drug is released onto the market, other drug companies get ready to rip it off as soon as the patent expires.

The first company wants to protect its investment, of course. So they often re-release the drug under a new name, simply to extend the patent period.

Between 1989 and 2000, two-thirds of all prescription drugs approved by the FDA in America were nothing more than modified versions of existing drugs. Only 15 per cent of the drugs approved during that period could be considered genuinely "new". For instance…
- Clarityn was recently reformulated in the US to become Clarinex.
- Prilosec (marketed as 'Losec' in the UK) has become Nexium in the UK and US.
- Sarafem (only currently available in the US), prescribed for relief of premenstrual irritability, is identical to Prozac. The manufacturer, Eli Lilly, simply made the pill prettier, got a new slogan, and forced users to pay patent prices for two and a half more years.

The National Institute for Health Care Management (NIHCM) Foundation has found that the so-called "new" drugs with modified formulas are priced much higher than the drugs they replace.

## Need help talking to your doctor? Your little-known rights explained

The average GP's consultation in Britain takes just 6 minutes. In the rush, many people dry up, and forget the troubles they have brought there. But taking a friend along as an informal 'advocate' is a great way to keep you focused.

It's common for pregnant women and their partners to use this technique. Your friend can prompt you if you forget something. They can also ask for clarification of a problem, or a description of the effects of a medicine. And when you leave, your friend can help by reminding you of what the doctor said.

## How to prevent 'abnormal' lab-test results

Always remind your doctor of existing conditions you suffer when arranging a lab-test. It can speed up diagnosis of problems, and prevent undue anxiety when test results are not 'normal'.

- If you're diabetic, your unusual blood sugar levels could affect laboratory results testing for other conditions.
- If you suffer from coeliac disease, an allergy to gluten in wheat, it can affect certain tests too.

Reminding your GP will prevent confusion about the results.

## Medical problem? This simple idea could save your life

According to the Medic Alert Foundation, one in three people in the UK – that's 20 million people – have a medical condition you can't spot just by looking at them. In many serious emergencies, these people won't be able to communicate their allergies or medical problems to the paramedics. This risks a terrible outcome.

Yet we're all familiar with the concept of bracelets warning "Allergic to penicillin". Medical alert necklaces go one step further. They contain up to 25 lines of crucial information in miniature. This keeps the necklace small and discrete. Visit www.medicalert.co.uk to order.

# Do you have 3 days' food – undigested – in your belly?

## Nine little-known tips for restoring a healthy balance 'down below'

An over-acidic diet, poor digestion and too many toxins in your blood can play havoc in your intestines, upsetting the whole balance of the natural bacteria in your bowels.

This can mean you are carrying up to 9 meals' worth of undigested food at any one time!

The battle of bowel flora, of bad bacteria versus good, must be won. If unfriendly bacteria take over, serious health problems such as Candida, chronic fatigue and IBS can develop.

**Enemies of good bacteria:**
- **Unfriendly bacteria positively thrive on yeast and sugar.** Limit bread, biscuits, chocolate, cakes, pasta and alcohol in your diet.
- **Dairy is very mucus-forming and acidic.** Cut out as much dairy produce as you can to give your colon a healthier environment.
- **Salt makes** the cells hang on to water, causing bloating and water retention. Cut out those salty crisps and peanuts.
- **Cut down on red meat.** It can be loaded with antibiotics (put into the animals' feed), is incredibly hard to digest and can take from four to nine days to move out of a sluggish system.
- **Unless antibiotics are life-saving, try and do without them.**

**Friends of good bacteria:**
- **Try to make sure your diet is composed of as much 'plant' food as possible.** You've heard it before, but a reminder is always good – make sure you eat your five portions of fruit and vegetables a day, they're high in water, and all the vitamins and minerals needed for a healthy gut. If you haven't got time, grab a fruit smoothie on your way to work.
- **Eat more chicken and fish, especially oily fish such as salmon and tuna.** It's less acidic and easier to digest.
- **Eat plenty of brown rice.** This is a really important weapon in your battle of the bulge as it will act like a broom sweeping away all those years of debris from the walls of your colon as well as providing plenty of B vitamins which are essential for the growth of friendly bacteria.

- **Eat more unsalted nuts and seeds.** They're packed full of nutrients, fibre and the essential fatty acids needed for a healthy heart, brain, joints and gut.
- **Consider a probiotic supplement.** You need to choose your probiotics carefully. Potency, quality and costs can vary considerably but don't go for the cheaper brands in health food stores – these cheaper supplements don't contain enough bacteria to make any difference to your body. **Best buy:** Biocare's 'Bio-Acidophilus', a daily vitamin supplement.

## Stop minor cuts and burns leaving you with unsightly scars

Use Calendula cream, a natural healer from your local health food and supplement shop, on all minor cuts and burns. It works best used with comfrey, which contains allantoin and speeds up the skin's healing process. Calendula contains triterpenes, encouraging new cell growth.

- First clean the wound with a tea tree wash.
- Then apply the cream.
- You will rid your wound of infection, and help even the deepest cut heal quickly.

This cream can also be used on burns, once the skin has begun to heal over. It will help to reduce unsightly scarring. But take note! Do not use immediately on burnt skin.

## Hum your way to easy breathing

According to a recent study by Swedish scientists, humming is an extremely effective way of increasing ventilation in the sinuses. It also reduces the risk of sinusitis.

## Eat crisps and drink lemonade to cure a sickness bug

If you're on holiday, and start feeling unwell with severe stomach trouble, eat some plain crisps and drink lemonade. The salt and sugar content works just as well as any normal rehydration sachets.

## The little-known medical use of clingfilm

Act fast if a serious burn requires hospital treatment. Doctors say you should cover the burn with a sterile gauze immediately. But if you don't have any gauze to hand, use clingfilm instead. Secured with a bandage, clingfilm won't stick to the wound. And it will keep the burnt skin airtight and safe from infection – a good temporary cover until you get to hospital.

## Drivers! Don't get killed by your airbag

A recent study in America revealed that while car airbags have saved 4,000 lives since their introduction, sixty drivers were actually killed by this safety device. In accidents they would otherwise have survived, the force of the airbag inflating crushed them to death. Don't risk injury or death from your airbag. Sit at least 25 centimetres (10 inches) away from your steering wheel.

## Honey – nature's own gentle antiseptic

Ancient traditions reveal the healing powers of ordinary honey. Now medical research proves it effective as a gentle antiseptic. Use it at home to treat cuts, grazes and minor burns.

## Why you should save your tea bags in summer

Cold tea bags can ease the pain of sunburnt skin. Cooled camomile tea bags are best. Dripping very cool strong black tea on the wound also works well. Alternatively, dab vinegar onto your skin to soothe it – or rub freshly sliced tomatoes onto the sunburnt area. It will ease the pain and prevent your skin from peeling.

## How tired and emotional celebrities relax from just £6

You can enjoy a celebrity-style spa experience in your own home using just salt and olive oil. This ultimate low-cost pick-me-up should cost you around £6.

First, choose a quiet day, take the phone off the hook and get in plenty of mineral water. The word 'spa' literally means "healing through water". Aim to drink at least two litres throughout the day, whilst following this programme.

- Eat only fruit and salad for the day.
- Avoid tea, coffee, alcohol or tobacco.
- Rub olive oil into your hair and cover with a hot towel to help

absorption.

- Then put on a mud-based face mask and relax in a bath with a mud, clay or seaweed-based product. Look for Dead Sea products at Boots.
- Revitalise your skin by massaging your body with olive oil and rubbing ordinary salt into your skin.
- For the true spa finish – but not if you have heart or circulatory problems – shower for three minutes, alternating hot and cold water.
- Then lie down, wrapped up warmly in hot towels, for at least 30 minutes.

## The ocean's natural stress-buster...

Our natural diet was once full of wild game, fresh salmon and walnuts. Now, studies on the modern populations of Eskimos, Japanese fishing communities and Australian Aborigines have revealed some startling facts about these foods.

- Eskimos with their diet high in fresh fish and omega 3 have among the lowest rates of heart disease – as do people in Japanese fishing communities.
- In highly stressed Hong Kong – where the diet contains a lot of fish – the incidence of depressive illnesses is startlingly low.
- The diet of the Aborigines is rich in wild game, high in essential fatty acids like omega 3.

Ask your local butcher about wild game, and make sure you buy fresh wild salmon instead of farmed fish.

## How to beat panic attacks with a bag of boiled sweets

Experiencing a panic attack is often the scariest part of having a phobia. During a panic attack, you may suffer from a rapid heartbeat, shortness of breath, excessive sweating and trembling – you might even imagine you are having a heart attack. Many people get nervous about flying, for example. It may only take one turbulent flight to trigger a panic attack in you every time you fly. Here are 3 tips for tricking your mind into relaxing when you are in a potentially frightening situation:

**1. Carry a packet** of wrapped sweets with you. If you begin to feel panicky, slowly unwrap a sweet and suck it, concentrating on the taste.

**2. Try counting down** from 100 in 7s (100, 93, 86 etc). This will give your mind an alternative focus to distract you from what makes you fearful.

**3. When your heart begins to race,** first tense and then release your thigh muscles. This burns adrenaline to reduce your feelings of "flight or fight". Also gently massage below one ear (not both). This alters the blood pressure to your brain, and can slow down your heartbeat.

## Warning! This 'Mediterranean myth' could kill you in your sleep

Research from Israel reveals that mortality rates amongst older people who take siestas are much higher than amongst people who don't take siestas at all. So don't take a nap in the afternoon, especially if you are over 70 years old. It is a myth that the traditional Mediterranean siesta lowers stress levels and lengthens life.

## Strengthen your body – at any age – with this ancient Chinese exercise

This simple qi gong movement from ancient China increases the production of enkephalins in your body. These anti-ageing growth hormones are crucial for fighting sickness and disease. And the exercise is so gentle, it's perfect for boosting health in later life.

- Start by standing up, with your hands at your side.
- Turn your hands so your palms face the floor.
- Now bend your elbows slightly, and bring your hands upwards to chest level – as if they are floating in warm water. Breathe in slowly during this movement.
- Then lower your hands slowly back to hip level, while breathing out.
- Concentrate on your breathing pattern and the elegance of your movements. Repeat six times for maximum benefit.

## Is your partner's snoring making your life unbearable?

These 5 simple tips could help your partner breathe better at night… so you can get a good night's sleep yourself.

- Tilt the head of your bed upwards by 10cm.
- Avoid sedatives and antihistamines before bedtime.
- Don't sleep with windows open.
- Use a humidifier in your bedroom if the air is too dry.
- Reduce bedroom allergens, like dust or pet fur, to alleviate nasal stuffiness.

## How to beat itching wrists with nail varnish

Paint the back of your watch with nail varnish if your wrist itches. It will prevent the metal irritating your skin, and it won't harm you.

## Beware the 15 biggest food allergy offenders

If you feel generally unwell and run-down all the time, check your diet. Certain foods and drinks could be contributing to ill-health. Check to see if you've eaten or drunk one of the 15 biggest food allergy offenders within the past two hours. Symptoms normally include a mix of headache, migraine, stomach cramps, lethargy and/or depression.

### Most likely to cause reaction:
Cow's milk, wheat, yeast, goat's milk, blackcurrants, kidney beans, eggs, prawns, soya, sun-flower seeds, oats, peas, salmon, barley, olives.

### Least likely to cause reaction:
Ginger, chicken, beetroot, carrot, cauliflower, plums, garlic, venison, avocado, celery.

## Beware goodbye kisses after eating peanuts

People with nut allergies can suffer a deadly reaction even from just a peck on the cheek. A recent survey found 5% of nut allergy sufferers had a reaction this way – up to six hours after their friends had eaten nuts. Simply brushing your teeth after eating nuts will protect your nearest and dearest.

## Dark circles under your eyes? You aren't tired... you're allergic

Contrary to popular opinion, dark circles under the eyes doesn't always mean you aren't getting enough sleep. They might point to a more serious problem. Dark circles and horizontal creases on the lower lid often indicate food allergies that can affect behaviour in both adults and children. Consult your GP, and try eliminating dairy products and refined sugars from your diet.

## Hayfever sufferers!

Beat hay fever – and stay awake – with this cheap, natural remedy. A Swiss study reported in the British Medical Journal reveals that butterbur is just as effective as antihistamines for treating hay fever. But it does not have the sedative effects associated with these drugs. Even the so-called "non-drowsy antihistamine", cetirizine, was found to make hay fever sufferers more sleepy than butterbur.

## The best time to check for signs of breast cancer

More than one in four women have never examined themselves for breast cancer, and of those that do, 70% don't do it regularly enough. They risk failing to identify breast cancer in its earliest stages, when medical treatment can prevent it spreading and save your life. Make sure you are doing monthly breast examinations. The best time to examine your breasts is about a week after your period ends.

Look in the mirror
- Any change in the shape or size of the breast or nipple?
- Any change in the position or colouring of the nipple, including inversion?
- Any dimpling, denting, scaling or discolouration of the skin?

Feel your breasts
- Anything that is not normally there?
- A lump or swelling, that feels different from the rest of your breast tissue?
- A lump or swelling in the armpit, arm or around your collarbone?

Be aware
- Any other changes?
- Discharge from one or both nipples?
- A pain in the breast, armpit or arm that is new for you?

If you notice a lump or any change such as tenderness, pain, or discharge, make an appointment to see your doctor. And if you're aged between 50 and 64 then you should be offered regular mammograms. If your GP's failed to arrange them for you, ask!

## Men! How to beat testicular cancer in 5 easy steps

Testicular cancer is rare. Only about 1,800 new cases are diagnosed each year. But it's the most common type of cancer in men between 18 and 35. And it can kill within weeks of developing. But 90% of cases can be cured if caught early. To stay safe, you should check your testicles for unusual lumps, bumps or swelling once every month. The best place to do this is in the bath or shower, as the water will soften the skin of your sac, making it easier to feel the  testicles inside.

1. Cradle the whole sac and testicles in the palm of your hand.

2. Feel the difference between the testicles. One is almost always larger, and hangs lower. This is completely normal.

3. Now examine each testicle in turn, and compare them with each other.

4. Use both hands to gently roll each testicle between your thumb and forefinger. No need to squeeze.

5. Then put your fingers behind the left side and your thumb in front, and start feeling the skin on the front and side, where the cancer is most likely to be found. The back and top of the scrotum is likely to feel very irregular. This is normal.

But one symptom of cancer is finding a lump in the testicles, about the size of a pea. Other symptoms include:
- a testicle growing or shrinking in size
- a feeling of heaviness in the scrotum
- a dull ache in the lower abdomen or in the groin
- a sudden collection of fluid in the scrotum
- pain or discomfort in a testicle or in the scrotum
- a more uncommon symptom is enlargement or tenderness in the breast area.

## Men! Demand regular prostate examinations over the age of 50

All too often though, you aren't. Not all doctors offer this examination automatically, so it's up to you to take responsibility for your health. Make sure you see a doctor straight away if you experience dribbling of urine during and after urination, poor stream and spray of urine, a feeling of incomplete emptying of your bladder each time you go to the toilet, a need to urinate more frequently, or waking up at night more than once in order to pass urine.

## Why women should drink more milk

Three glasses of milk a day can halve a woman's risk of breast cancer. Research in the International Journal of Cancer proves it. The study involved more than 48,000 women between the ages of 35 and 49, and showed how a natural fat in dairy products, called Conjugated Linoleic Acid (CLA) is a potent anti-cancer agent.

## Half of breast tumours vanish thanks to this new drug

Fighting breast cancer with chemotherapy? Ask your doctor about Herceptin, a new type of drug. Herceptin helps beat a dangerous gene found in some breast cancer tumours. The gene, called HER-2, produces a protein that speeds tumour growth – but Herceptin targets this protein. Taken in combination with chemotherapy, it causes tumours to shrink by up to half their size or disappear completely in more than 50% of cases. Chemotherapy alone produces similar effects in just thirty per cent.

## Spot skin cancer early with the "ABCD" test

Cases of skin cancer in Britain have doubled over the last 10 years. Caught early though, survival rates are good. Check your skin – and particularly any moles you have – once every month. Use this simple test, and if you are at all concerned, see your GP immediately.

**A**symmetry – a line drawn across the middle of the mole would not create virtually matching halves.

**B**order – the edges are uneven or unclear.

**C**olour – the mole is unusually dark or more than one shade.

**D**iameter – the mole has a diameter larger than that of a pencil eraser

## The little-known role of broad beans in tackling cancer

US studies reveal that a protein in broad beans significantly slows down or even stops the progression of cancer in the colon. Placing the protein next to cancerous cells in a laboratory results in the development of new, normal cells. Equally good results were achieved using fresh or canned beans.

## Don't let your barbecue give you cancer...

Beef cooked on a barbecue might taste delicious... But some of that flavour comes from burnt and charred meat, potentially leading to cancer. To reduce absorption of the carcinogens produced when barbecuing red meat, step up your intake of green vegetables in the same meal. Studies show the green pigment in vegetables, chlorophyll, seems to cut carcinogen absorption – if eaten at the same time. Include plenty of salad, broccoli and spinach on your shopping list in the summer.

## Why rinsing after brushing could give you mouth cancer

Look at the alcohol content in any mouthwash you may use. Those with an alcohol content of 25% or more have been implicated in mouth, tongue and throat cancers.

## Warning! Long-haul airflights could give you skin cancer

Icelandic research from the University of Reykjavik shows that pilots have a higher risk of developing skin cancer than the rest of the population. Flying over several time zones disturbs the body's biological rhythms, making it more susceptible to cancer.

Four hundred and fifty pilots were studied, and their cancer rates compared to the Icelandic Cancer Registry. Skin cancer rates were 15 times higher for those flying international routes.

## How the Spanish, Greeks and Italians fight cancer

Lower your risk of developing bowel cancer by increasing your olive oil intake. As well as lowering your cholesterol levels and reducing your risk of rheumatoid arthritis, research confirms that olive oil helps prevent bowel cancer. A survey of 28 countries found lower bowel cancer rates in regions with a high olive oil consumption.

## The smelly secret to beating Britain's heart bypass crisis

Last year, 28,000 people had to undergo heart bypasses in Britain. Fifty per cent of patients have to go under the knife again within 10 years. But eating just half a clove of raw garlic each day could save you from this distressing and risky operation.

Raw garlic has many health benefits for your circulatory system and cholesterol levels. It thins the blood, and may even work to destroy cancer cells. It adds to the health benefits of a traditional Mediterranean diet. And in Japan, where it's rarely used in cooking, it has been used as a medicinal herb for thousands of years.

Garlic must be taken regularly though. Start today for best results. And if the taste or smell of half a clove is too much for you, simply add 4 $\frac{1}{2}$ cloves to your cooking throughout the day.

## History of heart trouble? How 1 in 3 can protect themselves

Over 30% of all fatal heart attacks occur in the morning on waking and getting out of bed. The burst of adrenaline that gets you out of bed in the morning might just be the final straw to your system if you are at risk, and could even kill you.

Your best option is to find out about cardiopulmonary resuscitation training (known as CPR for short). Get yourself and your family educated about what to do if you become one of the 30% of patients suffering an attack first thing in the morning.

## The truth about red wine and cholesterol

Drinking alcohol helps produce HDL, the "good" form of cholesterol which reduces your risk of thrombosis. Any form of alcohol works better than being teetotal, but red wine appears most effective. Stick within the recommended limits though – 14 large glasses a week for men, 10 for women.

# What mobile phone companies won't tell you about heart attacks

To help safeguard your heart, keep mobile phone calls to under five minutes at a time. Latest UK studies show the mobile phone radiation created during longer calls can speed up heart rates. Long-term exposure could put you at greater risk of heart attacks.

# Painful piles? Apply a face mask quickly

You can soothe the pain of piles by applying a simple, fragrance-free face mask, from any pharmacy or beauty shop, to the afflicted areas. Face masks are designed to cleanse the skin. And they also have a slight tightening effect on the skin too. But their effect on large and inflamed piles is much more noticeable.

# Over fifty? Protect your eyes against the No.1 cause of blindness

Age-related macular degeneration (AMD) is the leading cause of blindness amongst the over 50s. It affects 600, 000 people in the UK alone. To avoid falling victim, eat foods high in the carotenoid, lutein. Studies have shown it helps fight this disease. Green vegetables, such as spinach and Brussels sprouts as well as egg yolks and sweetcorn, are high in this essential nutrient. Also ensure you get enough of the antioxidant zeaxanthin, available in red grapes, courgettes, pumpkins, peaches, corn, maize and orange peppers.

# The high-risk warning in the whites of your eyes

If the white part of your eye turns bright red with blood, you have suffered a scleral haemorrhage. This could be an early warning signal for hypertension, or high blood pressure. Have your blood pressure checked by your GP immediately and strengthen your blood vessels with foods containing flavonoids (berries, red grapes and citrus fruits) and vitamin C as well as deep green vegetables like spinach for vitamin K.

# An ancient Greek remedy to combat IBS

Artichoke's medicinal benefits were first recorded by a pupil of

Aristotle in the 4th Century BC. Artichoke extract has been shown to alleviate symptoms of IBS including flatulence, bloating, abdominal pain and nausea.

The recommended daily dosage for this is 320mg of standardized extract, equivalent to 8,000mg of dried artichoke leaf. Research also shows that artichoke extract stimulates the production of bile in the liver. This plays an important role in the digestion of fats, giving it a cholesterol-lowering effect.

## How to reduce the painful cramps of IBS

Take lemon balm in your tea or in a bath to stop painful bowel spasms, especially if your IBS is closely linked to your stress levels. You will find putting 4-5 drops of the essential oil in a warm bath will relax you. Or place a few leaves of the herb in boiled water. Leave it to stand a few minutes, and then drink.

## Men! Beat impotence before it strikes

By mid life there is little benefit to correcting impotence through quitting smoking or reducing alcohol intake. Cardiovascular damage from heavy drinking or smoking may not be reversible. Exercise is the best bet. To lower your risk of impotence, simply walk 2 miles every day. A US study has shown that middle-aged men who burned at least 200 calories a day in exercise (a brisk 2 mile walk) were less likely to suffer impotence.

## Why monkeys sleep tight at night

To stave off insomnia and enjoy a good night's sleep, eat a ripe banana at bedtime. The riper it is, the sounder you'll sleep, because the increased tryptophan in the banana is a calming agent. Have this banana with a warm drink of milk for double-plus calming effects.

## Get a good night's sleep with a hot water bottle

Heat loss from your body is the key to a good night's sleep. And vasodilation, as it's known, can be helped by putting a hot water bottle near your feet, and keeping the window open. This rapidly induces heat loss.

## How to flush flu out of your body in three days

- For the first two days of a flu virus, eat nothing but citrus fruits. Oranges, lemons and limes remove flu toxins and help your digestion too.
- Also eat grapes, apples, blackberries and dates.
- On day three, eat light meals containing mint, cinnamon, parsley and garlic – they all aid your digestive system.
- Turkish and other Mediterranean dishes will contain these herbs.
- Also eat plenty of onions, carrots, leeks, celery and cabbage. Avoid bread, potatoes, dairy products and sweet fatty foods. They encourage mucus to form, leading to added congestion in your lungs, throat and nose. Drink lots of fluids constantly, to flush the virus out of your system.

## The little-known cause of colds and flu lurking in your home

Common house dust can trap germs and encourage colds and flu in your family. Beat this hidden infection, by dusting with a vacuum cleaner and a soft attachment, rather than a duster and polish. These simply spread the dust around in the air, to settle elsewhere later on.

## When should you gargle with horseradish sauce?

Mix one tablespoon of horseradish, a teaspoon of honey, and one teaspoon of ground cloves in a glass of warm water, and use this little-known soother as a gargle, or sip slowly when suffering a sore throat.

## Never suffer a sore throat again

Gargle with warm salt water every morning and every evening to prevent catching a sore throat. This is the cheapest and most effective way of tackling the virus causing this condition. But don't swallow this mixture after gargling – it can cause a burning sensation in your gullet.

## Beat the common cold with oysters and oranges

Vitamin C and zinc are your best defence against catching colds. Eating just one orange a day will give your body more than the required amount of vitamin C. And zinc is found in high doses in oysters, pumpkin seeds, wholemeal cereals and pulses.

Alternatively, take one Zinc Gluconate tablet a day (around £3.50 for 50 tablets, from your pharmacy). Increasing the zinc in your diet prevents viruses binding in your nose.

## A healing soup to cure the common cold

Cut up half-a-dozen cloves of garlic and sauté in oil, being careful not to let them burn. Add 2 pints of stock (such as beef), and let it come to the boil for just a few moments. Then lower the heat. Separate two eggs and add the whites to the hot liquid, stirring rapidly. Mix the yolks with two tablespoons of vinegar and then pour them in. Add salt and pepper if you want and some croutons, if handy. This is a good treatment for the common cold or 'flu.

## Why your mother's good manners spread germs and disease

Forget what your mother taught you. Don't cough or sneeze into your hand. Put the inside of your elbow over your face instead.

Colds and germs are spread most easily by physical contact. So shaking hands, using door handles and even passing a newspaper to a friend could give them your cold if you've sneezed into your hand.

But the inside of your elbow? It rarely comes into contact with other people. If we all practised this, the rate of infection would drop dramatically.

## Why the Japanese wear surgical masks and gloves in winter

Give your body a winter break this year – wear gloves when you are out and about between October and March, to protect your immune system. Handrails, petrol pumps, cash machine buttons, public telephones, door handles, shopping trolleys… all are often crawling with cold and flu germs in winter. In Japan, many older people wear surgical masks and gloves throughout the winter, to ward off attack.

## Puffy eyelids? Frothy urine? Spot the early signs of killer disease

Lost your appetite recently, or feeling generally nauseous? These symptoms could be caused by many mild conditions. But if you also suffer from puffy eyelids and your urine is unusually frothy, you could be suffering from nephritic syndrome.

This little-known condition is a potentially severe type of kidney inflammation. Like many major illnesses, its range of symptoms seem unrelated and quite harmless at first.

Before you next visit your GP, make a note of every symptom or unusual change you notice in your body. You could help him spot the warnings signs of major illness early.

## Natural remedy beats the pain and discomfort of kidney stones

To increase urine flow and prevent kidney stones forming, drink three to four cups of coffee a day.

## Improve your memory and fight Alzheimer's with this natural extract

Chinese monks refer to gingko biloba as the 'fountain of youth', and with good reason. Studies have shown that taking 120mg of this supplement every day actually increases blood flow to the brain, providing much-needed oxygen to the brain cells and boosting your brain's performance.

Taken with ginseng, it improves mental well-being and can dramatically enhance your memory. It's also been shown to help people suffering from Alzheimer's Disease.

## Improve your memory with India's secret herb

Indians have used the herb bacopa monniera for over 3,000 years to help them remember the long and complicated verses of their sacred religious texts. Bacopa is now becoming known here in the West.

It can be used to consolidate new learning and improve intellect. Bacopa works by boosting the antioxidant defences of the brain and by regulating several neurotransmitters – brain chemicals which signal information from one part of the brain to the other.

# Reduce eczema and psoriasis with a bunch of grapes

Inflammatory skin conditions like eczema and psoriasis look sore and red because your blood vessels dilate, opening up to allow more blood through. But a substance called berberine, found in grapes, can help constrict the blood vessels. Eat more of this over the next three months to reduce inflammation and see a difference.

# What World War II soldiers knew about tea tree oil

Tea tree oil is so versatile as a health aid, it was issued as standard kit to the Australian army during World War II. It can deal with many first aid emergencies, from cuts and bites to fungal conditions like athlete's foot. It is very powerful, containing a natural antiseptic compound, terpinen-4-ol. Note! Tea tree oil must never be taken internally. For most purposes use just 4 drops diluted in half a cup of warm water, to wash wounds, as a mouthwash, in a foot bath to head off athlete's foot, and used sparingly – neat – on cold sores when they first appear.

# When should you wear tomatoes on your eyes?

Conjunctivitis is a painful infection of the eyes, caused by transmission of the staphylococcus bacteria from one person to another. Conventional treatment involves eye drops or antibiotic creams. But freshly-cut slices of tomato also work. The water in tomatoes contains a protein to destroy the bacteria. And the tomato's slight acidity resembles closely the acidity of your eye's natural, protective secretions. But careful! Do not use tomato juice. It is too concentrated and powerful.

# Women! Beat cystitis with a better-tasting fruit juice

To tackle cystitis effectively, try blueberry instead of cranberry juice. It has the same antibacterial substances that prevent urinary tract infections, but it tastes much nicer, with none of the "tartness".

# Hear better with warm olive oil

Get rid of earwax safely and naturally, with some warm olive oil. Pour some into a small bowl and then place this in a larger bowl filled with boiling water. Allow the oil to heat up to body temperature – warm, but not hot. Then apply a few drops into the affected ear. This will soften excessive wax, and help unblock the ear canal.

## What shampoo manufacturers won't tell you about dandruff

To eliminate dandruff easily, switch to a mild shampoo rather than an anti-dandruff one. Anti-dandruff shampoos are too harsh, and irritate the scalp. This worsens the problem. Baby shampoos are much milder. But note – a dry, flaky scalp at any age indicates a diet too high in refined sugars and lacking fatty acids. So before you change your brand of shampoo, start cutting out sugar from your diet and add unroasted nuts and seeds instead.

## Is this harsh industrial chemical hidden in your shampoo?

Before washing your hair or taking a shower next, check your shampoo and bodywash labels for sodium lauryl sulphate (SLS) and sodium laureth sulphate (SLES). Mainly found in harsh detergents and car engine degreasers, these chemicals are absorbed rapidly by your skin, and then retained in the eyes, brain, heart and liver. This may result in harmful long-term effects. And yet some beauty companies continue to include SLS and SLES in their products.

## The truth about curing hiccups

Recent US research suggests that swallowing a teaspoonful of sugar is effective in curing hiccups in 95% of cases.

## Eat this Italian herb to protect against brittle bones

Many people are now trying to avoid dairy products in their diet. But where to get calcium, vital for strong, healthy bones?

One teaspoon of ground basil contains 32 mg of calcium. Celery seed contains 38 mg per teaspoon, and one teaspoon of cinnamon has 28 mg of calcium. Other excellent food sources for calcium include dried apricots and figs, spinach, mustard greens, cabbage, rhubarb, broccoli and sesame seeds.

# Warning! Your moisturiser could actually be drying your skin

Study the packaging on your skincare and cosmetic products for propylene glycol. This is a cosmetic form of mineral oil found in automotive brake and hydraulic fluid, and also in industrial antifreeze – as well as in skin and hair products. It works to draw moisture from the lower part of your skin to the surface, giving only the impression of moisturising, rather than actually doing it!

Skin contact with propylene glycol can cause liver abnormalities and kidney damage. Yet this is still found in many skincare products.

# Why you should visit your dentist in the morning

Research suggests we are "hard-wired" to ignore pain in the early morning. Pain perception is much lower than in the afternoon or evening. So if you are expecting any kind of treatment, try to visit your dentist or doctor first thing in the morning.

# What the Japanese know about green tea and long life

Green tea is possibly the most healthy thing you can drink. Even though many Japanese smoke heavily, their national lung cancer rates are surprisingly low. Why?

The Japanese are big tea drinkers, commonly drinking an average of six cups a day. A chemical in green tea called EGCG literally shuts down the enzyme in cancerous cells responsible for cell growth and reproduction, without affecting healthy cells at all. Tea (both green and black) is also a mild anti-coagulant that keeps your arteries clot-free – and so prevents both strokes and heart attacks.

In fact, studies have shown that people who drink one or more cups of tea a day cut their risk of heart attack by a staggering 46%!

# Men! Beware the warning of wasted trips to the toilet

Minimise the risks of prostate and urinary problems in the coming years, by taking good care of your reproductive organs today.

- Take vitamin E. Latest US studies suggest that taking 50 milligrams of vitamin E each day can lower the risks of prostate problems by 32%.
- Make sure you can urinate properly at all times – palmetto berries have been shown to improve urinary flow.
- Take selenium supplements. Selenium is essential for preventing infections, but now difficult to get through diet alone.
- Wear a condom. US researchers in Seattle have discovered that promiscuity can increase your chances of developing prostate cancer in middle age, unless you wear a condom. Their study looked at around 1,500 men aged 40-64. Of these, 753 had been diagnosed with prostate cancer. Men who had over 30 sexual partners in their lifetime were shown to be at twice the risk of getting prostate cancer as their less-promiscuous and condom-wearing peers.
- Cut down on the amount of red meat and fat you eat.

## What the medical industry won't tell men under 50

If you're under 50, screening for prostate cancer can do you more harm than good. The test measures rising levels of prostate specific antigen (PSA), produced by the prostate gland and found in your blood. But older men tend to have higher PSA levels than younger men anyway – making the test less effective for under 50s. And a higher PSA doesn't necessarily mean you have cancer.

Plus, it's possible to have cancer without having a raised PSA, and there is no clear difference between the amount of blood PSA found in men with cancer, men with Benign Prostatic Hyperplasia (BPH) (or better known as enlarged prostate) or other conditions. Active screening and treatment can lead to psychological and physical harm, including impotence and incontinence. Wait until you're into your 50s, and then make it part of your regular annual check-up with your GP.

## Cut your risk of stroke by 30% this dinnertime

You can reduce your risk of stroke by up to 30%, simply by eating 5-6 portions of fruit or vegetables each day. But don't overdo it. Additional daily portions do not appear to reduce the risks any further. Best fresh food to eat includes broccoli, cabbage, cauliflower, citrus fruits.

# Sit down to ease any morning aches and pains

Try sitting in a rocking chair to ease any aches and pains you suffer when you wake up. A steady to-and-fro movement helps to increase circulation to the legs. And it is believed to prevent muscle cramps and spasms too. If you don't have a rocking chair, rock slowly back and forth on the edge of your bed before getting up.

# How a pencil could help relieve your aches and pains

Are you suffering from bruxism? This is the dental term for teeth-clenching or grinding that takes place at night, often whilst the sufferer is asleep. Sufferers tend to be high-flyers in lucrative but pressured jobs. But it can affect anyone of any age.

Stress is a key contributor. Some dentists believe it is a subconscious way of relieving work-related pressures. The habit becomes more comforting as teeth are worn down. And the problem is worsened by an incorrect bite. Many sufferers don't hold their teeth, mouth and jaw correctly.

Prescribed drugs could be a contributory factor too. Some doctors think that anti-depressants can cause teeth-grinding at night. The outcome? Head and body aches and pains.

To adjust your bite, hold your teeth, mouth and jaw correctly. Practise the old dental saying, "Lips together, teeth apart". Try holding something between your lips to keep the teeth apart – a pen or pencil is perfect. After 2 minutes, remove the pencil but continue to hold your lips and teeth in the same position. This is often enough to alleviate problems. Some sufferers also tend to chew their fingernails, pencils and the inside of their cheeks. Watch for these signs, and make a conscious effort to eliminate them. They're all trigger activities for bruxism.

# What Gypsy Rose Lee can reveal about your health

Palmistry is usually thought of in terms of gypsies, crystal balls and fairgrounds. But today, palm readings can give you information to help you make positive lifestyle changes. Daily examination of lines, patterns and bumps on your palms can indicate you are suffering from a health problem.

### 1. Reading the lines

The heart line runs across the palm from your first finger to below your little finger. Below that comes the head line. The life line is usually joined to your head line between the first finger and thumb.

### 2. Depth and strength

On either hand, look at how deep and strong the lines are. If the life line is strong it usually indicates physical stamina, so it will be less visible at times when you are feeling a lack of energy. If the head line is strong, mental energies are what drive you so you need to be aware of potential stress and take care of your body. If it's the heart line that is emphasised you can be impulsive which may lead to mental and physical exhaustion and a tendency to more accidents and injuries.

### 3. Spot women's problems early

Women should look for a triangle or diamond shape 3/4 of the way down your hand attached to outside of the life line. This can be anything from heavy or irregular periods to polyps or cysts. If seen on a man it can indicate urological problems or a predisposition to a hernia.

### 4. Check for ulcers

Stomach and intestinal problems like ulcers can be checked by drawing a diagonal line from little finger to thumb and looking in the centre of the palm between heart and life lines. If you see very fine lines there, like flames, it suggests your diet needs to be looked at.

## What the colour of your hands says about your health

- If your hands are a pinkish colour then you have a healthy constitution.
- Very red? Possible high blood pressure, liver dysfunction, and susceptibility to a stroke or diabetes.
- White hands could indicate possible iron-deficiency/anaemia, poor circulation, anxiety or shock.
- Blue or bluish grey: Circulatory, cardiovascular or respiratory problems.
- Yellow: Jaundice, hepatitis or an excess of beta carotene.
- The texture of your skin is also important. Delicate skin can indicate a weaker emotional and physical constitution and immune system. The rougher the skin, the more robust and resistant to disease you are.

# Five effective strategies to lower your blood pressure today

A staggering 10 million people in the UK are thought to suffer from high blood pressure. It becomes more prevalent with age and affects at least 40 per cent of the over 50s. Hypertension is not in itself a disease, but a serious condition that, over time, causes excessive force on your artery walls, and can seriously compromise many of your body's vital organs.

1. Losing just 9lb can bring blood pressure readings down to normal.

2. Walk for just 30 minutes a day, four or five times a week. But don't overdo it. Only start gentle exercise, and only with your doctor's prior approval and advice.

3. Cut 5 points off your systolic pressure, and 3 points off your diastolic pressure, by drinking less alcohol. And cigarettes, of course, must go.

4. Secret cause behind 10% of cases. Chronic illness, known as 'secondary hypertension', is behind one in 10 high blood pressure diagnoses, especially high cholesterol, diabetes, kidney, adrenal or thyroid disease. Once the underlying problem has been successfully treated, the high blood pressure can vanish too.

5. Beware certain medications. Birth control pills, cold remedies, decongestants, steroids, and non-steroidal anti-inflammatory drugs for arthritis can worsen your blood pressure.

# Four simple steps to opening a 100th birthday card from King Charles III

Most prescriptions for longer life make it sound so dreary, you'd rather not bother! But these simple steps can help you live to a ripe old age… without regretting it.

### 1. Floss your teeth
People with gum disease are twice as likely to suffer coronary heart disease as those with healthy gums. Infected gums release harmful bacteria into your bloodstream, triggering or accelerating furring of your arteries. In extreme cases, this can lead to deadly blood clots. Watch out for blood when you brush or rinse your teeth.

### 2. Have more sex

Levels of testosterone and oestrogen get boosted during sex, giving both men and women protection from heart disease. Plus, the exercise itself can burn off 150 calories every half hour.

### 3. Smile more often

It's true. A team of psychologists at Yale University in America has found that people who are positive about ageing live on average 7 $\frac{1}{2}$ years longer than those who regret the passing years. In fact, the effect on good health is greater than low cholesterol or low blood pressure.

### 4. Write a will

Studies have shown that people who take control of what happens to their assets after they die actually live an average of 7 years longer. Weird but true!

## One in 12 British men secretly suffers this 'old ladies' disease

Osteoporosis affects 3 million people in the UK. And the National Osteoporosis Society believes that as many as 1 in 12 men could be sufferers. The problem is, many doctors fail to recognise the symptoms. Of all the men found to have osteoporosis, 50% will be diagnosed as idiopathic – the cause is not known. However, specific risk factors only apply to men:

● Delayed puberty
● Low body weight
● Low muscle mass
● Hypo-gonadism with low  testosterone levels.

Plus, if you suffer from at least three of the following, see your doctor:
● Family history of the disease, poor diet (especially too much fat and protein), history of anorexia or bulimia, smoking, alcohol and lack of exercise, lack of calcitonin (from the thyroid), taking chronic anticonvulsant therapy, taking drugs which can cause dizziness, taking chronic steroid therapy, using antacids regularly, drinking more than two cups of coffee daily.

## 5 steps to reduce your risk of osteoporosis

1. Get regular bone scans if you have any family history of osteoporosis.

2. Weight-bearing exercise is crucial to maintain healthy bones; even a daily walk will help keep them strong.

3. Reduce all items in your diet that strip essential bone nutrients from the body. Cut down alcohol, smoking, carbonated drinks and caffeine as they are all linked to poor mineral absorption and can remove vitally needed calcium from the body.

4. Small amounts of protein are essential for bone health, but avoid high protein diets. These can lead to bone loss because of the way protein is metabolised in the body.

5. Consider nutritional supplements such as the minerals calcium citrate, magnesium, zinc, boron, manganese and vitamins C, B6, folic acid and vitamin A in the form of beta-carotene.

## Why you shouldn't waste your money on private health checks

Private medical check-ups are netting the industry more than £31 million a year. And it is not surprising that leading in the field are BUPA, who charge a staggering £425 for a ladies' health assessment, and £345 for men (based on the Classic assessment). They also recommend you attend this assessment once a year. If this was to continue for 10 years this cost would add up to a staggering £7,700! But you can save £410 on a medical check-up with these DIY tests. All are part of BUPA's annual health check-up. You can do them yourself for next to nothing.

- BUPA offer a fitness bike test to determine your level of fitness – your gym instructor can measure this and your pulse for free.
- BUPA offer a muscle strength test to determine the physical strength in certain muscle groups – this can be arranged at your local gym, for free.
- Vision test – go to your optician and pay £15 for an eye test.
- Height and weight measurements and body mass index calculations can be checked on the website http://www.bbc.co.uk/health/yourweight/bmi.shtml, or ask your gym to weigh you and work out your height:weight ratio.

## Scandal of Britain's ill-trained doctors

If your GP is aged 30 or older, beware his bedside manner. He underwent years of medical training, but he probably received no 'people skills' at all.

Today, at last, medical students do get some training in how to listen to their patients and how to communicate with them. But older doctors can often seem rude and brusque, simply because they're untrained in how to deal with people's emotions in a caring way.

## Avoid these three vegetables 7 days before an operation

Avoid eating tomatoes, potatoes and avocados in the week leading up to an operation. Research at Chicago University in the USA shows these foods can interfere with general anaesthetics and lead to increased feelings of grogginess and sickness after operations.

## Women! Why you should go to the toilet more often in summer

The chances of urinary tract infections double during the hot summer months. Here's how to stay healthy.

- Drink plenty of fluids each day.
- Empty your bladder fully every time you go to the toilet.
- Wear loose-fitting, cotton underwear to maintain ventilation.
- Avoid underwear that causes you to perspire, as moisture encourages bacteria to grow and flourish.
- Don't forget to change out of wet bathing costumes as soon as possible.

## Don't suffer from dry, chapped hands in winter

In cold and windy weather, always dry your hands with throwaway tissues, rather than a hot-air hand dryer. UK research reveals that increasing numbers of people who wash and dry hands with hot-air dryers are experiencing chapped fingers and hands. Why? Because it is difficult to dry your hands fully in this way. Tissues are more effective.

## A tablet to boost your brain power

Phosphatidyl Serine (PS) is a supplement that doesn't just enhance memory – it also stimulates your capacity to learn. This natural substance is found in most areas of the brain, but it decreases in concentration as you age. PS is thought to reverse memory decline, and research has demonstrated its role in improvements in memory, lucidity and in the general ability to cope with everyday pressures.

## Airline pilots reveal five easy ways to stay healthy at 37,000 feet

Pilots and cabin crew all know how to have a relaxing and enjoyable flight. Here are their tips for flying safely and comfortably.

### 1. Beware your bodily gases

At cruising altitudes, body gases expand by 30%. Here's how to reduce any discomfort.

- Wear loose clothes
- Avoid chewing gum, fizzy drinks and gassy foods like beans, cabbage and turnips before and during the flight.
- Have a pre-flight drink mixing one drop of peppermint oil with a teaspoon of honey dissolved in hot water.
- Colostomy patients should carry extra bags in case of leakage.
- Anyone with a plaster cast may wish to have a looser one fitted. Air trapped between the skin and cast will expand, causing pain.

### 2. Don't get dried out

The pressurization of aeroplane cabins leads to moisture loss in the air. Humidity levels fall from a comfortable 60% to a skin-drying 20%.

- Put a few drops of lavender oil into a spray bottle containing mineral water. Use this to cool and refresh your skin.
- Drink plenty of water and fruit juices to hydrate your body.
- Avoid alcohol, coffee and tea – all will dehydrate you even more.
- Don't wear contact lenses on flights lasting 4 hours or more.

### 3. Relieve painful cramping

Sitting up for lengthy periods results in swollen feet and ankles. This makes your shoes feel tight at the end of the flight.

- On long-haul flights, ask to reserve a seat by the aisles or emergency exits. You can then stretch out.
- Take hourly walks during the flight.
- Put 5 drops of lavender oil on a damp cloth, to make an ideal compress for swollen feet and ankles. Massage gently in an upward direction to the bottom of each calf, for 3 minutes on each leg.

### 4. Get over motion sickness

One in 3 people suffers travel sickness at some time. The best way to cure it is to avoid it.

● Try to book a seat above the wings, the steadiest part of the plane.
● Get plenty of fresh air through the air vents above your ahead.
● Distract your attention by reading, watching the in-flight movie, or playing a video game.
● Chewing a little raw ginger often helps. Or put three drops of ginger oil into a handkerchief and inhale.

### 5. Beat jet lag fast

● Travelling east and arriving in the morning? Try to stay indoors out of natural daylight and rest until the afternoon. This helps to advance your body clock.
● Travelling west? As soon as you arrive, follow the same waking, eating and sleeping timetables as the locals. Your body clock will adjust accordingly.
● A long soak in a bath of grapefruit and lavender oils, inhaling the aroma, helps you adjust to different time zones.

## The magic powers of cayenne pepper

Cayenne pepper, prepared from capsicum or chilli pepper, can be used as a stimulant, antiseptic and for relieving pain. It has even been used for the treatment of heart attack victims.

If the victim is still breathing, make them drink cayenne tea. Just mix a teaspoon of cayenne in a cup of hot water. This feeds the heart immediately and is one of the fastest-acting aids you can use. And if applied directly to a wound, cayenne will cleanse the wound, relieve pain and stop the bleeding.

## Why you should wear suntan lotion this winter

A week in the mountain sun is the equivalent of three months' beach exposure – even in mid-winter. At 2,500 metres altitude, the sun's ultraviolet intensity is 40% greater than at sea level. And for every 1,000 metre height increase, the sun's rays are 15% more intense. If you're going winter skiing, add extra sun protection factor the higher you go.

## Alleviate earache with chamomile tea

Steep 1-2 teaspoons of chamomile flowers in boiling water for 10-15 minutes. Strain out the water, wrap in a clean cloth and apply this hot compress to the ear for natural relief of earache.

## Vinegar loosens blocked sinuses and chest colds

Add 1/4 cup or more of vinegar to a vaporiser, or a bowl of hot water. Breathe it in and feel the relief.

## Settle your stomach with cinnamon

Dissolve 4g of ground cinnamon in 1 cup of warm water, cover it for 15 minutes, and drink it like tea. This remedy can also ease diarrhoea and flatulence.

## How to get rid of wrinkles with vodka

Give your skin some vodka to reduce the appearance of wrinkles. Combine 2 tablespoons of vodka, 1 tablespoon of fennel seeds, and 1 1/2 teaspoons of honey. Stir well and allow to sit for 3 days. Strain mixture. Use full strength or add 2 tablespoons of water to dilute. Use a cotton ball to apply to face. This is also an excellent home-made toner.

## Fight hay fever by changing your diet

Studies show allergic reactions are much more severe and frequent if your immune system is weak. The best way to prevent hay fever is to detoxify your body in time for the May-June onslaught. Aim to start this a month before the hay fever season starts.
● Eliminate dairy products, fish, wheat, citrus fruits and chocolate from your diet to see if there is an improvement to your suffering.
● Boost your diet with foods to help you detoxify: asparagus, carrots, grapes, beetroot, onions, broccoli, cabbage, peppers, sweet potatoes, brown rice, tomatoes, live natural yoghurt and green tea.

## The trick to removing insect bites with a credit card

If you get stung by a wasp or bee, and the sting won't come out, then scrape the area gently with a credit card. The edge will tease the sting out of your skin. If you're at home when it happens, use dental floss – just as effective.

## How lovemaking can unblock a stuffy nose

Sex releases natural antihistamines in your body. It can therefore help combat asthma and hay fever, and will unblock a stuffy nose.

## Sunbathe more safely with orange and yellow fruits

German research from the University of Düsseldorf confirms sunbathers can boost protection from the sun's harmful, ultraviolet rays by increasing their intake of certain foods. The 12-week study involved fair-skinned men and women taking daily doses of 25mg of carotenoids, a vitamin A-like substance found mainly in brightly coloured fruit and vegetables.

Findings revealed those taking carotenoids reduced their sunburn reaction by a sun protection factor of 2.4. To boost your protection, eat dark green, leafy vegetables such as broccoli, as well as brightly coloured orange and yellow fruit and veg. And add vitamin E to your diet as well, proven to further increase sunburn protection.

## At last! A sane look at hormone replacement therapy

Is it any wonder most of the recent scare stories about hormone replacement therapy come from male doctors and researchers? It's easy for them to say "Stop taking HRT". They will never have to go through the menopause.

But what do female experts say about HRT's health benefits and long-term risks?

Firstly, the menopause is not an illness or disease. It is a natural – if uncomfortable – change in the hormones your body produces as you reach middle age, or recover from a hysterectomy. Hormone replacement therapy puts man-made versions of these chemicals into your system instead.

● The fertility hormone. Oestrogen is crucial to the monthly cycle in women of child-bearing age. Its levels ebb and flow as the body releases eggs and fertility is achieved.

- The energy hormone. Progesterone drives your body's energy levels. Actually a form of the male hormone, testosterone, it gives you the energy needed to carry a growing baby and then give birth. But production drops to zero during the menopause, leading to fatigue, memory loss and mood swings.

It is commonly thought dropping oestrogen levels cause hot flushes. But in fact, lowered progesterone causes most of the physical and mental symptoms – night sweats, lack of energy, mood swings, vaginal dryness, loss of sex drive and irritable bladder problems.

HRT will alleviate all these problems, as long you continue taking it. Plus, research links it to improved long-term defence against brittle bones, heart disease, Alzheimer's and even hair loss.

But recent research shows these long-term health benefits outweighed by dangerous side-effects. The US Women's Health Initiative studied thousands of women between the ages of 50 and 79. Its findings revealed the effects of 5 years' HRT given to 10,000 women.

- BENEFITS: Twenty-five extra women will avoid hip fractures and 30 will avoid colonic cancer
- DANGERS: Thirty-eight extra women will suffer coronary thrombosis, 37 will suffer non fatal strokes, 44 extra embolisms will be caused by blood clots, and 42 extra women will suffer invasive breast cancer.

Overall, these risks are small. Just 1 in 62 women will be harmed by 5 years of treatment. But only 1 in 180 women will avoid a hip fracture or colonic tumour as a result of taking HRT.

So where does this leave you? The British government's Committee for the Safety of Medicines believes these reports of increased cancer risk should not stop you taking HRT. If you find the daily benefits of HRT have changed your life for the better, just be sure to check regularly for unusual lumps or tenderness in your breasts.

But what if you don't want to increase your risk of cancer? Can you continue replacing your body's lost hormones, yet avoid these potential side-effects?

Many alternative doctors think so. They question the way HRT is made in laboratories, and recommend using natural progesterone and oestrogen instead.

- Natural oestrogen can be found in supplements available without prescription from your local health food shop. Ask about dong quai, siberian ginseng, garden sage, chaste berry, sasparilla, unicorn root, wild yam and St. John's wort. They prove most effective taken in combination. And add tofu to your diet. It's made from soya beans, rich in phyto-oestrogens (also known as 'plant oestrogens'). They trick your body into thinking it's still receiving oestrogen, and helps maintain adequate levels. But because they don't encourage cell proliferation, they don't pose any of the cancer risks associated with oestrogen.
- Natural progesterone is only available on prescription from your GP. Don't believe the myth it is contained in wild yam products. Yet many UK doctors don't know natural progesterone exists, let alone that they can prescribe it for you.

These natural alternatives remain unlisted by most medical pharmacies. Yet incredibly, they are actually the source of all the laboratory chemicals prescribed by hundreds of British GPs every day!

Pharmaceutical companies are not allowed to patent chemical structures found in nature – like the natural oestrogen in siberian ginseng, for instance. So instead, the big pharmaceutical companies take natural sources of progesterone and oestrogen… and turn them into artificial man-made forms.

There is an alternative to all HRT treatments, of course. Allow your body to go through the menopause, and tackle the symptoms caused by reduced oestrogen and progesterone instead.

For example, the herb black cohosh used to be seen as a form of oestrogen. But recent research suggests it may reduce hot flushes by acting to regulate your body temperature. This increases the chances the herb can offer a safe HRT alternative.

PLEASE NOTE! If you are considering coming off your HRT programme, or switching to natural hormone replacements, you must consult with your GP first. Ending the treatment suddenly and self-prescribing other treatments can prove very dangerous. Work with your doctor's advice – not against it.

## Eight steps to surviving the menopause without taking HRT

If you want to meet the menopause head on, and beat the symptoms of hot flushes, memory loss, mood swings and night sweats, there is a 'whole body' approach you can adopt to help you cope with the changes your body is going through.

1. Take daily supplements to support you: 100mg vitamin C, 300mg calcium, 350iu vitamin D.

2. Monitor your diet. Eat more fruit and leafy green vegetables to give yourself a health boost.

3. Drink less alcohol, fizzy drinks, coffee and tea. They only add to that 'wired' feeling.

4. Go organic, especially with meats. Added growth hormones in cattle feed will prolong your menopause.

5. Cut back on processed foods, high in sugar and fat. They add to physical stress.

6. Avoid plastic-wrapped food. Plastics contain molecules that are similar to oestrogens, leading to a drawn-out menopause.

7. Cut down your intake of fluoridated tap water, and rinse thoroughly after brushing your teeth. Fluoride is bad for your bones, especially when falling oestrogen levels increase your risk of osteoporosis.

8. Drink a cup of peppermint tea if you feel a hot flush coming on. It will stimulate your nerve endings to sense the actual, cooler temperature around you.

## Suffering menopausal night sweats? Make a cup of tea...

Research shows that a cup of sage tea can eliminate menopause-associated night sweats. Add four heaped tablespoons of dried sage to one cup of hot water and cover and leave for four hours. Then strain out the herbs and drink. This dries up perspiration and alleviates sweats for up to 48 hours at a time.

# YOUR WEALTH & RETIREMENT

**Discover the little-known techniques to slash your tax and build your fortune while others miss out**

# 109 secrets of the Square Mile revealed (including 37 unbeatable tax-saving tips!)

Britain's investment industry is a joke. Everyone involved might mean well, but they've got more important things to worry about than helping you provide for a comfortable future:

- Your bank manager pays you less interest on your savings than you fork out for your mortgage.
- Investment fund managers only worry about losing less each year than their competitors lose.
- Financial journalists simply reprint 'buy' recommendations from the stockbrokers and banks who pay their wages through advertising fees.

But you don't have to pay 5% commission upfront, plus 1% fees every year, just for the pleasure of watching your money evaporate in an Equitable Life, with-profits bonds or pension misselling scandal. The simple strategies and tactics revealed in the following pages will put the only person who really cares about your money in charge of growing your wealth…YOU!

## Urgent tax query? This insider's trick gets it answered within 3 days

Do you have an important query for the Inland Revenue? Don't wait 6 weeks for a written reply to a letter… and certainly don't waste time 'holding' on the telephone. Simply write "For the attention of an inspector" on the top of your envelope. If your query is important and urgent, this guarantees a speedy response.

## Seventeen little-known and proven ways to cut your tax bill

The tax system in Britain is now so complex many people miss out on perfectly legal ways of saving tax. And according to TaxAction, hard-pressed Britons each pay £114 too much on average, every year.

## Here are 17 top tips you can use to minimise your bill, and maximise your allowances.

**1. Give to charity.** It can save you tax. The Gift Aid scheme deducted your donation from your total income when working out how much allowance you get. Ask your Tax Office for details.

**2. Cut your taxable income.** You get a higher tax-free allowance for any tax year in which you are aged 65 or over, but the extra allowance is reduced by £2 for every £3 of total income above £18,300. So anything you can do to keep your total income below £18,300 will allow you to hang on to more allowance and save you tax.

**3. Invest for tax-free income to cut your bill.** You can enjoy 5% of with-profits or unit-linked bonds as tax-free income, for instance. A one-off pension contribution has the same effect.

**4. Turn losses to your advantage.** Keep a record of any loss you made on selling shares or other investments during the recent stock market downturn.

**5. Avoid penalties.** You must tell your tax office about any losses within five years and 10 months of the end of the tax year in which you suffered them. So if you act before 31 January 2005, you can notify losses made in 1998-99).

**6. Carry losses forward.** Once you have told your tax office about any losses, you can carry the loss forward indefinitely to set against future capital gains.

**7. Insure yourself "in trust".** If you have an insurance policy that will pay out on your death, ask your insurance company about getting your policy 'written in trust' for someone else (your children, say). The payout on your death will go immediately to them without forming part of your taxable estate.

**8. Negotiate with your employer to save National Insurance.** Your own contributions to your  pension scheme are liable to National

Insurance, but your employer's are not. You save National Insurance if, instead of a pay rise, you can persuade your employer to pay extra into your pension fund. But this only works if your employer makes the contributions. If you get the money and pay it in, you will be caught for National Insurance.

**9. Employ your spouse.** Self-employed people can employ a family member, and claim the money they pay as an allowable expense. This means your spouse (or whoever) gets the money tax-free if it's below the threshold for deducting National Insurance and PAYE. This is currently £89 a week. But paying them at least £77 a week will protect their right to state retirement pension.

**10. Pay your kids to clean.** Letting out a property? Paying a partner or child to do the cleaning or the gardening has the same advantages. Note, though, that they must actually do the work, and be paid a realistic wage for it.

**11. Get a tax boost for your new business.** Claim tax relief on business expenses incurred before you actually start trading. Make sure you keep records of all possible expenses.

**12. Don't forget!** If you register for VAT, you can also claim back VAT on some pre-registration expenses, but you will need a receipt showing the supplier's VAT registration number.

**13. Check your diary.** If you were a single parent, lost your husband (only available to widows), or were married before 6 April 2001, you should have received additional personal allowance, widow's bereavement allowance or married couple's allowance. These allowances were abolished on that date (apart from married couple's allowance for people born before 6 April 1935. But it is not too late to claim for earlier years, as long as you do so within six years of 31st January of the tax year in question.

**14. How old are your kids?** If you had children aged not more than 16 (or not more than 18 and in full-time education), make sure you received children's tax credit for the 2001-02 and 2002-03 tax years.

**15. Keep records of your costs if you're in dispute with the Revenue.** You have the right to complain if you think your tax office has made a mistake or is being unreasonably slow. If so, you can claim the costs of sorting out the problem, such as the cost of phone calls, or a tax adviser's professional fees, so hang on to relevant receipts.

**16. Seek redress.** If you have had a lot of inconvenience or distress, the Revenue may pay some compensation. See Inland Revenue Code of Practice 1, "Putting things right when we make mistakes" (from your local tax office).

**17. Plan carefully to reduce tax on a property you do not live in the whole time.** You may have to pay capital gains tax when you sell a property you did not live in for the whole time. There are exemptions, but some only apply if you have lived in the property for at least some of the time, so if you can, it is worth living there to start with and before you finally sell. See Inland Revenue help sheet IR283, "Private Residence Relief", available at www.inlandrevenue.gov.uk or by calling 020-7667 4001.

## How to earn an extra £81 per week tax-free

You can rent a room in your home and be exempt from the first £4,250 of rent you receive. That means you can charge £81 a week and pay no tax whatsoever on this additional income.

Plus, you can calculate the income less expenses and, if you have made a loss, this could be claimable against other property income you have made in the same year. To keep tax as low as possible, keep a record of all relevant expenses such as letting agent fees, redecoration, maintenance, ground rent, buildings insurance, accountancy fees, stationery and postage, bank charges, telephone calls, travel expenses. Keep records of these for up to six years.

## How shareowners can beat the taxman by gifting their gains

Maximise your annual capital gains tax allowance by transferring shares between yourself and your spouse. The capital gains tax allowance for 2003/04 is only £7,900 per person. But there is no capital gains tax on gifts between spouses.

Be aware though! An immediate transfer and subsequent sale will likely fall under tax avoidance legislation. It's illegal for the purchase and sale of shares by a spouse to form part of a tax avoidance scheme.

So simply leave some time between transfer and sale of shares. If possible, sell in a subsequent tax year. Consider transferring now and selling after April next year.

## Retiring soon? Three tips to turn your new situation into big tax savings

When you retire, your income and your personal allowance changes. Here's how to take advantage of your new situation.
- Avoid cashing in any of your investments. Wait till you have retired and your income has dropped before you realise your gains.
- Higher-rate tax payer? Pay pension premiums up to the limit in the years before you retire. You will enjoy higher-rate tax relief on them.
- Few capital gains? If you are a higher-rate taxpayer with few capital gains to show this tax year, look for investments that pay no income – such as zero dividend preference shares (known as 'zeros') or unit trusts. Use these instead of taxable bank accounts and income bonds.

## Tax-payers! How to ensure your advisor works for your benefit

When seeking personal advice on tax matters, make sure the person you talk to is a Chartered Accountant or a Certified Accountant. They are insured to cover claims against them and are members of professional bodies regulating their conduct and training. This means their advice will be professional, informed and secure.

## Seven tips to turn a tax investigation upside down

If your latest tax return has been selected for investigation, you need to prepare and turn the tables. It can be done. Here's all you need to know and do:

### 1. Ask why
The inspector might hide behind the 'random selection' wheeze. But most will indicate a broad reason.
- You sent in your return late, implying the figures don't add up.

- Income, expenditure or profit figures don't match those for comparable taxpayers.
- Contradictory evidence from different sources – bank, employers, ex-partners etc.

### 2. Get help
Ask your local Inland Revenue office for a copy of the Taxpayers' Charter – so that you know what they can and can't do to you.

### 3. Be prepared
Always keep a copy of everything submitted to the Inland Revenue. Otherwise, you can't hope to defend yourself properly. Any taxpayer who has to ask for copies looks unprofessional and disorganised. Support all your income, expenditure and profit figures with documentation.

### 4. 'Guess'timate better
Contrary to popular belief, the taxman will accept estimated figures, albeit by negotiation. Where gaps exist, recalculate your estimates and retain a note of your calculations. Be prepared to justify your reasoning during any meeting.

### 5. Assume they know everything
Potentially, the taxman has full financial data about you from your bank, building society, employers etc. But don't be surprised if he has also spoken to customers, suppliers, friends, relatives and neighbours.

### 6. Check your lifestyle
The inspector will work hard to check your declared income and lifestyle match. Satellite dishes, cars, boats, and other unexpected signs of affluence could all spell trouble. Beware buying discounted luxury goods if you can't get receipts.

### 7. Good cop, bad cop
Just like in a cops'n'robbers film, some inspectors play the 'good cop, bad cop' routine. One tries to establish a rapport, to lull you into a false sense of security. The other one tries to intimidate you with threats of big fines and further investigations. Don't fall for either. Every question the taxman asks has a motive. Listen carefully, work it out, and give as straight and honest an answer as you can.

## What nine out of ten British taxpayers don't know about claiming a rebate…

Latest research reveals between 75% and 90% of taxpayers pay more than they should. So if your accounts are accurate, and you adopt a positive approach, you can claim a nice cash rebate, or even come out of a tax investigation with money in your pocket.

As the taxman goes through each line of your accounts, ask: "Did I claim the full allowance there?", "Am I entitled to any benefits for this?" The tax inspector will not tell you how to pay less tax unless you ask. Be sure you do!

## Warning! Why you must keep your tax receipts for the next 6 years

Don't be tempted to throw out all your paperwork when the tax year ends. If you are self-employed, you must keep all your tax papers for 5 years and 10 months after the end of the tax year. Your claim for this year can be investigated at any time up until then. The taxman has the right to demand all the relevant paperwork. Make sure you keep it

## This 10-second test cuts hours and days off filling in your tax return

When your tax return forms arrive in the post, flick through to make sure you check you have all the relevant pages straight away. Call your local tax office if there are any missing. This will ensure you can get on with completing your details in your own time – without risking a late submission through the taxman's incompetence.

## Scandal! Banks cheat 80% of overdraft customers…

If you're regularly in the red, reduce your overdraft charges simply by asking your bank to explain how they were calculated. Latest UK research indicates that 80% of all overdraft charges are calculated incorrectly. If your bank cannot justify its charges on your account, you should be entitled to an appropriate refund. Make sure you get it.

# These 7 simple steps will improve your credit rating today

### 1. Make sure you are on the electoral register

This is the first place lenders and credit reference agencies look to check your home address. Contact your local council and ask for the Electoral Services Office.

### 2. Check your family's rating

A lender will see information relating to everyone living at your address when you apply for credit. Even family members who have moved elsewhere may affect your rating! If you are estranged from your family, you can ask the agency to separate the files.

### 3. Don't apply for too many loans

Be selective when applying for credit. If you are turned down once and then apply to lots of lenders hoping one will give you money, the information will appear on your file. It may look as if you are trying to commit fraud.

### 4. Always pay your bills on time

Don't wait for a final reminder – that red letter might be your way of making the most of your cash flow, but it sends the wrong signals to the utility companies and the credit reference agencies.

### 5. Say why you fell behind in the past

If you failed to make payments on a loan in the past, tell one of the credit reference agencies why. For example, illness, redundancy, relationship breakdown. Your statement will be added to your file, helping you get credit in future.

www.equifax.co.uk
Tel: 0845 600 1772.
www.experian.co.uk
Tel: 0870 241 4297.

### 6. Don't let late payments end up in court

Council tax debts and unpaid bills can get out of hand. If you fall into financial difficulty get in touch with your local Citizens Advice Bureau (in your Yellow Pages). If you end up with a County Court Judgement (CCJ) against you, there will be problems in getting credit in the future.

### 7. Never go to a credit repair agency

These companies charge between £50 and £200 to improve your credit rating but are often just loan sharks. You don't need to pay to correct the details on your file – it can usually be done for free after you have paid to see your file.

## How to manage your credit cards better

Typically, credit cards mean you can take goods and services now and pay for them up to 56 days later. You can 'borrow' this money up to a set limit without arrangement fees and/or having to provide security. Also you can repay any outstanding borrowings at your own speed (subject to a small monthly minimum requirement). Having a credit card normally makes it easier to arrange other borrowing facilities too. But which one to choose?

- Seek a no-annual fee card with a low introductory rate and a competitive rate at the end of the discount period.
- If you're not 100% confident you'll be accepted for a card, apply for one with a slightly higher rate offer. These are generally easier to obtain.
- Don't move credit cards too often – if you do this more than once or twice in a two- to three-year period, credit card providers will stop offering you cards.
- Avoid immediate interest charges – check the small print to make sure interest is charged from the day cash is debited from your account, rather than from the day of purchase.
- Ignore payment protection insurance. There are usually so many exclusions and disclaimers, this expensive form of insurance is nearly worthless.

## Financial scandal! Beware these journalists' 'best-buy' advice

Don't be conned by popular financial magazines and newspaper reports. View their 'best-buy' reports with scepticism. These magazines and newspapers are part-funded by advertising revenues. Indeed, the advertisers often pay more attention to the publisher's bottom-line than the readers do.

This compromises the journalists' independence. How? Because if the magazine criticizes an advertiser's products, it may lose that advertising contract.

For each product praised in a financial review – such as mortgages, credit cards, pension schemes or ISA investments – check to see if the product provider has an ad elsewhere in that issue. Even better, look at product surveys in publications that don't accept advertising, like Which? magazine for example.

## Big City con! Why you should never believe your newspaper on New Year's Day

Don't trust the national newspapers' share tips of the year. It's a fact that most financial journalists have little training in accountancy or investment analysis. But do you have any idea how bad their share tips can be?

Look at these results, achieved during 2002 by share tips given for the coming 12 months over the Christmas and New Years' period 2001.

- The Sunday Telegraph
  Average Loss:   -52%
- The Independent
  Average Loss: -41%
- Midas in the Mail on Sunday
  Average Loss:   -59%
- The Sunday Times
  Average Loss:   -54%

What's worse, the market makers who control prices for individual shares ramp prices after a hot newspaper tip. Buy a share the day after a newspaper has tipped it, and you could be asked to pay up to 40% extra or even more.

## Use this finance insider's secret to find the best investment deals every time

Get the very best deal on mortgages, credit cards, bank accounts and ISAs. Simply go to the professional advisers' "bible" at www.moneyfacts.co.uk. It's where the newspapers and magazines go to get the data they use in their articles. Now you can cut out the middleman, and access this information direct too, for free.

# How to turn your credit card into a mortgage

Having trouble getting a mortgage? Use this clever strategy to boost the finance world's trust in you.

- Use your credit card more often, not less.
- Make sure you can afford to pay off the monthly bills.
- Clear all balances before they come due.

Once finance companies can see you are a responsible credit card holder, they will upgrade your creditworthiness. This will make getting a mortgage or other big loan much easier.

# Little-known tip to beat county court judgments

Avoid having damaging county court judgments on your credit reference agency files. Try to agree to an out-of-court agreement formalised using a little-known 'consent order'.

This is a legally binding agreement that's simply endorsed by the relevant court – and isn't registered anywhere else unless its terms and conditions are broken. Outcome? The claimant receives their money, and the defendant isn't blacklisted.

# Serious debts? Four steps to tackling your problem today

### Step #1: Work out where you are
- Take a sheet of paper and write down every penny you owe – loans, overdrafts, credit cards, store cards, HP agreements, and any other creditors.
- Do not include your mortgage. It is a form of investment.
- Add up your debts – this is your personal deficit.

### Step #2: Release easy cash instantly
Ask yourself these three questions about every recent purchase you've made:
- Does it add practical value to my life?
- Do I really need it?
- Is the item beautiful?

If you can't answer a resounding "Yes!" to these questions, sell it. Use the extra money to start repaying your debts fast.

### Step #3: Stem the flow of outgoing cash

- Right this instant, take every credit and store card in your possession and destroy it.
- Get out of the 'buying crap' trap. Quit buying expensive treats to make you feel better. These quick emotional fixes only add to your financial burden.
- Buy only what you need and what you can afford.

### Step #4: Pay cash – always

If you need to buy a household item, paying cash is the cheapest way possible. If you can't afford what you need, save until you can.

## Warning! Beware putting all your loans into one big debt

Avoid increasing interest repayments on your debts. Be wary of consolidating small debts into one big loan. Do your sums, and you may well find a single loan involves arrangement fees and a higher interest rate. They all add to your overall debt.

## What your bank doesn't want you to know about the '6-year rule'...

By law, bad debts can only be pursued for six years from the last written contact between creditor and debtor. For mortgage shortfalls, this periods rises to 12 years. So mortgage lenders are now pursuing ex-mortgagees for early 1990s' debts, for instance.

This means you can ignore any debts you have now outside the 6- or 12-year limit. There simply needs to have been no written correspondence on the matter for the appropriate period of time.

To help get your old loans safely through the 6- or 12-year anniversary, deal with all your other debts by telephone. Any written correspondence triggers a new six- or 12-year period, don't forget.

## Drowning in debt? How you can stay afloat for just £1 a week

Work out what you can afford to pay your creditors, and offer a nominal sum. For instance, one pound a week is more trouble to collect than it's worth. But if you've shown willing and made an offer, the courts will look more favourably on you if things get legal.

## Creditors chasing you? What you should know about 'full and final' offers...

If you have problems repaying debts you owe, and your lenders are pressing for you to repay quickly, it's good to know this valuable secret.

You should refuse your lender's 'full and final settlement' offer. Contrary to the title, it is always negotiable. If pressed, offer a settlement of 10% of the demand maximum. You will force your creditor to accept your situation, and work to resolve it more amicably.

## What the government won't tell you about stakeholder pensions...

Stakeholder pensions are not the best way to save for your retirement. Don't buy into one if you are still working. Personal pensions are poor value compared to final salary schemes – and they are also poor value compared to personal pensions ten years ago, when your money bought twice as much annuity.

Annuity returns are so poor right now, you will be better off investing in competing retirement savings schemes such as Individual Savings Accounts. ISAs don't have the upfront income tax breaks of pension schemes but are incredibly flexible.

Be wary of stakeholder pensions if you are still working, and make other savings arrangements to help fund your retirement.

## Already retired? How to turn £1,908 into £3,600 overnight

Stakeholders are not the best way to plan for forthcoming retirement. But they're great for a high-income return if you have already retired. You can get an income from your personal pension immediately!

Anyone between the ages of 50 and 75, who is not working, should consider investing in a stakeholder. For starters, 22% of your investment is paid by the government in the form of tax relief. So to get your annual limit of £3,600 in your pension you only pay £2,808 (under 2003/04 limits). If you then draw a pension immediately, you can take out a quarter of the £3,600 as tax-free cash. That gives you cash back of £900. In total, this strategy makes the net cost of an annual £3,600 pension contribution just £1,908.

Talk to your financial advisor about "immediate vesting". You won't get large sums of money to spend for free. But in percentage terms, it's a great way to offset falling bank and building society interest returns.

## Don't get fleeced by financial cowboys

Here are 3 simple steps to assess an independent financial advisor's honesty and quality.

- Ask your IFA about the commission they receive. The Financial Services Act states that commission must be disclosed to the client before any sale – don't let anyone tell you otherwise.
- Consider paying a flat fee. Ask your IFA to reinvest any commissions he might receive on your behalf.
- If you decide on a product (like a pension, insurance policy, mortgage or ISA for instance) on the strength of your IFA's advice, ask them to confirm in writing the reasons why they've recommended it to you. This will deter anyone trying to missell you a product. You'll have written evidence if you choose to complain.

## These 3 questions uncover bad financial advice

There's no guarantee of performance from any financial product. Investments may go down as well as up. But if you feel you've been ripped off by a financial advisor, there are 3 simple questions you can ask yourself to judge your claim before you start proceedings to decide whether your claim is worthwhile.

- Was your attitude to risk not taken into account?
- Were your circumstances not factored properly?
- Did the IFA fail to ask you about your financial goals in enough depth?

Answer "yes" to one or more of these questions, and you could have a good case for compensation from the dodgy IFA who ripped you off.

## How to get compensation from a dodgy financial advisor

If you believe you have indeed been sold a poor or inappropriate product, follow it up with a formal complaint. You may be eligible for big compensation. Make your complaint effective, by complaining to the right people at the right time.

- Firstly, complain to the advisor who sold you the product. Write to them, stating you wish to make a complaint, and explaining what you're complaining about.
- You should receive a written reply within 7 business days, saying that your case is being dealt with.
- You should receive another letter within 2 months explaining the outcome of this internal investigation.
- You can accept this explanation or, if you are still unhappy, take your case to the relevant ombudsman.
- Send them photocopies of any correspondence between you and your advisor. You have six months to bring your case to the relevant regulatory body if you fail to reach an agreement with the service provider.
Financial Ombudsman Service, tel: 0845 080 1800 or visit www.financial-ombudsman.org.uk.

## Professional investor's secret tracks the FTSE with no stamp duty and no management fees

This great investment idea acts just like an index tracker, but without charging you management fees. And it can be traded easily and quickly, just like a share – but without costing you a penny in stamp duty!

Exchange Traded Funds aren't widely recommended by the investment industry. The sales commission isn't attractive to IFAs and banks. But each share in an ETF invests in a range of shares, giving you cheap and easy access to broader exposure, with lower risk, than buying individual shares. Finance professionals use them instead of tracker funds. Visit www.ishares.net today to see what they could do for you.

## Why is your IFA hiding this low-risk, high-return investment from you?

There is a form of investment anyone can access, that pays up to 7% interest risk-free. But don't expect your bank or building society to recommend it to you. Nor will you hear about it from your financial advisor.

Permanent Interest Bearing Shares (Pibs) do not pay any commission to salesmen promoting them. Essentially, Pibs are building society debt, issued when societies want to raise money for acquisition or expansion. They pay a fixed rate of interest and are much safer than shares or corporate bonds. At the moment they are paying a rate of 6% to 7% – nearly double the best rates in a deposit account.

- You get a better deal if you hold Pibs for the longer term.
- Watch the FTSE. Pibs cost less when shares have had a good run.
- Put your Pibs into an ISA to get the dividends tax free.
- You usually have to buy in blocks of £2,000 or more.
- Currently, there are ten Pibs in issue. You can buy them through a regular stockbroker.
- Check prices in the weekend national newspapers, including the Financial Times and The Times Money.

## Big City con! Why so-called 'ethical' funds are anything but...

Don't be conned by 'green' fund managers. Fair-traded, organic, honest and renewable they ain't. Most of these advisers do little more than pick the most green from the top 200 UK companies. But this just means they will pick Vodafone over BP.

Plus, the "no go" areas you might expect to find excluded from an ethical fund are often still in there. To build an honest fund, campaigners ask fund managers to screen investments for 11 nasty habits – alcohol, tobacco, nuclear, arms, gambling, animal testing, pharmaceutical, fur, environment, endangered species and human rights. Yet the biggest funds screen for only 5 of these 11 categories! If you want to build a truly ethical investment portfolio, it's better to research and select the shares yourself.

## Your step-by-step guide to safety-first investing

Here's a sensible, low-risk strategy that should generate decent returns on your hard-earned money:

### 1. Beware free advice
If you're offered free financial advice, ask yourself "What's in it for them?". Con-artists use internet newsgroups and chat rooms to ramp shares by talking up their prospects.

### 2. Don't get befuddled

Beware any investment you can't understand. If it's too complex, or you know nothing about the industry it operates in, stay away.

### 3. Low returns, low risk

And vice-versa. But many investors lose out because they want to believe they can invest with low risks and high returns. The classic hallmark of a scam.

### 4. Spread your risk

If you put all your cash in one investment, you're risking every penny if it goes belly-up. Spread your risk across different investments instead. A wise allocation will include:

● Rainy day protection – at least 3 months' spending money stashed in an easy-access account.
● Bricks & mortar – your own home could be the best investment you ever make.
● Government gilts – rock-solid but boring investments, made as a loan to the government and paying guaranteed interest each year.
● Blue-chip shares – big-name companies might not offer much growth for your money. But they are safer and often pay good annual dividends.
● Smaller company stocks – AIM and Ofex-listed shares offer greater risk, but greater possible rewards.

### 5. Use your tax-free limits

You can hold almost any investment in an ISA. This special account simply does away with tax on any gains you make. Be sure to use your maximum limits every year.

### 6. Avoid overseas investments

If you do want exposure to overseas markets, buy into a fund run by a UK company. Laws in other countries are designed to protect investors living there. If things go wrong or you get ripped off, you won't have the legal fallback you enjoy as a British investor buying financial products here in the UK.

## Not started saving for your pension yet?

Research by Legal & General suggests that every hour you delay pension savings could mean £2 less in your pension fund. Industry experts say you should save a percentage of your salary equal to half your age.

## How to buy the UK's safest investments with no commission

The Bank of England's Debt Management Unit is now responsible for selling government gilts direct to UK private individuals. Visit www.dmo.gov.uk to read the Private Investor's Guide and access the necessary application forms.

## Seven simple tools City professionals use to find bargain stocks and shares

Using nothing more than a daily paper and a pocket calculator, you can join the investment world's sharpest minds in uncovering unloved shares, set to soar. Use these key ratios in a company's accounts next time you go bargain hunting in the City:

● **Dividend yield**
Published daily in the Financial Times, for shares listed on the London Stock Exchange. A dividend is the money paid on each share from the company's net profits. Small companies often don't pay dividends – they plough their profits back into growing their business. But if a large company doesn't increase its dividend, or cuts it, you can bet it needs the money simply to survive. As the share price falls though, the dividend yield (dividend compared against share price) will rise. This could make the stock a relative bargain.

● **Earnings per Share (EPS)**
The most important ratio in the City. Represents a company's post-tax profits divided by the total number of shares in issue. Generally, an EPS higher than the cash flow per share (shown on the cash-flow statement in the company's annual report) indicates a company with strong value. A steadily rising EPS indicates financial health and growth.

● **Dividend cover**
This tells you whether a company can afford to pay its shareholders their dividend or not. Divide the EPS by the dividend announced by the company. The result should be 1 or higher. If it's less than 1, avoid it. The firm hasn't got the cash to pay its dividend, and is digging into cash reserves.

- **Price-earnings ratio (PE)**

The PE is often referred to in financial journalism, and it's quoted daily for each company in the FT. It's calculated by dividing the share price by the earnings per share. If you're investing for the mid to long term, look for shares with a low PER compared with other firms in its sector. If you want a fast profit though, you could buy a stock with a high PE. Although these shares are overvalued, the price will have upwards momentum. Investors who move quickly can make money. But you must sell the stock before it rebounds.

- **Price/sales (PSR)**

Use this ratio for new companies with fast growth, but no profits yet. Divide last year's sales figure by the market value of a firm. Buy if a stock has a low PSR compared to others within its sector – especially if it's less than one. For market leaders, the PSR will be around 3 or 4.

- **Price/research ratio (PRR)**

For companies with high research expenses, such as pharmaceuticals and biotech, the PRR is a good cross check to the PSR. The PRR is the market capitalization of the company divided by its research expenses for the past year. This number should be low.

- **Return on capital employed (ROCE)**

This measures management performance. The ROCE is calculated as profits before tax and interest on loan repayments, divided by capital employed. In sectors like retail, the share price will increase if there is a rising ROCE. A company can improve its ROCE by buying back shares from the stock market. This can also improve its share price. Buybacks are a definite buy signal for you – but you have to buy as soon as the buyback is announced to get the maximum financial gain. Watch out for news of buybacks in the FT and on financial websites.

- **Compare ratios**

A stock may appear good value on the basis of one ratio, but poor value on another. Use a number of ratios in analysing a stock, and look for consistency.

## How to become your own local bank manager

Credit unions are a little-known revolution in the banking and insurance world. These co-operatives, owned and managed by their members in much the same way as a building society, give each member voting rights independent of their level of savings.

Members take an active role in running the union, attending the AGM, proposing policies, debating policies, and electing persons of trust to manage the union. As a saving and borrowing member of a CU, you get access to free life savings insurance (LSI) and loan protection insurance (LPI) cover.

Credit union shares are withdrawable but, if you leave your savings alone, they can earn interest or annual dividends. Some of the larger, longer established CUs pay annual dividends of up to 8%. And by law a credit union may not charge more than 1% per month of the unpaid balance of a loan. This makes them a great source of cheap credit.

To find your nearest credit union, visit www.abcul.org or call the Association of British Credit Unions on 0161 832 3694. They can also give details on setting up your own credit union.

## London art gallery owner shares 9 top tips for investing in beautiful pictures, sculptures and prints

When you see the work of an artist you like, and you find he or she is in the area, ask the gallery if it is possible to visit the artist in his or her studio. Many artists have regular open calling hours.

**1. Always call ahead to make sure it is all right.**

**2. Never just drop in on a working artist,** unless you have been invited to by them.

**3. Trust your eye –** buy what you like and not what you think you should be buying. Never buy anything you don't like, even if you think it might turn out to be a worthwhile investment. Remember, you will be living with it for years yet.

**4. Don't be afraid of asking** for more information about the artist and about their techniques. But don't feel that you have to understand what they "mean" by a particular painting.

**5. Get extra value** when buying something. Ask the dealer (or the gallery) to give you a copy of the artist's CV with it.

**6. Make a note** on the back of the painting of when and where you bought it, and for how much. When your grandchildren inherit it they will know all about it!

**7. Beware of reproduction prints,** which are worthless. They may be dubbed "limited edition prints, signed and individually numbered by the artist". But these are different from artists-made prints (etchings, screenprints etc) which are great to buy (and often cheaper than paintings). Make sure any prints you invest in are original and one of an edition of only 75 or less.

**8. Go to art fairs** and seek out galleries that have the kind of thing you like. The Affordable Art Fair can be a great place to start (see www.affordableartfair.com). There are three of these held each year across the country and they can be a great place to see a lot of art on sale at one event.

**9. Visit degree shows at art colleges.** But bear in mind that often the artists' styles will still be developing and many students make their ' finals' pieces too big or too wacky for people to live with in their own home!

## Scam warning! Why 'wine investment' leaflets should go straight in the bin

Like all alternative investments, there are no regulations to cover wine or investments in other drinks. Over the past ten years there have been plenty of smooth-talking sharks attracted to gaining easy money by conning people into buying unsuitable drinks investments. In the UK alone, these sharks may have turned over £150 million over the past decade. But so far, only five people have been jailed.

## Watch out for these six warning signs...

- Any cold call from a slick operator trying to interest you in wine investment. Don't give them the time of day.
- Letters offering free confidential reports on companies you hold shares in and then go on to push wine investments. This approach succeeded for companies like Boington & Fredericks, City Vintners, Goldman Williams, James Hewitt Associated and Liquid Acquisitions. People

thought they were making a sound wine investment buying wine from them. But they actually paid 100% or more over the odds.

- Sole traders or partnerships, rather than limited companies. You can sue sole traders and partnerships for any money lost. But you have to find them first. The government DTI only has responsibility for registered companies.
- Lies such as being told fine wine is not affected by economic cycles. This is rubbish. Fine wine prices may not suffer the volatility of stocks and shares. But the price and demand for fine wine follows normal economic and wealth cycles.
- Pushy sales techniques. If you're told this is a special deal, and you have to make your mind up now, ignore it.
- Incomplete price lists. A company that cannot give you a price list of the wines it is offering. All legitimate companies will be able to supply full details.

## Also be sure to check...

1. How long has a company been trading?
Find out for free at www.companieshouse.gov.uk.

2. Are you paying the right price for the wine?
Find out for free at www.wine-searcher.com.

3. Does this wine investment company have a history of defrauding clients?
Find out for free at www.investdrinks.org.

# YOUR PERSONAL SAFETY

## Beat the thieves! 107 tips for keeping your home, your family and your wallet safe!

# Professional thieves, the SAS and Los Angeles Police Department reveal 107 tips for beating crime and staying safe

The British government claims we now have more police than ever before. But try telling that to the four million householders who suffered the upset and loss of burglary, vandalism and car theft last year.

And what about the 20,000 crimes involving guns (up more than 30% in just 5 years)…or the shocking fact that 4% of us were violently attacked last year…or the soaring number of muggings, break-ins and credit card frauds committed by Britain's ever-growing mob of drug-crazed criminals?

We each have to take responsibility for our own protection today. And in these pages, ex-burglars, SAS soldiers, the Los Angeles Police Department, and professional bodyguards share little-known secrets you can use to make your wealth invisible to aggressive criminals. Plus, their expert training also reveals simple steps you can follow to protect your life and liberty should you become a target.

## Warning! Thieves are targeting your name, your date of birth and your credit card details right now

Identity theft is the robbery and misuse of your personal data. The Public Interest Research Group calls it the "fastest growing crime in the Western world". Using details such as your name, date of birth and mother's maiden name, a professional criminal can impersonate you and commit serious financial crimes in your name.

You won't know you've been targeted until police or unknown debt-collectors are banging on your door, demanding explanations or payment.

Now, the number of reported identity frauds in Britain has doubled in the last two years. It costs law-abiding citizens and companies £1.3 billion each year. Here's how to defend your name, your date of birth and your credit card details.

## 1. Keep an eye out for these danger signs

- Bin bags mysteriously ripped open outside your house? It might be stray dogs or foxes at work... or it could be an ID thief after your credit card slips and bank statements.
- Carefully review all financial statements, utility and phone bills for accuracy. Inexplicable transactions or activity may indicate the presence of ID thieves.
- Report inaccuracies immediately and ensure such entries are amended.

Regularly obtain copies of your credit report from credit agencies. Check these for discrepancies – references to accounts you don't own, credit checks made by institutions you've never sought credit from, and strange addresses. Report problems immediately and have credit agencies amend your records. Obtain your credit records from:

www.equifax.co.uk
Tel: 0845 600 1772
www.experian.co.uk
Tel: 0870 241 4297

## 2. Guard against intruders and opportunists

Take precautions with sensitive paperwork and data. ID thieves are particularly interested in obtaining these details:

- your full name
- address
- phone number
- national insurance number
- drivers licence number
- bank account details
- credit card numbers
- telephone calling cards
- birth certificate
- passport

Store this information and sensitive paperwork in a secure place known only to you.

### 3. Beware! Your rubbish tells tales

Don't leave sensitive paperwork out for the dustman. All unwanted paperwork relating to financial and personal matters should be shredded or burnt before disposal. A shredding machine can cost less than £80 from your local stationery shop.

### 4. Don't get mugged for sensitive data

Carry as few ID documents and credit cards around with you as possible. Never carry pin numbers along with credit cards.

### 5. Safeguard your personal post

Your letterbox offers a goldmine to the professional ID thief. If you live in a residential block and everyone's post is left by the front door for collection, exposed to scrutiny of other residents and visitors, then foil possible interception by using an accommodation address. For a small monthly fee an accommodation address will receive post on your behalf and forward it or hold it for personal collection. Consult your Yellow Pages under "Accommodation Addresses" or "Secretarial Services".

### 6. Computer and email files

These hold financial and personal data, leaving it vulnerable to house-breakers and ID thieves. Protect your computer's data from further crimes by ensuring all sensitive files and documents on your computer are encrypted. Without your private key, snoops can't access encrypted files. Download Pretty Good Privacy (PGP) encryption free of charge from www.pgpi.org.

### 7. Stop giving out personal details

These days more and more people want as much information about you as they can get. Avoid revealing personal information about yourself or your financial affairs unless you are legally obliged to do so.

### 8. Never reveal your mother's maiden name

It's commonly used by banks as a security phrase to verify who you are. As good as a skeleton key to an ID thief.

### 9. Don't create online profiles on the internet

If you must provide information to register at a website, give fictional details. Ensure emails containing sensitive data are encrypted. Never send credit card payment details over the internet without ensuring that the connection is encrypted. Look for a locked padlock icon at the bottom right-hand corner of your screen.

## What the police won't tell you about making your home 14 times more secure

The most common home security systems are 'bells-only'. But due to the cost of false alarms, the police are no longer obliged to act unless there's evidence the offence is still in progress. Plus, only one in ten house alarms get reported to the police. There are as many complaints about the noise made to Environmental Health Departments!

But the police must attend a monitored security system that has a maintenance contract. A signal goes to a control room where false alarms are screened out. Information on file gives directions to your property, whether to expect a dog, and who you've entrusted with spare keys. Less than 3% of households adopt this system, even though it's not expensive. An alarm system costs up to £500 and maintenance costs around 82p a day.

Burglars often know which alarm systems are monitored and stay away from houses that have them. For example, you are 14 times less likely to be burgled with a monitored security system installed. Experienced criminals know what brands of system are monitored and move on.

## Going away for 3 days or more? Act on these 5 security measures right now

**1. Cancel all milk,** newspaper and other deliveries.

**2. Make sure your garage** is secure and alarmed if necessary.

**3. Invest in some timer switches** and programme lights or appliances such as TVs and radios to switch on and off throughout the day and night. To the casual observer, and potential thief, it will seem as though your house is occupied.

**4. Let trusted neighbours** know you'll be away, and ask them to keep an eye on your property. Notify them who they should get in touch with in the event of an emergency.

**5. For real crime protection** value if you will be away for two weeks or more, ask if friends are willing to drop by a couple of times a week, to clear post from the doorway, water plants and generally make the place seem inhabited.

## A professional burglar writes...

Make sure your home isn't burgled in your absence. Tell as few friends and neighbours as possible that you're going away. Many break-ins can be linked to these people, either directly, or because they've talked to others. Teenage children especially can give away your absence to clever con men. Also install these deterrents to ward off attack when you're away:

- Gravelled driveways and gardens. Would-be burglars don't want to be noisy.
- Lock the garage door (even if it's empty). Burglars often check to see if the car's not there. If they can't see, they can't be sure and will go away.
- Put a handmade 'Danger: New Doberman' sign on the back door. Most burglaries take place at the back of properties, and many burglars will go elsewhere rather than tackle a large, dangerous dog.

## Stay safe from road rage and carjacking with these top eleven SAS tactics

Drive safely – day and night, in rural and urban areas – using the skills of defensive driving taught by Britain's security services.

### 1. Think ahead to minimise risk

Motorists are most vulnerable when the car is stopped, especially when they've broken down. To stay safe, plan your route beforehand. Carry a map to avoid having to ask directions. If you do get lost, ask at a garage, pub or shop rather than a stranger in the street. Always carry a torch, a filled petrol can, and jump leads.

### 2. Ensure your car is well serviced

If you haven't already, join the AA or RAC breakdown recovery service. Even the most basic roadside cover will get you driven or towed home safely.

### 3. Keep a mobile phone in your glove compartment.

This way, you can call for help without leaving the car.

### 4. Allow plenty of time for your journey

This means you can drive defensively and safely. Use major roads wherever possible. Many carjackers and thieves target stationary cars in quiet minor roads.

### 5. Be wary of overtaking on remote roads

Drivers may interpret this as a challenge, and respond aggressively.

### 6. Avoid using the right-hand lane

Except for overtaking, be wary of straying into the fast lane. Even if you're driving at the speed limit, another driver may want to go faster still. Let them.

### 7. Beware young male drivers

And don't be provoked by them. Men under 25 are a major source of road rage  aggression. Many of them feel they have to prove their masculinity when driving. And they often try to antagonise other drivers into competitive driving, especially at traffic lights and long stretches. Do not respond.

### 8. Always keep a safe distance from the car in front

Keep at least two car lengths between you and the car ahead – even when you're travelling slowly or stationary. If you sit too near the car in front, the driver behind can pull up close and box you in. This is now a common tactic for aggressive carjackings. Give yourself room to drive away if you feel uneasy.

### 9. Don't invite carjacking

Car jackers and thieves operate most often at traffic lights. Cars are stationary, and drivers relax for a moment. Stay on guard. Keep all doors locked, and any valuables out of sight. Never switch off the ignition or open your window to anyone. There have been recent cases in London and Yorkshire of carjackers posing as windscreen cleaners. You have been warned.

### 10. If you're scared, use this VIP bodyguard's trick

If someone appears threatening, shift your body to the centre of the car and sound your horn continuously. You will draw attention from witnesses. Drivers of celebrities and VIPs are taught to use this trick in emergency situations.

### 11. Carry a camera to protect yourself

It's rare, but if your car does come under attack, point a camera at your assailant. Most will back off when faced with potential photographic evidence of their actions.

## Are you being stalked by an ex-spouse, business partner or ID thief?

Imagine if your ex-spouse, business partner or ID thief wanted to uncover details of your financial and personal life. It wouldn't be difficult. Any cowboy telephone engineer could supply them with the basic equipment to keep you under surveillance… and you'd know nothing about it.

In fact, it could be happening to you right now. Take these four simple precautions to defend your privacy if you have cause for concern.

**1. Make sensitive phone calls from public payphones.**

**2. Get a 'pay-as-you-go' mobile phone deal.** No contracts, no credit checks, no line rental agreements and no ID requirements to buy one. But beware. The government is likely to crack down on the anonymous purchase of mobile phones at some point. So buy now, while it's still possible.

**3. Stay invisible.** Switch off your mobile phone when not using it. It transmits location data when switched on – enabling investigators to pinpoint the location of the phone and track your movements.

**4. Keep unexpected incoming private calls private.** Set up an anonymous voicemail service. This is useful if there are calls you can't take at work or home. For example, maybe you are looking for a new job. Premier Voicemail Ltd provides London numbers or local rate 0845 numbers (£80 and £120 per annum) and accepts postal order prepayments. Visit www.premiervoicemail.co.uk for details.

## Women! Are you in danger from the 10 early warning signs of an abusive relationship?

Studies show women in abusive relationships often remain in denial until it's too late. By the time they accept their partner is manipulating, controlling and threatening them, he has already become violent and dangerous.

If you're at all uncomfortable in your current relationship – or your friends keep warning you about your partner's behaviour – check whether you're at risk from these 10 early warning signs.

1. Does your partner make you feel afraid simply by using threatening looks or gestures?

2. Does he regularly smash and break things when he loses his temper?

3. Does he ever blame you for making him angry?

4. Has he hidden or taken any of your things away from you as 'punishment'?

5. Does he call you names, upset you on purpose, or belittle you at every opportunity?

6. Does he demand to know your every movement when you're out of the house?

7. Has he told you not to go out when he's not at home?

8. Has he cut you out of any big decisions you should have taken together recently?

9. Does he take the money you earn from you as soon as you receive it?

10. If you're not working, has he stopped you from applying for jobs or attending interviews?

## The sad truth about 'Have-a-go heroes'

If you are the victim of a mugging, don't resist. Try to stay calm, and view the situation as a business transaction. They want to get as much from you as fast as they can. You want to hand over as little as possible, and remain safe. Muggings usually involve violence only when the victim puts up a fight.

## Why you should always carry a worthless wallet

If you've nothing to give to a street robber, you're more likely to be assaulted in retaliation. But give them low-value and worthless items that appear valuable, and they'll think they've hit the jackpot, and will run away.

So to get rid of bagsnatchers fast, hand over a wallet full of expired cards, low-value foreign currency, supermarket loyalty cards, old membership cards, and useless bits of paper.

## This diplomat's secret could save your life

Your passport is a prime target for thieves operating at airports. And in some countries (Bolivia, Israel and Peru as examples), you have to take it with you at all times. So carrying a 'camouflage passport' may save you losing your real British passport. You can hand them this fake instead.

Even more importantly, a camouflage passport could save your life. If you are the victim of a hijack, your false passport could be used to persuade terrorists you are not from Britain, and are not a supporter of American foreign policy.

A camouflage passport looks exactly like a real passport, but is issued by a non-existent country. It contains your photo, exit and entry visa stamps, a registration number, official seal, and a security hologram. It can also be issued in an alternative name.

For details, search the internet. Prices for camouflage passports are high, and you must make sure you are comfortable dealing with the shadowy organisations willing to produce them.

## Car thieves' secret for safer parking at night

Safeguard your car by parking only in well-populated areas at night. Don't bother parking in car parks. Opportunist thieves are less likely to operate in full view of passers-by. And don't assume a CCTV car park is safer. They rarely have anyone in attendance. And you will find it impossible to claim negligence against the car park owner in the event of theft. Legal precedents ensure that cases are dismissed by county court judges.

## Who's accessing your PC when you surf the internet?

To surf the net in privacy, turn on 'cookie notices' in your browser. Cookies are small pieces of data sent and stored by your computer, containing passwords and other useful information. They enable you to access your favourite sites more quickly. But they can also be used by unscrupulous sites to trawl for data; tracking where you go, and what you look at. This data can be used to create a profile about you for marketers.

## "Recently divorced 43-year old woman seeks a caring man..."

Women! Beware when placing personal ads. If you are genuinely seeking someone to help you put the pain of the past behind you, stating it in your ad could prove dangerous. An ad like this sounds as though you may need counselling, not a new friend. Plus, it puts you at risk of attracting predatory charmers or chronic manipulators looking for a new project.

## The little-known truth about spam emails

Don't ever reply to an email sender you don't recognize. Unsolicited emails are used by spam marketers to find out whether your email address is active. By replying, you alert them that it is – adding to the value of your address on marketing lists, and guaranteeing more junk emails in future.

## Warning! Your work colleagues could be reading your private emails

Choose a combination of letters and numbers for your computer password at work. Make it completely nonsensical to other people. But ensure it's simple enough for you to remember. Avoid using the name of your partner, pet or favourite football team. These are the commonly used passwords. And it is advisable to change your password regularly as well, just to be safe.

## Eight little-known ways the super-rich avoid being robbed

If you own your own home, have more than £5,000 in savings or investments, and have two or more cars on the drive, then con men and thieves will consider you a very good target. To them, you are wealthy enough to make robbing you worthwhile.

Britain's super-rich know how to protect themselves though. Here's how millionaires defend against theft and robbery:

1. Keep a low profile on a day-to-day basis. Crooks are constantly on the look out for visibly wealthy individuals.

2. Dress in high street (rather than designer) fashions.

3. Don't wear expensive jewellery

4. Drive a less sophisticated car for day-to-day travel

5. Pay cash (rather than by credit card)

6. Keep expensive cars, your boat, luxury caravan etc stored away from your home.

7. Avoid personal publicity. One Suffolk man who talked publicly of using his wealth to restart his son's private school was burgled shortly after appearing on television. Better stay out of sight. The rich do

8. Don't trust strangers with your status. Today's friend, colleague or casual acquaintance might be tomorrow's fraudster or informer. As far as your financial status is concerned, work strictly on a need-to-know basis.

## Warning! How supermarket loyalty cards can betray you to the taxman

If you'd rather the taxman didn't snoop on you, beware using supermarket loyalty cards. They allow the store to record detailed information about your spending habits. And the Inland Revenue is now requesting access to supermarket records as part of its latest tax investigation strategy.

## The secret timebomb in your GP's filing cabinet

Information about your health can affect your job prospects, your ability to get a mortgage or loan, and insurance claims. And with advances in genetic technologies, you could soon suffer discrimination for diseases you don't even have yet.

You need to make sure that this sensitive and potentially damaging information does not fall into the wrong hands. It could explode to ruin many areas of your private life and future health.

### 1. Protect your career

Medical discrimination is illegal, but it happens every day. Taking anti-depressants or seeing a psychiatrist can prejudice your employers against you and make you the subject of office gossip. Don't reveal any treatment. Similarly, don't discuss plans to start a family at work – employers have been known to transfer women to less desirable jobs in anticipation of maternity leave.

### 2. Only reveal the bare minimum

Everyone assumes a complete health record is necessary to obtain the best and most specific health care – but they are wrong. In the vast majority of cases, past medical information is not taken into account when reaching a diagnosis. And in emergency situations doctors don't have time to access a patient's medical records.

### 3. Beware your psychological profile

Even if you have never suffered a serious illness, your record gives your GP a psychological profile of you. Frequent consultations about minor illnesses could label you as neurotic. Past abortions or smoking will suggest a tendency to carelessness or risk-taking. Depression can imply someone struggling to cope or emotionally incompetent. And having no health record at all could signal that you are not careful or responsible at all.

### 4. Check your record is accurate

Book an appointment with your GP today, and review your health record in detail. Have him explain anything you don't understand – and amend any inaccuracies on the record. Look out for incomplete information. Maybe you had a cancer scare and were sent to a specialist, only to be given the all-clear later.

### 5. Set privacy standards with your doctor

Inform your doctor that under no circumstances are test results to be left on voicemail, email or faxed through to you. Many workplaces routinely access email and phonecalls. Call your GP yourself for results on a private line and always verify your identity. Make sure your request for privacy is recorded in your medical file.

### 6. Don't settle for second-class private healthcare

The only information your doctor is obliged to share with a health insurer is an actual diagnosis. Having had hundreds of tests that never led to a diagnosis of a specific disease or condition should not prejudice your right to quality healthcare. When you make an insurance claim, you must sign a release form to authorize release of medical information. Note on the form that your authorization is limited to just one year. Your insurer always has to have your permission before it can get this information – so the less they know the better.

### 7. Insist on confidential treatment

Today, you can go online for healthcare – anonymously. There are many simple medical tests you can do yourself at home. Tests for cystitis, bowel disorders, diabetes, digestive disorder, menopause or prostate disorders can be bought online at www.homehealth-uk.com along with detailed instructions of how to carry them out. The site is a secure environment, and all identifying information is deleted from the system afterwards, so you can be assured of your medical privacy.

## Business travellers! How to check your destination's security status

Do your homework before you jet off to an exotic location. Visit the Foreign Office's website at www.fco.gov.uk/travel/countryadvice.asp. Check the 'Travel Advice Notices' posted there to assess the current conditions in the specific country you'll be visiting.

## How 5 minutes with a photocopier could save you 7 days of hell on holiday

Before you travel abroad, photocopy any travel and ID documents, and credit cards. This will speed up the process of replacement if lost or stolen. It can take up to days and even weeks to arrange replacements otherwise.

Carry these copies separate from your originals. And keep another set for emergencies with a friend back home too.

## How to protect yourself against aeroplane hijackings and security alerts

Here are two little-known secrets about staying safe when flying overseas.

- Book yourself into the VIP waiting lounge. It might cost you £15 for a year's access, but security incidents usually happen in areas of easy access. Membership of the International Airline Passenger Association carries the right to wait in specially reserved lounges with extra comfort and facilities (visit www.iapa.com).
- When flying, book a seat on wide-bodied planes like the Boeing 747. According to the US Overseas Security Advisory Council, hijackers tend to avoid these aircraft as they carry too many passengers.

## Six simple tips to stay safe on overseas holidays

1. Be careful when choosing a cab at the airport. Only use those vehicles with official markings.

2. When your driver delivers you to your destination, leave the passenger door open until you've checked all your bags have been unloaded.

3. If your hotel uses electronic keys, ask the clerk to re-swipe the card when you check in. This way you know you are starting with a fresh key code.

4. In your hotel room, use a cable lock to secure your luggage into one big bundle before you go out. It's difficult for a thief to walk off with three or more items of luggage tethered together!

5. Lock your door, use your security chain and use the peephole to identify people who knock at your door. And use a doorstopper alarm to alert you if anyone tries to enter your room. You can buy this and other travel security tools from www.magellans.com.

6. When driving in a hire car, be very wary of damsels in distress, "accidents" or people flagging you down. Criminals have been known to stage situations in order to ensnare victims.

## The little-known reason why pickpockets shout "Thief!" in busy crowds

It's an old trick, but it works. Pickpockets often shout "Stop thief" before they strike in the middle of busy markets and crowded High Streets.

Why? It makes everyone feel for their wallets, to make sure they've still got them. And they look towards the noise, putting them off guard against personal attack. Meanwhile, the pickpocket's mate watches where people have felt to check their wallet… and steals it by sneaking up behind them as the hubbub dies down.

## Four hot tips for safer travel from the Los Angeles Police Department

- Self-ticketing machines for airport bus tickets etc. Thieves love them, because you have to concentrate on dealing with the machine.

- Coat hooks on toilet doors. After hooks were removed from all rest-area stalls at the Pennsylvania Turnpike, it hurt thieves' business so much they put the hooks back up themselves! Keep your bag on the floor between your legs instead.

- Security X-ray machines. Don't get separated from your bag at security checkpoints. Wait until your route through the metal detector is clear before putting your bag on the conveyor belt. Thieves can take your stuff while you're stuck behind someone who sets off the metal detector.

- Tag your bags. Always put your ID tag on the outside and inside of your bags. Handles can come off during baggage handling.

# TRADE SECRETS
## How to get FREE holidays, FREE travel... even FREE money right now!

# 197 insider tips for living the high life... without breaking the bank

It is well known that the super-rich tend to be tight with their money. How else do you think they stay rich? But few people realise the tricks used by famous celebrities and millionaire businesspeople can bag you big discounts on the finer things in life, too.

Staff working inside the entertainment, travel and restaurant trades reveal that, every day, thousands of ordinary people 'upgrade' their way to free holidays, books, DVDs, first class airline seats, and free meals in top restaurants. Their secret? Knowing when and how to ask for more than you can afford.

Plus, if you've ever suffered bad service or cheeky staff, this chapter shows how you can get your revenge. These hot tips come from deep inside the country's leading businesses...where serious complaints can cause havoc   delivering the results you want, straight away.

## How the super-rich avoid this 15% restaurant rip-off

Watch out for a new trick being played on unwary diners by some of London's most expensive restaurants. On the menu, it states that a service charge of 15% will be added to your bill. But the bill itself doesn't remind you of this. Then, on the credit card slip, they leave a space for your "Gratuity".

Result? Unwary customers pay the service charge twice. Always check the adding up on your restaurant bill (as do the truly wealthy whenever they dine out). Make sure nothing has been added in "error" –increasingly common at larger Christmas and New Year parties.

## This little-known trick ensures you only eat in the very best restaurants

It's ironic, but the greater the choice in a restaurant, the worse the food usually is. Simply check the menu in the window. Better restaurants offer fewer dishes. They order limited daily supplies of fresh food to avoid wastage.

Oriental food is different though. Even the best Chinese restaurants offer more choice, because they use the same basic ingredients, mixed with different sauces.

## Why you should never eat out on a Monday

Monday is a terrible day to eat out. Fresh deliveries haven't come in, and any advertised "specials" are likely to be leftovers from the weekend. Never, ever eat fish or seafood in a restaurant on Monday – unless you want to get sick. Make your reservations for special occasions on a Tuesday instead. The kitchen will be freshly stocked, and the chef will be well rested after taking Sunday or Monday off.

## How come the Germans always get good holidays?

When researching an upcoming holiday, German tourists ask to know the size of the hotel room – down to the exact square metre. They also demand to know exactly what they will get for their money before booking. If you're looking for an apartment that, say, sleeps six, do what the Germans do. You don't want to end up with three people sleeping on a sofa-bed!

## The best ways to get 'bumped' and enjoy free flights, free hotels and up to £200 in cash

Airlines routinely overbook all their flights by 6% because they expect a certain number of "no show" passengers. But this causes mayhem if everyone does turn up, especially on busy routes and during the summer.

To solve this hiccup, airlines routinely ask if anyone wants to wait until the next seat becomes available on an upcoming flight. Volunteers usually get to negotiate the compensation they receive. But if too few volunteers come forward, the airline then has to choose who to 'bump' at random.

Obviously, most people find it very inconvenient, and hate being bumped against their will. The European Union now demands airlines offer larger compensation packages to anyone 'bumped' in this way. For short-haul flights, it may be £125 cash, plus free flight and hotel accommodation. For long-haul, the cash compensation may reach £380. You can bet the airlines don't like being told how much compensation they should pay!

This situation offers you a great chance to enjoy free travel and free hotel accommodation, plus a cash payment if you wish.

- Make a reservation only if a flight is almost full. If there are less than eight seats available, some people will most likely be bumped.
- Look for flights on heavily travelled days. Fridays are especially good for short-haul flights in Europe.
- Identify routes flown by small-bodied aircraft like 727s and 737s.
- When the airline asks for volunteers, step right up.
- Be careful not to seem over-eager for compensation. Volunteering means you're willing to get bumped in return for compensation. The airline would rather not know it can mean a free flight, free accommodation and a cash payment to you!

## These three magic words uncover the cheapest airline tickets

These three words will ensure your travel agent gives you the cheapest deal available for your airline tickets. Simply specify you want the "lowest possible fare", because they may have special deals available that do not fall under "economy" or "APEX".

But beware. Not every travel agent will be equally competent or motivated to find you the cheapest possible ticket for your flight. So a good strategy is to book the best-value, fully refundable fare early, then continue looking for something better to pop up. Be sure your first ticket is 100% refundable before you book another ticket.

## How to rent a hire car at 15% off... and enjoy a free extension on your time too

Stop hiring cars directly from the rental companies. And don't simply assume 'preferential rates' deals from airlines, tour operators or hotels are cheapest either. To get anything up to 15% off the list price of a good hire car from Hertz, Avis and all the other leading rental firms, book via www.carhire4less.co.uk instead.

And when you collect your car, ask when it is due back – exactly when. Some 24-hour hired cars are allowed an extra hour's grace. Others can be returned at any time during the appropriate morning or afternoon, as long as they've not been previously booked out. But some rented cars must be back strictly within the 24-hour period, or late returns are charged at the full daily rate. If you are offered leeway when you next hire a car, get it in writing to avoid any confusion.

## How to live the "Florida Life" without breaking the bank

For a cheap holiday to the United States, simply swap your home with an American family's house for two weeks this year. Americans love Britain, and – while you might be itching to go somewhere hot and spacious – you'll easily find someone keen to live in your house and "go local" in Britain. Find holiday-swap agencies at www.home-exchange-network.com.

## Get paid to live in a luxury Scottish castle

A great way to enjoy a change of scenery in Britain – and get paid up to £100 a week or more – is to sell your services as a house-sitter.

More and more home owners are employing people to live in their house while they are away as a security measure. You could find yourself looking after some amazing properties, all over the country. To become a house-sitter, visit www.homesitters.co.uk.

## What travel agents won't tell you unless you ask

Next time you 're booking a holiday, ask the travel agent to show you The Gazetteer. This is the "truth book" for the travel industry, usually kept under the counter at travel agents. But you should not be denied access to this information. For every destination and hotel promoted, it gives the unedited version of the travel agent's brochure. Most travel agents won't freely suggest you look at this book.

## Cut the cost of your next holiday abroad by up to £150

Eliminate the cost of unnecessary travel insurance. Simply study your home contents policy before travelling. Often, it will cover property lost or stolen away from home. So taking out travel insurance would mean you're effectively double covered.

Plus, any claim for lost property against your travel insurance could affect your home contents insurance premium. The travel insurers would be entitled to ask your contents insurers to share the cost of your losses. And if your home contents policy has an in-built no claims discount, you would lose this and see your annual premium rise anyway.

## Holidaymakers! Haggle with confidence in exotic foreign markets with these 8 'money-off' techniques

Use these "delaying tactics" to beat down prices when buying in overseas markets where haggling is tradition.

1. Point out imperfections.

2. Say you don't have enough money.

3. Say you want to shop around.

4. Walk away.

5. Offer no more than half of the opening asking price.

6. Push for a '2 for 1' or '3 for 2' deal.

7. Get a last-minute discount, by carrying small notes and change, and counting out 10% less than the agreed price. Make it your final, take-it-or-leave-it offer.

## Holidaymakers! What to do if your bags are lost at the airport

Don't panic if your luggage doesn't show up on the conveyor belt after arrival. Some suitcases are taken off the plane by hand, and left somewhere else. Here's how to deal with the situation.

- Check at the over-sized luggage desk.
- Then ask an airport official to look for you.
- If it still can't be found, ask to fill in a PIR (Property Irregularity Report), describing the bag and its contents and an address to send it to.
- If your luggage won't arrive until the next day, be sure to ask for some money towards essentials such as toiletries, underwear and nightclothes. Even if you've packed spares in your hand luggage, you may be entitled

to claim immediate compensation.

● Some airlines will promise to compensate you later if you hang on to receipts, but if this is the case, make sure you agree on an acceptable budget.

## Hunting down cheap airline flights? Buying direct could be your best strategy

To get the cheapest flights on the internet, don't neglect the airlines themselves. Most people simply log onto www.lastminute.com. But airline websites can update their deals to fill vacant seats very quickly. Buying a ticket on the internet is not the same as getting the cheapest price. Often the best deals are offered directly by airline websites. These include:
www.british-airways.com
www.lufthansa.co.uk
www.klm.com
www.flybmi.co.uk
www.easyjet.com

In some cases you sign up with the airline and they notify you via email of hugely restricted but incredibly cheap specials a few days before the flight. For example, £190 return to New York… £69 to Venice… and just £29 to Dublin.

## Free concerts, theatre tickets and cinema trips

Set yourself up as an Arts Critic. Contact the editors of all your local TV and radio stations, plus newspapers and magazines, and offer to provide them with a weekly Arts column. Then contact all your local cinemas, theatres and concert venues. Introduce yourself as the Arts Critic for 'Radio Whatever' and ask for press tickets for events. They'll normally be pleased to have you as their honoured guest for the first-night performance of the next big release.

## Enjoy free meals in top restaurants, plus £200 cash per night

Set yourself up as a Restaurant Reviewer. Contact the editors of all your local newspapers and offer to provide them with restaurant reviews at no cost to themselves. Then contact all the local restaurants you fancy eating in. Introduce yourself as the Restaurant Reviewer of whatever paper you've linked up with and ask for a complimentary meal.

Make sure the editor writes you a letter of introduction. Once your name gets known, you'll probably find that restaurateurs will actually invite you to dine in their establishments and – because your reviews will bring in extra advertising – your editor will probably be more than happy to pay you from £50 to £200 for your review!

## How to get a free bottle of wine every time you eat out

Get a good table, better service, and maybe even a free bottle of wine or dessert next time you eat out. Simply say "We're celebrating" when you book. Repeat this when you arrive. The restaurant will expect you to spend more on your celebration – and so give you better service.

## How to get all your favourite cosmetics for free

Save money by asking for free make-up samples at cosmetic counters in larger department stores. They keep a wide range of samples under the counter and will provide you with them on request.

## Enjoy a free night out watching TV live!

Unknown to many TV fans there are ticket agencies whose job it is to pack TV studios with audiences. All the ticket agencies can be contacted by phone or via the web. To find out which shows have empty places, and enjoy a fun-filled night with your friends, click on the following sites or give them a call for a full list of shows.

Standing Room Only
Tel: 020 8870 0111
Email: Nick@standroom.com

Powerhouse Film & TV
Tel: 020 7287 0045
www.powerhousetv.co.uk

BBC ticket unit
Tel: 020 8576 1227
www.bbc.co.uk/whatson/tickets
Email: tv.ticket.unit@bbc.co.uk

## Winner's secret for prizes and cash from TV and radio

If you want to be picked to take part in television and radio phone-in competitions, have a happy voice. TV and radio stations want viewers and listeners to think they've all got a fair and equal chance of being selected to win that big prize – but they haven't.

Reality is, all incoming calls are monitored. Anyone who sounds slow, nervous or tense – or just isn't to the presenter's liking – will not get picked. Best approach? Sound relaxed and cheerful. That's what they want to hear.

## If you pay for your prescriptions, beware this government-sponsored scam

250mg penicillin costs £2.70 for 28 tablets via private prescription, but £5.90 for an NHS prescription. Ask your pharmacist if the medicines you need are cheaper via NHS or private prescription. A private prescription is normally issued without charge by your GP, and costs you a variable amount at the pharmacy – depending upon drugs' costs and dispensing charges. Often, it will cost much less than the NHS charge.

## Savvy shoppers! Get big sale news, cut-price mobiles and household savings all in one

If you like shopping and saving money, make www.buy.co.uk your home page. It offers an email alert service, to update you on forthcoming store sales, plus newspaper offers on goods and services of interest to you (based on a self-completed checklist).

You can also compare electricity and gas tariffs easily, by entering your current supplier's name, your average annual bill and payment method (standard quarterly or direct debit). The online calculator will work out how much you could save by switching, and lists three suppliers offering the biggest savings.

This site also helps you to compare mobile phone tariffs, and it has a water calculator to reveal whether you'd save money by switching to a meter.

## Four hassle-free tips to cut the cost of your household bills

You can make a real difference to your household bills without cutting back on the warmth and light you enjoy at all.

1. It costs you nothing to switch all your household appliances off stand-by when you're not using them. But leaving that little red light on costs you just as much as when the TV, stereo or DVD player is in use!

2. Turn your thermostat down just 1° C (around 0.5° F), and you won't notice any difference – but you will save money on your bills.

3. Move furniture, especially upholstered chairs, away from radiators. You will get the heat circulating around your house better.

4. Lower the thermostat on your water heater. Water heaters sometimes come from the factory with high temperature settings. But just 115°F (46°C) provides comfortable hot water for most uses.

## Claim fridge-freezers for just £25, free light bulbs, plus £2,000 cash!

Thousands of pounds worth of grants are available to help you save energy in your home. If you're a homeowner, pensioner or currently in receipt of state benefits, call 0800 5120212 to find your nearest Energy Efficiency Centre. They will help you find out what grants and free products you can qualify for. For example free low energy light bulbs, new fridges for only £25, or insulation grants of up to £2,000.

## Save up to £307 on your insurance costs this year

Simply by shopping around for better insurance deals saved our researcher £307 a year on his premiums. Don't just accept the first quote you get, or automatically renew with your current insurer. Competition is high amongst insurance companies right now. Use an internet broker such as www.screentrade.co.uk, and you'll be able to find the cheapest quote quickly.

## This little-known fact will save you 25% or more on your travel insurance

Many holiday-makers automatically buy expensive insurance through their holiday company. But form E111 from your local Post Office gives you NHS-standard medical treatment in any EU country. You don't need to have this cover in your travel insurance.

What's more, your home contents insurance already covers your baggage whilst travelling (but check your policy). Also, holiday companies over charge for your insurance cover as their hefty commission charges are included within it.

But take note. Form E111 does not pay for ambulance journeys, repatriation, and other, out-of-the-ordinary costs though.

## Seven clever steps to cutting your insurance bills

1. Join an approved Neighbourhood Watch scheme. To get more information call the National Neighbourhood Watch Association on 020 7772 3348. Norwich Union is one insurer that offers discounts for members of these schemes.

2. Fit approved locks to windows and doors. Check with your insurer which products are approved – and fit a burglar alarm too.

3. Opt for a voluntary excess. It could save you up to 50% on some policies.

4. Decide whether you need cover for accidental damage. This is often optional but can add to the cost.

5. Make sure you have the right amount of cover. Don't over-insure.

6. Pay for your insurance in one lump sum. Monthly premiums result in higher charges overall. Making just one payment could save you between £10 and £28 a year.

7. If you are moving house, check that your new property is not in an area affected by flooding or subsidence. You can find out whether there are any local hazards by keying the postcode into the search on

www.homecheck.co.uk. It identifies potential problems due to flooding, subsidence, radon, coal mining, landslip, landfill, waste, historical land use, air quality and pollution.

## Injured in an accident? Not your fault?

If you have been injured as a result of someone else's negligence, you have a potential "personal injury" claim. For example, a car crash caused by the other driver going through a red light or talking on their mobile phone. You are entitled to a cash payout for the pain and discomfort you have suffered – as well as compensation for any loss of earnings, medical costs, or insurance excess. Here's how to get the money you're owed.

1. First, make sure you really do have a claim. Check whether the accident was in any way your fault, or the other person warned you of potential dangers.

2. Don't let 'No Win, No Fee' smallprint rob you. This kind of solicitor still has to make his money somehow. So if you don't win, you may be obliged to pay your opponent's fees!

3. Watch out for other costs, such as medical report fees that you will have to pay for regardless of the success of your claim.

## How to pay 80% less for designer clothes, fridge-freezers, cut glass, and much more!

Buying direct from the factory isn't just for wholesalers and shopkeepers. You can save a massive 80% on all types of goods – from designer clothes to electrical products – if you know where to go, and how to shop. These are a bargain hunter's little-known tricks.

1. Look for single-stock outlets near your home. Those stores stocking more than just one type of product won't offer you such good deals. To find addresses, simply type "factory shop" into a good search engine like Google.co.uk.

2. Shop when no one else is there. 80% of customers visit at the weekends – so any remaining bargains will disappear fast, and queues will be longer. Also avoid high profile sales. They attract heavy crowds. Go mid-week instead.

3. Know your rights. Most factory goods are perfect. But some seconds are sometimes mixed in with these stocks. You can claim a refund on defective goods that are sold as perfects. You're still covered by all of the consumer protection laws. But this can prove easier said than done at some outlets, especially if you've had to travel. So always view all items in daylight.

4. Don't be afraid to ask. If you want more money off the price shown, ask! Smaller, owner-managed businesses are most likely to agree to further discounts.

## Misled by a salesman, abused by a waitress, ignored by a big-name company?

19 tips for causing havoc and getting your money back – quick

1. Make your complaint as soon as possible.

2. Stop using whatever you are complaining about. If it's a meal, stop eating it. If it's a service, put it on hold.

3. Prepare your complaint. Stick to one or two main problems. "The more specific and thorough the information is the easier it is to act quickly" reveal Customer Service experts at Abbey National.

4. Decide what you want. A refund? A replacement? Cash compensation? A personal apology from the Chief Executive? This way, you know what you're aiming for.

5. It's usually best to start by asking for a refund. Never ask for a replacement unless you really want one. Stores don't want to lose a sale so they often drag their feet over a refund, but will be quick to replace the item.

6. Make your complaint in person. They can't ignore you if you're standing in the middle of their shop. It may be a little embarrassing, but they'll soon listen to you.

7. Complain about the product but praise the service. Getting staff on your side will help get your complaint dealt with quickly.

8. Set a deadline. There is no such thing as a standard response but you should ask for a specific time.

9. Don't accept a deadline longer than a month.

10. Make a nuisance of yourself. Call them regularly. The more annoying you are, the more likely they are to deal with you quickly.

11. Repeat your shock and disappointment at your treatment.

12. If you're complaining about a person then speak to their manager.

13. Remind them you have been a loyal customer for many years.

14. Do not, ever, say you are going to take your business elsewhere in future. The company will have no reason to fix the problem if they've already lost your custom.

15. Don't take 'no' for an answer. If your first letter meets with a rebuff, there is no reason why you should not
- challenge the points made in response
- write to another main-board director for a second opinion
- involve a third party such as Trading Standards or an official watchdog; or
- continue corresponding until the company gets so sick of you that it finally surrenders.

16. Go to the boss.

17. If the company is a member of a trade body complain to them. They can often sanction or fine a company if they do not act properly.

18. If your claim is for less than £5,000 you can go to small claims court. You do not need a solicitor. For more information contact the Citizens Advice Bureau at www.adviceguide.org.uk.

19. If you're complaining about a financial service you should talk to the Financial Services Authority. Call: 0845 606 1234 or visit www.fsa.gov.uk/consumer.

## Computer users! The little-known law that protects your health at work

If you're employed to use a computer or view a TV screen as part of your job, you're entitled to protection under the Display Screen Equipment Regulations of 1992. Here are your little-known rights:

- Free eye tests. You can ask your employer to pay for an eye test at any time. This right is covered by regulation 5 of the DSE regulations.
- Order a wrist rest. These padded rests can help prevent the aches and pains of repetitive stress injuries, caused by typing.
- Check your desk, chair and footrest are appropriate. Chronic back, neck and headaches have become commonplace thanks to people sitting for long hours on unsuitable furniture. Your chair should allow you to adjust its height and tilt its back-rest position. Plus, it should have a five-star wheel base for stability and ease of movement.
- Your employer should provide you with a foot rest if requested.

## Don't let them get away with it!

Use your consumer rights to beat bad service, shoddy goods and rip-off refund lies.

If you've complained about shoddy goods or bad service, but the company is ignoring your problem, show you've done your homework by citing your rights.

Under the Sale of Goods Act 1979:
- Goods must fit their description.
- They must be of satisfactory quality.
- They must be fit for the purpose for which they were sold.
- You have a right to a refund.
- This law applies to the retailer of the good. You do not have to deal with the manufacturer or distributor.
- It also applies to sale items and second-hand goods.
- It does not apply to property and goods bought privately.

Under the Supply of Goods and Services Act 1982:
- This says that a service provider must carry out the service with "reasonable skill and care".

- They must complete it within a reasonable time (unless you have both agreed a specific time).
- They must make a reasonable charge for the service (unless you have agreed a charge in advance).
- They must use materials which are "fit for the purpose".

## Airline flight from hell? How to complain effectively and quickly

Claiming compensation from an airline can be difficult if you don't know how the system works.

- Write to the airline's Customer Relations Manager and send a copy to the travel agent you booked the flight from.
- Double-check crucial flight details such as date, flight number, arrival and departure locations. Plus, state where the incident you're complaining about took place.
- Don't let your complaint drop if they don't pay up. Contact the Air Transport Users' Council at www.auc.org.uk (tel: 020 7240 6061). They are often successful in getting compensation for dissatisfied travellers.

## How to borrow £2,000 worth of contemporary art to decorate your home

A unique scheme has just been set up enabling anyone in England to buy original artwork from selected galleries, with favourable loan conditions. You never know, you might just get lucky and end up with a piece that is highly valued in a few years' time.

An original painting can breathe life into your home and right now is perhaps the very best time to consider buying. Many local arts councils are operating special schemes where you can buy a painting (or a sculpture, ceramics or textile originals) with a special interest-free loan over 12 months.

Your loan could be for up to £2,000 depending on your area. To find out, ask your local arts council if they have these instalment or part-payment schemes, and which galleries are part of it. If you are not sure which council you come under, contact Arts Council of England at www.arts.org.uk.

## Clever trick for getting up to 20% off electrical goods in high street stores

If you want to save up to 20% off the cost of a DVD player, home computer, television or hi-fi system, tell the shop assistant you want to pay by credit card. But then ask if they'd give a discount for cash.

Using this trick recently, it was possible to get a £239 television reduced to just £200 in a well-known high street store. The reason? Credit card payments, credit instalment plans and similar schemes all cost time and money for the store. Additional paperwork, delayed payments, finance companies' charges all add up. You can save money by making life easier for them with a cash-only deal.

## An ex-Member of Parliament reveals...
## How to make your MP sit up and bark like a dog

Got a problem you feel the government should fix? Get your MP working for you with these little-known tactics:

### 1. Write to your constituency MP
Your local MP has vested interest in resolving your problem. They want you to vote for them at the next election! So write to them c/o the House of Commons, London SW1A 0AA.

### 2. Challenge their reply
If you write direct to a government department, you'll receive a bland, non-committal reply drafted by a faceless civil servant. If you write to your MP, you might get the same reply. But at least it will be signed by the MP or the minister responsible for that department. Write back, and ask if they actually read their reply before it was sent. This attracts the MP's interest who'll pass on your comments to the minister who'll refer it to that civil servant who drafted the reply. This increases the attention given to your problem.

### 3. Telephone the House of Commons
For urgent matters, call 020 7219 3000 and leave a message for your MP to call you back. This way, you'll get a faster response. And when you speak, ask for a personal meeting to discuss the issue.

### 4. Ask your MP about the next surgery

MPs hold surgeries in their constituency – usually on a fortnightly basis – where they meet constituents. But most fail to publicise them widely. You'll need to ask. Phone the local political party in the telephone book. Make an appointment.

### 5. Supply full details

You'll get a more practical response from the MP if you've supplied some background details before your meeting by letter.

### 6. Lobby 200 MPs to get things done

Ten constituency letters sent to one MP on the same subject discloses a serious issue that should be followed up. But if 200 MPs each receive ten letters on the subject from their constituents, the government is alerted to the issue. So get your friends and family involved. Set up a website to find other people with the same complaint. Upgrade your complaint to a lobby group.

### 7. Don't make this classic mistake

Any lobby group using pre-printed forms to write to those 200 MPs is wasting its time and money. They are usually treated with contempt by MPs, because these printed forms suggest your lobby has no real interest in the issue. People can't even be bothered to write a personal letter!

### 8. Scare the Whitehall bureaucrats witless

Ask your MP to table a Parliamentary Question. This can have an electrifying effect on resolving your problem. Your request will almost certainly be passed to a minister who will ask a bureaucrat to deal with it. And nothing disturbs a civil servant more than having to prepare a PQ for oral answer.

It's not only necessary to provide an initial reply, but to counter every conceivable supplementary question as well. This is why ministers bring such big books to the despatch box at Question Time.

There may be several pages of notes and comments for each PQ that's been tabled. Civil servants are the same as everyone else. They're not keen on extra work. When they're faced with a constituent who knows how the system operates, they'll usually do all they can to bring matters to the speediest possible conclusion.

# Eight steps to overturn your local council's stupid decisions

Are you passionate to stop something happening in your local area? From a school closing to a garage being built on a local beauty spot – if you're not happy with a future plan, then it's up to you to try and overturn the council's decision. With these 8 proven steps, it really is possible:

**1. Do your homework.** Read up on the council's plans, get books from the library, find other organisations that have dealt with similar situations, and read the coverage in the local press.

**2. Get the word out.** Gather support from friends and neighbours. And ask local printers about joining your cause – you could get a reduction on the cost of flyers and posters.

**3. Keep your message simple.** You need to provide a strong snappy upbeat and positive message, clear for everyone to read and for the media to pick up on.

**4. Write press releases** and send them to your local paper and businesses. Make sure you outline your issue and any events you have planned.

**5. Don't exaggerate, ever**. Keep to the facts, but be bold in getting further information. You have the right to attend most local council meetings.

**6. Share tasks to boost results.** Assign different tasks to different people: designing leaflets on a computer, writing letters, talking to people in your local shopping centre, finding a good lawyer, making high-profile contacts. Also be sure to talk to local councillors, MPs, MEPs, libraries and even journalists.

**7. Set up a public meeting in a small room.** You could gather names on a petition by setting up a stall in a popular area of town (like outside a local supermarket), or you can knock on people's doors. Remember to gather email addresses too. Try and get an expert to come and talk. Hold your meeting on a Saturday, so people can attend.

**8. Organise a demonstration.** Make sure you have enough people on your side, or it could be a wash-out (especially if it rains). Tell the local authorities about your campaign demo, and always tell the media. Beware. You do need police permission.

For further information, go to www.amnesty.org.uk and www.citizensconnection.net.

## Warning! Is your medical insurance policy really worth the premium?

Before taking out private cover, make sure you read the small print clearly to find out exactly how much cover you really have. Some insurance companies don't cover you for extensive diagnostic testing, surgical intervention, long-term hospital stay, outpatient consultations etc, which could all run into thousands of pounds.

The last thing you want to hear if you're suffering from a debilitating illness is that you've run out of cover and your private treatment is no longer available.

## Computer users! Scandal of the rip-off printer ink cartridges

Don't replace printer ink cartridges for your computer just because the light is flashing. Many printers are programmed to flash after a certain period of time, or when the ink drops below a certain level. But there may still be plenty of ink left in the cartridge.

Why this rip-off? Because most printer companies also produce ink cartridges too. So they set the machines to warn of low-ink levels early… costing you money but boosting their profits.

To beat this scam and save yourself money when the little red light starts flashing, access the ink cartridge and lift the lid up and down three times. Replace, and then continue using the printer. This little trick usually eliminates the flashing lights, and allows you to keep printing for twice as long.

## Four phrases to make a double-glazing sales rep shut up… and offer you a 60% discount instead

Most people get stung on new window deals because they don't know how much they are worth in the first place. Windows are often marked up about 60% for the first price. Here are four phrases that will cut the toing and froing of time-consuming haggle and cut to the chase.

"I've had a quote half that from another (named) company and their quality is just as good."

"It's too much. I can't afford it. I had half that much in mind."

"They said I'd get 40% off on the phone and that's a price I'd be willing to consider."

"I like your product but if that's your best price, I'll have to get a few more quotes."

## Scam warning! The old courier loophole is dead

Gone are the days when you could simply call around courier companies and get them to subsidise your travel plans by footing the bill for your air ticket. Modern technology means packages can be electronically tracked across the world today. On-board couriers are rarely needed anymore.

So don't fall for the claims of so-called 'courier clubs' in national newspapers and on the internet. They promise to help you find cheap courier flights. To access these deals, they tell you, you need to join their club, or buy their directory – usually for a fee of around £50.

Save your money for your holiday. No courier company in the country deals with these outfits regularly.

## How to get the latest books delivered to your door – free

Don't go to a bookshop and pay top price. Instead, write to the publishers of the books you want, and say you're looking for books to sell in your new bookselling or mail order business. Ask for sample copies. Alternatively, set yourself up as a book reviewer for your local newspaper. You'll be amazed how many publishers are desperate to give away free copies – with no obligation – if they think there's a chance of getting their book reviewed in the press.

## Nine professional bargain-hunting tips for buying household goods at auction

**1. Check lots** carefully before bidding.

**2. Steer clear** of goods that are broken, damaged or have missing parts, unless you know you can personally repair or replace them.

**3. Be cautious** of any goods offered for sale 'as is'. This means the auction house isn't prepared to specifically describe a lot's age or condition.

**4. Play safe,** and don't buy electrical or computer goods unless you can plug them in and test them. These are notoriously dodgy.

**5. Also avoid last-minute entries.** They're often entered late so they can't be inspected, because they're faulty or sub-standard in some way.

**6. Get goods at lowest prices.** If several lots offer you similar goods, wait for the later ones to come through before bidding. Many dealers will have drifted away by then, and you'll face less competition.

**7. Stand against the back wall** when bidding, so you can see everyone, but they can't see you. This prevents unscrupulous auctioneers artificially pushing up bids by pretending someone is bidding at the back of the crowd.

**8. Avoid being ripped off** by the auctioneer's other favourite trick. Never accept their opening price. It's a try-on to catch naive bidders.

**9. Keep quiet** and wait until the bidding slows to £10, £5, or even £1 increases.

## Four steps to avoiding the heartbreak of ruined holiday photographs

1. Don't put your camera films into 'checked baggage'. The high-power x-ray machines used to scan your suitcases could destroy your pictures. Carry them in your hand luggage instead.

2. Always take your treasured holiday snaps into your high-street

chemists to be developed. These are usually dealt with on-site and are unlikely to go astray.

3. To safeguard your film, put a tiny sticky label stating your name and postcode on each film. If they are lost, you will be entitled to compensation as retailers have a legal duty to take reasonable care of customers' goods.

4. Avoid low-cost postal services. At busy times of the year, like August, September and New Year, an increasing number of films are sent to these services. You will find it impossible to claim if films are lost in transit or even on arrival.

These services put a small print disclaimer on their clip-out adverts which absolves them of all responsibility for your films. County court judges uphold this, and dismiss claims by angry customers whose films have been lost.

## Get extra memory to surf the net faster – instantly and free

Your computer stores various web pages and images on your hard drive as you surf the net. Increase the amount of hard drive space used for storing these, and you'll surf faster! How? Simply click on:
● Start, settings, control panel
● Internet options, temporary internet file, settings.
● Move the 'amount of disk space to use' slider to 300MB for optimum browsing performance.

## Make effective legal complaints from just £2.99

The excellent website at www.desktoplawyer.co.uk offers many legal letters you can buy and download for a range of consumer, employment and property problems. If there's a complaint you've been meaning to make – whether it be cancelling a mail order because it has arrived too late, or seeking compensation from a travel company for unrealised holiday expectations – you can get a professional to write the letter for a fraction of the cost of a solicitor's fees. Letters are priced from £2.99 and can be customized to suit your exact circumstances.

# Get important letters taken seriously every time

If you want a letter of complaint or grievance taken seriously, write "3rd copy" on the top left hand corner. This gives the impression that you have kept a copy for yourself and sent another copy to someone else. You often get better results when making complaints if you use this great tactic.

# Why taking a nap on a long drive could save your life

In Britain, an estimated 300 deaths and thousands of injuries a year are caused by drivers falling asleep at the wheel. The government urges drivers to stop for 15 minutes every 2 hours, if on a long journey. But 69% of consumers surveyed feel that Britain's motorway service stations do not have adequate facilities for drivers who want to rest, although 19% believe that the monotony of motorway travel is to blame. Beware driving at abnormal speeds, yawning, tired eyes and not remembering the last few seconds. All signs of deadly driver fatigue.

- Be well rested before long trips.
- Try not to drive between midnight and 6 am since this is when you are normally asleep.
- Drink 2 cups of coffee or a high caffeine drink as a short-term boost.
- Remember that opening windows and turning up the stereo is of little use.

# How to spot a liar

Ask a simple, direct question. Listen for the giveaway response: generalised comments accompanied by vague speech patterns such as 'yeah', 'well', 'you know'. And watch for the tell-tale body language such as loss of eye contact, and hands touching the mouth.

# Owed up to £5,000? The hassle-free route to getting your money quickly

You do not need a solicitor. Simply go to small claims court. For more information contact the Citizens Advice Bureau at www.adviceguide.org.uk. If you're complaining about a financial service, you should talk to the Financial Services Authority first. Call: 0845 606 1234 or visit www.fsa.gov.uk/consumer.

# Gameshow insider's hot tips for bagging Bruce's £136,000 bonus

Ever find yourself sitting in front of the TV shouting the answers to the contestants on a game show? If you fancy your chances of walking away with a handful of wonderful prizes, it really couldn't be easier.

- Find out about getting on: Just watch the rolling credits at the end of the show. You'll see a name and address of who to write to and a telephone number. Plus, the web site at www.ukgameshows.com has a listing of all game shows on every channel and how to enter.
- What happens next: You'll be sent an application form. Make sure you fill in the  whole form, and not just your name and address. Write full answers to questions like "Do you have any hobbies?" and "Name something funny that has happened to you".
- Send in a picture: When applying for a game show like Family Fortunes, make sure you can see all of the faces clearly in a group photograph. No passport photographs – this isn't a customs inspection. Look happy and approachable. Good looks are irrelevant. And no need to do anything wacky. Just smile and look friendly.
- Practise before the audition: Play your own version of the programme at home. Learn how the format works.
- If you get invited, be human! If you're picked for an audition you'll play a bit of the game and will have to talk a little about yourself. Try not to mumble, but do sound enthusiastic. A bubbly personality is useful. But enjoying yourself is key.
- Never sulk: Do it for a laugh! Go in with the attitude that you don't care if you win or not. You won't get far if you hint that you're only in it to win.

# SEX & BEAUTY

**Look great, feel beautiful,
and enjoy the best sex of your life
with these sizzling tips**

# 136 tips, tricks and techniques for looking young, feeling sexy, and enjoying a better love-life

Time and again, research proves that a satisfying sex life is vital for good health. It boosts the 'feel good' hormones we need to stay happy. It helps maintain better physical and mental health in people over fifty. And for every 100 extra orgasms you enjoy per year, your chances of suffering an early death plummet by 36 per cent!

And yet 22% of men and 40% of women have had to ask their GP for help with difficulties in their sex life in the last 12 months. And the more you worry, the more difficult it is to relax and enjoy good sex…which only serves to worry you more…and a vicious cycle begins.

This is why we have selected the 136 tips and techniques in the pages that follow. These simple techniques can help anyone become more attractive to the opposite sex…recover from loss of sexual desire…overcome problems associated with growing older…and enjoy great sex at any age.

## Looking Good/ Feeling younger

### A simple tip for younger looking skin

Vitamin C is the only antioxidant you can use directly on your skin which is proven to prevent oxidation of tissue – keeping it young and supple. So take a vitamin C tablet (the strongest you can find) and dissolve it in half-a-teaspoon of boiling water. Let the water cool until comfortable to the touch. Add it to a small amount of eye cream and pat gently under your eyes and around your mouth.

### Reverse the ageing process with a cupful of blueberries

Improve your balance, co-ordination and short-term memory – eat a cupful of blueberries each day. The antioxidants in the fruit act to protect you against harmful free radicals in your body. This slows and even reverses the degeneration associated with growing older.

## Beat the stigma of rosy cheeks and broken veins on your nose

People might assume you are a heavy drinker if you have rosy cheeks or suffer from broken veins on your nose. But they don't realise the strong connection between red facial skin and low stomach-acid production.

As we get older, production of hydrochloric acid slows down, leading to this visible condition. But supplemental HCL and pepsin can correct this simple digestive disorder. Take one capsule of betaine HCL pepsin just before meals (made by Lamberts and available from www.expresschemist.co.uk).

Make sure your doctor is aware of this treatment and that he monitors how it goes with you.

## What soap manufacturers don't want you to know about their moisturising creams...

Your average bar of soap has had the most beneficial part of it removed. Glycerin is a natural by-product of the soap-making process and is a natural moisturiser. But commercial manufacturers remove the valuable glycerin and use it in their more profitable lotions and creams. Look instead for handcrafted soaps that boast a high glycerin content and your skin will no longer dry out and itch from regular soap.

## Treat hair loss with folk remedies from Russia and Scotland

Add kelp to your regular diet. This seaweed contains properties that make your hair richer and full-bodied and it contains essential minerals, such as iodine, that are important for hair growth. Many folk remedies for baldness use the humble onion. Russian barbers recommend mixing a tablespoon of honey, the juice of one onion and a shot of vodka – then rub this mixture into your scalp every night, cover and rinse off in the morning.

## The smell of ice cream could help you lose weight

Decrease your appetite and lose weight easily – sniff some vanilla. A study shows how overweight people given vanilla-scented skin patches significantly reduced their intake of sweet food. This suggests the smell of vanilla may help assuage cravings for sweet snacks. Try carrying some vanilla essence with you next time you are on a diet.

## Get a flatter, firmer stomach – sitting down!

Strengthen your abdominal muscles with this easy sitting exercise. Strengthening your muscles like this is also a great way to promote good skin tone all over your body.

- Sit on the floor, knees bent, arms around knees.
- Lean backwards slowly, using your arms around your knees to support your weight.
- Use your arm muscles to pull back into sitting position.
- Rest for five seconds.
- Repeat ten times.

As your abdominal muscles gain in strength you can reduce the effort made by the hands and arms until you can perform the exercise ten times without holding your knees.

## Look 10 years younger with these delicious summer fruits

Reverse the signs of ageing – eat plenty of berries, especially blueberries, blackberries and strawberries. They are high in antioxidants, which fight the free radicals that cause ageing and damage your body.

## Five beauty clinician's tips to find the right perfume for you

1. Wear stronger scents in cold weather. Cold reduces a scent's strength.

2. Purchase a new scent late in the day, when your sense of smell is sharper.

3 Try scents on your own skin, as everyone's skin chemistry is different.

4. Apply perfume right after you shower or bathe. Your pores will be open and soak up the scent.

5. Don't use perfume near pearl or costume jewellery. The alcohol in perfumes can cause pearls to yellow.

## Cursed with acne? Improve your skin in just 13 weeks using these 3 proven techniques

### 1. Change your diet
Include more zinc (beef, lamb), vitamin A (carrots, broccoli) and vitamin B complex (fish, beans).

### 2. Eliminate existing spots
Put ten drops of tea tree oil in a bowl of hot water, cover your head with a tea towel, steam your face, then dab blemishes with ice cubes.

### 3. Cleanse your skin effectively
Wash with a one-part purified water/one-part lemon juice mix three times a week.

## How ice cubes help to tackle acne

Latest American research indicates that rubbing ice cubes over your face for three to five minutes before applying medication can help dramatically. Benzoyl Peroxide is an effective treatment available in various formulations and strengths.

## What cosmetic surgeons will never tell you about wrinkles, crow's feet and puckered lips

Many plastic surgeons know how important facial exercise can be. Yet they fail to recommend it to their patients. Why would they promote a simple exercise that achieves a firm, young, ageless-looking face for free?

As we age, gravity pulls everything down, giving the drawn 'careworn' look that makes us appear older. With a good facial workout, this can be reversed.

● Place an index finger at the outer corner of each eye, with your middle fingers at the inner eye corners.
● Squint strongly with your lower eyelids, trying to move them up.

- Squint and release ten times, keeping your upper eyelids open wide. Now hold the squint and think UP, maintaining the strong squint with your lower eyelids as you count to 40, focusing on the outer and inner eye muscles flexing.
- Repeat the entire exercise.

Perform this exercise once a day for two weeks. After that, twice weekly workouts are fine. Facial muscles are small, so you'll see improvements quickly. Try this simple exercise for a non-surgical facelift today.

## To strengthen and lengthen your neck, kiss the ceiling

- Sit upright, tilt your head back looking at the ceiling, lips closed and relaxed.
- Start puckering your lips together in a kiss and stretch the kiss, as if you were trying to kiss the ceiling.
- Keep your lips puckered for ten counts, relax, bring your head back to normal and repeat five times.

## Smooth worry lines on your forehead easily

- Cover your forehead with the palm of one hand, holding it firmly.
- Try to push the forehead muscle toward the top of the head, pushing against the resistance of your hand.
- Hold for a second, then relax. Repeat ten times.
  This exercise not only tightens skin on the forehead. It also helps smooth frown and worry lines, training the forehead muscles to work together, instead of rippling.

## Stop your double chin showing with this simple exercise

- Lie on your back, with your knees slightly bent and feet flat on the floor.
- Slowly raise your head and tuck your chin against your chest.
- Hold this position for a second, then slowly lower your head.
- Try to repeat it ten times at first... and gradually work up to 50 repetitions.

## These 'forehead push-ups' eradicate frown lines quickly

- In a sitting or lying position, place both your index fingers on the forehead so that they are parallel to the top of each brow.
- Now pull the fingers down so that they're half an inch above the brows.
- While fingers are pressing down, concentrate on pushing the eyebrows up.
- Push eyebrows up and release ten times.
- Now hold eyebrows in up position, continuing to keep fingers pressed down – and do mini-eyebrow push-ups until you feel a tight band of pressure above the brows.
- Hold them up and count to 20.

## This simple daily exercise can smooth out crow's feet

- Place your ring and middle fingers of each hand at the outer corners of your eyes.
- Pull the corner towards the hairline and hold. At the same time squeeze your eyes shut and hold.

## Smokers! Prevent your lips from puckering as you age

- Sit upright and purse your lips together.
- Lift your pursed lips towards your nose and keep them there for five counts.
- Relax and repeat five times.

## How to keep your smile wrinkle-free

- Sit upright, lips closed and teeth together.
- Smile as broadly as possible, without opening your lips.
- Keep them there for five counts.
- Relax, and start puckering your lips in a pointed kiss.
- Keep it there for five counts and relax.
- Repeat ten times.

## Women! Slow the ageing process with tofu and sofa milk

Soya contains phyto-oestrogens (also known as 'plant oestrogens'). They trick your body into thinking it's still receiving oestrogen, and helps maintain adequate levels. Now UK research shows soya offers protection against osteoporosis and senile dementia, by mimicking the health benefits of hormone replacement therapy – but without the increased risk of cancer.

## Invest in a satin pillowcase to keep your skin smooth

Research findings in the UK show some wrinkles are formed at night when you're lying on either side of your face. Slippery satin discourages this wrinkling effect.

## Women! How to maintain your health after the menopause.

A recent study in Boston, USA, reveals those older women supplementing their diet with vitamin D were better protected against osteoporosis.

## The natural facelift in your fridge

Tighten the skin around your eyes by applying egg white and leaving to dry. As it dries, your skin will tighten, visibly reducing the signs of ageing.

## A quick and natural moisturiser for under £1.00

Moisturise your face with mashed avocado. It contains vitamins B and E to improve your skin. Margarine is a good, inexpensive moisturiser too.

## How to have healthy-looking hair – instantly

Give your hair a beautiful and instant shine. Smooth almond oil into your palms and rub lightly through your hair.

## The little-known use of mashed potato

Eliminate cracks and rough patches on your hands or feet. Apply a mashed potato mixed with a teaspoon of olive oil, and leave for 15 minutes before rinsing with cool water.

## Your kitchen cupboard's cheap and effective bodyscrub

Scrub your body clean and fresh with a mixture of caster sugar and cool water.

## A relaxing bath to keep you young and beautiful

The best beauty treatment of all? A good night's sleep. Achieve it tonight by adding a few drops of orange blossom and meadowsweet to a warm bath. Relax in it just before going to bed.

## Boost your bra size in just 3 months... without expensive surgery

These simple weekly exercises will increase your "muscular platform", the group of muscles supporting your breasts.

- Modified Push-Ups: Kneel on the floor with your arms in front of you, just wider than shoulder-width apart. Bend your arms at the elbow, and – keeping your body in a straight line – lower your body straight down to the floor. Then pull back to upright.
- Standing Push-Ups: Stand about 25 centimetres (10 inches) from a heavy desk. With your arms straight, place your hands on the desk, slightly wider than shoulder-width apart. Bend your arms at the elbow, and lower your trunk to the desk. Do not bend your knees. Now push back up again.
- Dumbbell Stretch: Lie on your back on the floor, with your arms outstretched. Grip a five-pound dumbbell in each hand, with your palms facing upwards. Bending your elbows slightly, extend your arms straight over your chest until the weights touch each other.

## Get larger breasts in 30 days with this natural herb

Wild yam extract is both a breast enlarger and a sexual stimulant. Called Diosgenin, it contains DHEA – the source of all sex and steroid hormones in your body. You can buy it in combination with Black Cohosh and Soy Isoflavones too. They mimic the action of oestrogen, to help boost breast size. Take 2 or 4 tablets a day. They cost £20-40 for a 60-day supply. Some women see improvements within just 30 days. Others take three to nine months to achieve best results.

# Feeling Sexy

## Two Tantric shortcuts for heightened sexual pleasure

These mystical sex tips come from the Tantra tradition of ancient India.

- Next time you make love, keep the tip of your tongue on the roof of your mouth, towards the front.
- Also, try and breathe deeply as you approach orgasm. If you can relax into your experience, it will be much more intense and enjoyable.

## The everyday aphrodisiac in your fruit bowl

Bananas are surprisingly effective aphrodisiacs. Use as much of each banana as possible – including the white pithy substance underneath the peel.

## The sexy secrets of sesame seeds

With no less than eight sex-related nutrients, sesame seeds help prevent infertility, raise sexual drive and give good overall health. They are one of the highest sources of the trace element selenium, essential for optimum immunity – and a higher sperm count. Grind the seeds in a blender before eating them to release their mineral content.

# Sex

## Men! Try this herb for stronger, firmer erections

Ginger has a great reputation as a love tonic. Crystallised ginger is not as strong as fresh ginger, so eat it straight or combined with hot tea. Hot, mixed green and black tea with plenty of crystallised ginger root is a medieval romantic remedy. Take stronger-tasting ginger the easy way – sprinkle it on a refreshing fruit salad that's eaten as a starter. This stimulant thins blood and encourages prolonged and firmer erections.

## Women! Heighten your partner's sexual ecstasy

Put two drops of water-based lubricant inside the tip of the condom. KY-Jelly is perfect. The condom will rub more against his penis during sex, causing increased stimulation and pleasure. Careful though – three drops or more can cause slippage.

## Men! How to have a larger penis… just when it matters most

Does size really matter? Not if a woman is fully aroused before sex. Women experience most sexual pleasure in their clitoris and the first couple of inches of the vagina. If your partner's vagina is aroused through foreplay, the blood vessels around it become engorged and sensitive – making your penis feel bigger to her.

## Men! Protect against prostate cancer with pumpkin seeds

Pumpkins are seen as a symbol of fertility in many cultures. And now science is proving superstition right! The seeds protect the prostate gland in men – as well as being a great source of calcium, magnesium, zinc and B vitamins and essential fatty acids. Add seeds to soups and salads on a frequent basis.

## How to maintain a healthy sex drive long into the future

Pine nuts are one of the richest dietary sources of zinc, the most important mineral for sexual behaviour and fertility. Zinc is vital for sperm production and ability to move, and is also essential for production of all enzymes that govern the senses of taste and smell – required for sexual arousal.

## The sexual value of a man's "million dollar point"

The Million Dollar Point, as it's known in America, was first identified by Taoist spirituals. It can help delay ejaculation and prolong sex, without decreasing pleasure at all.

The spot lies behind the testicles, just in front of the anus. Press on it firmly with the index and middle fingers of one hand to delay ejaculation. Your partner will be amazed at 'his' sexual prowess!

## Two steps to a stronger penis

Strengthen your erection and muscle control with these simple exercises.

● Try weightlifting. Hang a face flannel over your erect penis and see how far you can raise it. As your strength improves your can progress with a small towel.

● Try squeezing the shaft of your penis until it becomes hard a couple of times a day. Repeated squeezing produces increasingly firm erections.

Men! How does your penis compare with the national average?
12% of men: 10.2cm to 12.3cm
20% of men: 12.7cm to 15cm
45% of men: 15.2cm to 17.6cm
20% of men: 17.8cm to 20cm
3% of men: 20.3cm or more

## Men! Ignore so-called penis enlargers... and never put your penis in a vacuum

Magic herbal or hormone creams combined with massage techniques claim to increase length. Trying these methods shouldn't cause personal damage unless applied too enthusiastically. But genuine improvements are non-existent.

● Don't get conned by metal rings that supposedly increase size either. They constrict blood circulation out of the penis, and can seriously damage the delicate vascular network of your penis.
● Steer well clear of vacuum pumps too. These glass cylinders fit over the penis, and are sealed at the base. The air inside is then partially removed, and a weight of about one-half stone is hung on the outside of the device. This increases the suction and can produce a temporary engorgement. But a severe vacuum can damage the inner vascularity of the penis. And as pressure mounts, the glass can shatter onto your penis.
● Cosmetic surgery is the only proven method of penis enlargement. It involves a modified liposuction technique, putting fat cells from your thigh or hip, washed in saline, stuffed into very small incisions on the sides of the penis... rather like cutting open and stuffing more meat into a sausage. This difficult four-figure procedure is potentially very painful, with stitches and extensive bruising occurring for many weeks. In the end, only minimal lengths and circumferences are added to your penis in most instances.

### Men! How big is big enough?

A woman's vagina is around 8-9cm long when unaroused. This expands to 11-12cm on arousal. So even a 'short' penis of 10cm length will fit perfectly during love-making. Plus, only the first third of the vagina is sensitive. Any-sized penis can generate pre-orgasmic and orgasmic pleasure simply by stimulating the crucial first-third of the vagina.

### Are you at risk from sexual arthritis?

Many arthritis sufferers do not realise they're actually experiencing sexually acquired reactive arthritis. SARA can be identified easily by a number of symptoms.

- Women: pain on passing urine, vaginal discharges.
- Men: redness of eyes, pain on passing urine, urinary tract infections.

Sexually acquired reactive arthritis (SARA) can be triggered by catching chlamydia bacteria during sex, resulting in tender and swollen joints. But simply wearing a condom can prevent transfer of this bacteria. If you're already suffering from SARA, it can be eliminated by GP-prescribed antibiotics.

# Fertility

### Trying for a baby? This vitamin cocktail boosts sperm count in just two months

Decreasing sperm count and damaged sperm are vital factors in male infertility. A recent Japanese study involved giving an antioxidant cocktail to men producing damaged sperm.

The cocktail contained 200mg vitamin C, 200iu vitamin E and 400mg gluthione. One dose was given daily for two months, and results showed the antioxidants worked effectively to increase sperm mobility and concentration.

All these ingredients are available from health food stores.

# How chicken eggs can help you get pregnant

Double-plus your prospects of success by spreading egg white over your penis and vagina before sex. This increases sperm mobility, increasing your chances of conception.

# Why porn films boost your chances of falling pregnant

US research on men with fertility problems reveals masturbating whilst watching X-rated videos produces double-plus sperm counts, and healthier sperm too. Sperm quality and potential increase in line with greater sexual excitement.

So if you're trying to conceive, concentrate on foreplay and abstain from penetrative intercourse for as long as possible to boost your chances.

# Men! Why you should have sex twice a week or more

Having two orgasms a week is a health plus for men. The British Medical Association did a ten-year study. It showed men having an orgasm less than once a month had double the death rate of those having orgasms twice a week.

This is because at orgasm the level of the hormone DHEA increases in response to ejaculation and this hormone helps boost the immune system and acts as an antidepressant.

# Do you have 3 days' food – undigested – in your belly?

### Nine little-known tips for restoring a healthy balance 'down below'

An over-acidic diet, poor digestion and too many toxins in your blood can play havoc in your intestines, upsetting the whole balance of the natural bacteria in your bowels.

This can mean you are carrying up to 9 meals' worth of undigested food at any one time!

The battle of bowel flora, of bad bacteria versus good, must be won. If unfriendly bacteria take over, serious health problems such as Candida, chronic fatigue and IBS can develop.

**Enemies of good bacteria:**

- Unfriendly bacteria positively thrive on yeast and sugar. Limit bread, biscuits, chocolate, cakes, pasta and alcohol in your diet.
- Dairy is very mucus-forming and acidic. Cut out as much dairy produce as you can to give your colon a healthier environment.
- Salt makes the cells hang on to water, causing bloating and water retention. Cut out those salty crisps and peanuts.
- Cut down on red meat. It can be loaded with antibiotics (put into the animals' feed), is incredibly hard to digest and can take from four to nine days to move out of a sluggish system.
- Unless antibiotics are life-saving, try and do without them.

**Friends of good bacteria:**

- Try to make sure your diet is composed of as much 'plant' food as possible. You've heard it before, but a reminder is always good – make sure you eat your five portions of fruit and vegetables a day, they're high in water, and all the vitamins and minerals needed for a healthy gut. If you haven't got time, grab a fruit smoothie on your way to work.
- Eat more chicken and fish, especially oily fish such as salmon and tuna. It's less acidic and easier to digest.
- Eat plenty of brown rice. This is a really important weapon in your battle of the bulge as it will act like a broom sweeping away all those years of debris from the walls of your colon as well as providing plenty of B vitamins which are essential for the growth of friendly bacteria.
- Eat more unsalted nuts and seeds. They're packed full of nutrients, fibre and the essential fatty acids needed for a healthy heart, brain, joints and gut.
- Consider a probiotic supplement. You need to choose your probiotics carefully. Potency, quality and costs can vary considerably but don't go for the cheaper brands in health food stores – these cheaper supplements don't contain enough bacteria to make any difference to your body. Best buy: Biocare's 'Bio-Acidophilus', a daily vitamin supplement.

## Eliminate body odour once and for all

Many people suffer from excess perspiration leading to unwanted body odour. This can linger even after washing. But this natural solution really works. Just add two cupfuls of tomato juice to a warm bath, and bathe in it for 15 minutes. This can neutralise embarrassing body odours for several days.

## Suffering from boils? New research reveals a quick and simple cure

Latest US studies suggest that many people suffering recurrent boils have low blood levels of zinc. Take 45mg of zinc twice daily to prevent further outbreaks.

Or apply a raw onion slice or a heated tomato slice compress to a boil. Change the compress every three hours.

## Make your eyes bright and beautiful with these 6 beauty experts' tricks of the trade

1. Soothe tired eyes quickly by applying raw peeled potato to them.

2. Cucumber juice contains high levels of moisture-retaining potassium to prevent water evaporation from your skin.

3. Apply cotton wool pads soaked in witch hazel or chilled milk. Milk reduces inflammation, and is a great, non-irritating moisturiser.

4. Apply cold teabags. Avoid herbal teabags – they don't usually contain all-important tannic acid. Ordinary tea bags are better.

5. Refresh tired eyes instantly. Cover them with your hands for two minutes, and look into the dark.

6. Freshen up puffy eyes. Run a spoon under cold running water, and then apply to each eye.

## Quick and easy massage to revive tired-looking eyes

Reduce puffiness under your eyes. Massage gently around the eye area to promote fluid drainage and oxygenate cells. Tap lightly around the eye socket and brow bone with your index finger. Do this 10-20 times a day for each eye.

## What's really causing those dark circles under your eyes?

Constipation is a major cause of dark circles around the eyes. To eliminate eye shadows, increase the amount of fibre in your day-to-day diet.

## Men! Does your penis pass the 'postage stamp' test?

One in ten UK males over the age of 21 suffer from impotence at some point in their lives. But this is usually a short-term difficulty caused by stress or worry. To check whether you are suffering a more serious problem or not, wrap a strip of postage stamps around your penis before going to bed. Moisten the stamp on one end of the strip and stick it to the stamp at the other end to make a snug-fitting band. In a typical night, you should have three to five erections. So if you find the strip has torn when you wake up, you are still having erections – and everything is in full working order.

## Men! How to find and stimulate your partner's G-spot

The G-spot – named after the sexologist Dr. Ernst Graffenberg – is a highly sensitive area on the front wall of your partner's vagina, about two thirds of the way towards the cervix.

It feels like a muscular crossroads, a small group of muscles that resist firm but gentle pressure. By slowly increasing this pressure, you can trigger an orgasm, almost at will.

Simply thrusting with your penis is ineffective. Instead, you men should lean back so that your penis is pressed firmly against the uppermost side of your partner's vagina. In fact, if you press there long enough without moving, you can bring your partner to the most intense and powerful orgasm she's ever experienced.

## Women! Seven proven ways to reduce monthly headaches, bloating and mood swings

Sex hormones such as oestrogen drive the production of prostaglandins, the substances that come from traces of fat stored in cell membranes in the uterus. These prostaglandins cause pre-menstrual pains and mood swings.

But there are simple ways you can overcome this hormonal change, and smooth your way through the monthly pre-menstrual stage.

### 1. Eat a low-fat vegetarian diet

US medical researchers have discovered that a low-fat vegetarian diet reduces the length and severity of pre-menstrual symptoms. It lowers oestrogen production, thus reducing prostaglandin production. Plus, eating a vegan diet with no animal produce whatsoever can boost levels of a protein in the blood called sex-hormone binding globulin. This can help the body to excrete oestrogen, easing pre-menstrual symptoms further.

### 2. Add more vitamin C and E to your diet

Also eat more starchy carbohydrates. This will help rid your body of oestrogen, a major factor in. Recommended foods are pasta, rice, potatoes, fruit, garlic, onions.

### 3. Avoid sugary foods and fats

These can be sources of extra oestrogen, and are known to worsen symptoms. Avoid cabbage, sprouts, cauliflower and broccoli too.

### 4. Restrict salt 7-10 days before the start of your period

Salt makes your body retain extra water, leading to that bloated feeling. Eat little and often to prevent food cravings. Exercise more during this time – walking, swimming, cycling. Regular exercise boosts energy levels by producing endorphins. These natural opiates produce a feeling of well being. And exercise helps to fight fluid retention too.

### 5. Take calcium supplements regularly

In a recent UK study, women took 1200mg of calcium daily for three months. Just under 50% reported a noticeable reduction in mood swings and depression. Also, 50%+ experienced fewer pains and cramps. But don't rely on milk as a source of calcium though. PMS may be linked to lactose intolerance. Check your reaction to dairy products, to make sure they're not worsening your symptoms. Milk and dairy foods are a source of oestrogen too. Avoid these as much as possible during this time.

### 6. Limit alcohol and caffeine intake

Ideally, eliminate these altogether. US research shows that coffee drinkers are five times more likely to suffer from PMS. And any caffeine-containing drink is known to increase irritability as well.

### 7. Mix and match other supplements to suit your body

A daily dose of one to three tablespoons of flax seed oil in fruit juice should improve general health and energy levels. Up to 200iu of vitamin E taken daily pre-menstrually has been proven to relieve breast symptoms and depression. Six to eight 500mg capsules of evening primrose oil taken daily for a minimum of three months is reported to ease breast discomfort too. A daily 300mg supplement of magnesium taken from 14 days before the start of the period has been shown to ease general PMS symptoms. But take care. Doses of 600+mg may cause diarrhoea.

## Men only! This DIY treatment can prove 100% effective in fixing premature ejaculation

US studies into "satisfactory intercourse experiences" reveal most woman need between four and ten minutes to reach orgasm after penetration. But premature ejaculation usually occurs after just 30 to 90 seconds.

So gaining control of your ejaculations is the key to fixing your problem. It will enable you to bring your partner to orgasm again, just like you want to.

### Possible physical causes
- Bladder and/or urethral infections can affect ejaculatory control. Antibiotics such as trimethroprim may be prescribed by your GP.
- Sensitive penis tip. Wearing a condom can dull sensations. The thicker the condom, the better.

### Practical causes
- Hurried intercourse is a common trigger. Reschedule sex to an undisturbed time and location to rectify this.
- Work-related stress or concerns over the relationship itself can encourage premature ejaculation.
- Over-excitement in the first few weeks of a new relationship. The brain and penis are simply out-of-sync with the body. Use a condom, and try a less exciting position. Be aware that time should resolve this.

### Most common cause
- Vicious cycle of anxiety. Once a man becomes concerned about premature ejaculation, it leads to greater sexual anxiety… leading to premature ejaculation… leading to greater sexual anxiety. Here's how to beat your problem:

### 1. Don't take drugs for this temporary problem

Anti-depressants such as Prozac and Seroxat are sometimes prescribed by GPs. But these drugs are rarely successful. They have well-known side effects of decreased libido and delayed ejaculation. This effect can provide greater control. Dosage varies, and the tablets need only be taken just before sex. But premature ejaculation usually returns as soon as the treatment is withdrawn.

### 2. Don't resort to creams and sprays

Special creams and sprays can be applied to the penis to deaden and delay ejaculation. But these can irritate the penis. And the effects are short-lived. In reality, drugs, creams and sprays are not long-lasting treatments.

### 3. Practise the 'stop-start' technique

This DIY exercise is almost 100% effective. Find some undisturbed time when you can relax. Masturbate towards climax, and stop. Grip the penis just below the glans to lessen orgasmic sensations if need be. Allow these sensations to fade away, and then start masturbating again. Repeat this exercise as many times as you can without climaxing. This takes practice, but masturbation is a crucial step in fixing your problem. It takes away all the worry of performing well during intercourse.

### 4. Take control of ejaculation

Using the 'stop-start' technique, many men can soon control masturbatory ejaculations. This shows the problem is resolvable. And when you've mastered masturbatory ejaculations, involve your partner. Tell them to arouse you manually, and say 'stop' as you approach a climax. Rest, calm down and start again. Practise this technique over several weeks.

### 5. Finally, return to intercourse

Once you and your partner have taken control of your ejaculations, you are ready to have full intercourse again. But as you reach climax, withdraw your penis and lie down. Rest, calm and start again. Repeat this exercise over several weeks, until you and your partner are in full control of when you ejaculate.

## Women! The true sexual power of your vagina revealed

To heighten sexual pleasure, contract your vaginal muscles more tightly around your partner's penis. Practise strengthening these muscles on a daily basis. To identify the right muscles, pause the flow several times when next urinating. These same muscles need developing to give you and your partner maximum arousal.

- First, contract for three seconds, then release for three seconds.
- Repeat ten times.
- Next, alternate between contracting and releasing ten times as quickly as possible.
- Finally, contract and hold for three seconds. Then push down for three seconds.

Alternate these exercises for as long as possible up to five minutes. Do them three times a day – and you'll soon experience greater sexual enjoyment.

## Men! Exercising this forgotten muscle will give you firmer erections, greater sexual control, and improved health in later life

The pubococcygeus muscle (PC muscle) is crucial to the strength and longevity of your erections. It is the same muscle you squeeze shut to stop urinating in mid stream. It pumps semen when you ejaculate. But having a weak PC muscle causes weak erections, weak ejaculations, impotence, premature ejaculation and more.

To regain control and boost your erections, flex this muscle whenever you have a couple of moments to spare. You don't need an erection to work your PC muscle. Sitting down, with a straight back is perfect. Waiting for a bus, for instance.

These exercises can soon give you better control of your ejaculations, firmer erections and a healthier sex life as you age. Here's how:

### 1. Locate your PC muscle

Go to the toilet, and standing up, urinate. Stop yourself mid-flow, completely. It may take several attempts to find your PC muscle. But once you have, you'll be able to exercise it at will. You can also find your PC muscle by getting an erection, and trying to move your penis without using your hands. This movement is controlled by your PC muscle.

### 2. Perform simple Kegel exercises

You don't need an erection to perform Kegels. But it is more effective if you do. Simply squeeze and release your PC muscle. Repeat 20-30 times. Work your way up to repeats of 100-200.

### 3. Practise the Long Squeeze

Just like it says, the Long Squeeze means squeezing your PC muscle, and holding for as long as you can. Aim for a slow count of twenty. Repeat 10-20 times, and build up to 100 sets per day.

### 4. Stair Steps

As with the Kegel, tighten and release your PC muscle. But do it in tiny stages. Feel the small increases and decreases in pressure as you step up and step down. Repeat 10-20 times, and aim to build up to 100 sets a day.

## Women! Release your Kundalini energy with pelvic bouncing

According to experts in the ancient Eastern sex art of Tantra, we all possess a potent form of sexual energy, called Kundalini energy. It can help us reach our latent potential. To release this energy within yourself start by making yourself comfortable and lie on your back.

- Rest your arms by your sides, palms facing upwards and bend your knees so your feet lie flat on the floor, your hips' width apart.
- Relax your neck, jaw and shoulders and then raise your pelvis from the floor.
- Bounce your pelvis up and down for a few minutes.
- You will rapidly feel charged up with energy all over your body.

## How to reach an orgasm without any physical stimulation

- Make yourself comfortable and lie on your back.
- Rest your arms by your sides, palms facing upwards and bend your knees so your feet lie flat on the floor.
- Relax your neck, jaw and shoulders, and then raise your pelvis from the floor.
- Close your eyes and imagine drawing in energy, picturing it as golden light, from the bottom of your spine.
- Tighten your PC muscle (the muscle you would use if stopping yourself urinating) each time you breathe in.
- Then as you breathe out, picture the energy moving upwards along your

spine.

● Repeat this until your energy is at the top of your head.

## Eight ways to beat sexual boredom and love your lifelong partner again

"To have and to hold til death us do part" is all well and good when you first get married. But what about in the middle of raising kids, work stresses and growing older? How do you keep the sexual spark alive?

1. Enjoy a natural endorphin high by flirting with each other. Experts say flirting sends natural amphetamines and endorphins surging through your body, stimulating an instant emotional "high" similar to orgasm. And the key to successful flirting is anticipation.

2. Imagine you have just met and remember that intense awareness of your partner's eyes on you. It will have a terrific effect on how you carry yourself – you'll look your partner straight in the eye when they talk to you, and be aware of your body when you move in front of them.

3. The written word is also powerful. Plant notes everywhere; on the fridge, in his briefcase or her make-up bag. Each one should describe what you find sexy about your partner. Or write notes telling him or her ten things you'd love to do to them right that second.

4. Enjoy the thrill of an affair – by arranging a surprise trip for you and your partner. Many people end up in affairs, not because they are unhappy, or out of love in their marriage – it may seem strange, but part of the attraction is simply the feeling of uncertainty that is felt by everyone at the start of a new relationship that gives everything a greater intensity. Long-term relationships often lose this element of uncertainty and spontaneity, which can lead to sexual boredom.

5. Meet up outside your home so you don't fall into your normal roles so easily. Surprise them with an unsolicited lunch invitation; arrange to meet them at lunchtime in the bar of a plain but presentable hotel. Book a room, buy a bottle of champagne and have wild sex.

6. Feel sexier than ever – make the first move. If your partner is always the one to initiate sex, the message you're sending is this: I do it to please you, not because I want to. This leaves both of you feeling cheated. The

person who initiates sex feels sexier because they're taking control and giving themselves power. Be the boss by suggesting sex and taking the lead role during love-making as well. Let your partner lie back while you do all the work.

7. Don't forget kissing – it's what you used to do when you first met! Many couples find that kissing stops once the relationship gets going or dwindles to a quick prelude before getting down to business. A long, passionate kiss can be more intimate than intercourse.

8. Have a steamy night in – enjoying a sensuous dinner party for two. Dedicate a night to your partner. Let them know of your plans by sending a note to them at work explaining why they are your No.1 desire and as a postscript, detail what you're aching to do that night. This will increase their anticipation and desire throughout the day. Splash out on some champagne and plenty of foods you can eat with your fingers (such as fresh fruit, crudités, dips and chocolate) and get ready for a picnic in bed. Or you could plan a delicious meal to cook together – it can be one of the most sensual things you can do together as a couple.

## Is your GP stopping you from having sex?

Many prescription drugs can have a devastating effect on your sex drive. For instance, beta-blockers, used to lower blood pressure, reduce stimulation to the erectile centre and can cause men problems in maintaining an erection. ACE-inhibitors, such as Lotensin, have fewer sexual side effects. But as they are more expensive, many doctors may not initially prescribe them. If you are at all concerned, ask your GP to review your prescription.

And although a lack of sexual desire is often a symptom of depression, evidence suggests that SSRI anti-depressants (such as Prozac) can interfere with sexual response in men and women, affecting ability to achieve orgasm. Always ask your doctor what sexual side effects may be caused by any medication you may be taking.

## Fifty plus? Two great ways to enjoy a better sex life

### 1. Take time to stimulate your partner
Whereas just seeing your partner naked might have been enough to turn you on when you were younger, you may now need to be a little more hands on.

- Spend time talking, touching and caressing.
- Some women need constant clitoral stimulation in order to become fully aroused. This can be accomplished through manual or oral stimulation – or by using a vibrator.
- Women often suffer from vaginal dryness as they get older, which can lead to painful sex. So use a lubricant like KY-Jelly.

### 2. Make love in the morning

Now, without the commitments of kids and work you don't have to squeeze sex into your routine last thing at night. You have all the time in the world to enjoy yourselves – so make the most of it.

- You may find that the early morning is the best time to make love, after a good night's sleep.
- Or try the afternoon, when your hormone levels are sharper than at the end of day..
- Also, you may no longer share a double bed, maybe for health reasons such as a bad back. You could keep your larger bed for lovemaking and have a separate bed for one of you.

## How the French over 50s beat illness and maintain their healthy sex lives

For many couples lovemaking may be limited by health concerns. A heart attack or other illness may require you to abstain from sex and all activities causing exertion for some time.

Try the French 'Chalon' position. The woman lies flat on her back while the man lies crossways to her, facing her on his side. She puts her legs over his and he curls his thighs under her bottom and enters her softly. This position not only reduces stress, it also allows you to see one another.

## What porn stars do when they want to last longer

Ron Jeremy, 'king of porn', is approaching 50, still loves sex and is still highly successful in the adult entertainment industry. Despite the fact his fans call him the "Hedgehog" – short, fat and hairy – Ron's ever-pressing determination to get into mainstream films has landed him in over 1,600 adult movies. When Ron is performing in front of the cameras and has to prevent ejaculating too soon, he thinks "of dead dogs and Vietnam casualties" to dampen his mood. This may be a bit severe for most people, but I think you get the idea!

You may not like the idea of Ron's tip. So why not try an ancient secret from the East. This simple exercise discovered by the Taoists of China will help you perform for longer. Practise injaculation: This technique can be achieved by pressing the 'Jen-Mo' point (an acupuncture pressure point on the perineum, halfway between the anus and scrotum). This reverses the ejaculation. The man experiences greater pleasure as the orgasm occurs in very slow spasms – and may last for up to 5 minutes.

## The 12 facts of secret sexual body language revealed

1. Looking longer than usual into another person's eyes shows your interest. And it can make that person feel special.

2. Widen your eyes a little. Research in the US shows sexual interest is revealed by wider-opened eyes.

3. But be careful not to gaze at someone for too long, if it is not being returned. An intent gaze is alluring only when it is welcomed by the other person.

4. Avoid closed signals, even if you feel nervous in the other person's presence. Arms folded, hands clasped, legs crossed together. These body signals say to the other person you don't want them near you.

5. Face them directly, and put your arms at your sides.

6. Keep your shoulders back and lean forward slightly. This shows attentiveness.

7. Sitting down? Rest your arms on the arms of the chair. This indicates you're very receptive to the person in front of you.

8. Keep your legs uncrossed.

9. If you can sit in a chair that's lower than their one, the other person will feel more comfortable with you.

10. Subtly mirror the other person's position and movements. This reinforces the sense of being well matched. If they're standing in a relaxed manner, adopt the same position.

11. When the person shifts position, copy that movement as naturally as you can. Try to move closer as you do so. This adds to that sense of intimacy.

12. Once you're tuned into their body movements, you can start slowly altering your own, so you become more open and receptive. The other person is then more likely to start copying you without knowing it!

## Why men go crazy for the smell of fresh pizza

Lovers have always used scented preparations to attract and arouse each other. Ancient civilisations made use of perfumes based on animal substances such as musk, amber-gris and civet. And today, artificial musk is now found in most aftershaves because it resembles the smell of male sex hormones and appeals to women.

But now, US research indicates that the smell of certain foods attracts men more than some women's perfumes do. Melted cheese, tomato and onion sauces are known to excite many men!

To arouse someone you want to attract, try this proven technique. Look for perfumes containing alpha-androstenol, and colognes that include alpha-androstenone. These are the most powerful attractors of all. The back of the packaging should tell you if the ingredient you want is included.

## Five simple beauty tricks to keep your skin younger-looking

1. Cleanse skin by rubbing with a warm-watered, muslin cloth.

2. Avoid soap, flannels and cotton wool that dry and age your skin.

3. Tone with orange flower or rose water.

4. Don't use alcohol-included toners which are too abrasive.

5. Eat more pomegranate. It contains a fatty acid (punicic acid) that slows body cells' ageing rates.

## What the French won't tell the Americans about beating middle-aged spread

To stay the same weight as you get older, eat several small meals each day rather than one or two large ones. Research at Tufts University in Boston, USA has found people in their 50s and older can still burn up small meals successfully, but their bodies find it harder to cope with larger meals. This leads to unnecessary weight gain and associated ailments and illnesses.

Aim for 400-500 calorie meals – about the size enjoyed by most French people at mealtimes. Avoid big blow-outs of 1,000 calories at a time. They are the No.1 cause of America's obesity epidemic.

## Feel ten years younger in just five minutes with these five ancient rites

Indian Lamas claim to have discovered the secret of eternal youth. It's based on little-known exercises called the Five Rites. Devotees say these are the simplest and most effective way to remain healthy and happy well into your retirement years. Some claim they can help you feel 10 years younger in just 5 minutes!

But you can't just begin these exercises right now. First, experts advise you check your current physical state to ensure you're ready.

- For the first week, and only if you are relatively healthy and fit, do each exercise three times.
- If you are inactive, overweight, or have health problems, do not perform rites 4 and 5 until you have built up some strength by practising rites 1-3.
- If you have any concerns whatsoever, consult your GP.
- If you have not exercised for some time, prepare by walking daily, for a half hour each day.
- Only do what you feel comfortable with. That may be only one of each exercise for the first week.
- Build up to two of each exercise the second week, three of each exercise the third week, or at a faster pace only if your body does not hurt when you do these exercises.
- Twenty-one is the maximum of each exercise you should ever do. If you want to enhance your programme, do the exercises at a faster pace,

but do not do more than 21 of each exercise each day.

● The Five Rites may stimulate detoxification, creating many unpleasant physical symptoms. So increase the number of each exercise slowly.

### 1. The Rotator

This stimulates all your energy sources and mobilises your spine.

● Stand erect with your arms outstretched level with your shoulders.
● Turn your whole body in a clockwise direction as far as you comfortably can.
● Return to the original position to start again.
● This exercise may make you feel slightly dizzy to begin with. If so, slow it down and continue at a more comfortable pace.

### 2. The Leg Lift

This speeds up your solar plexus energy centre and strengthens abdominal muscles.

● Lie full-length on your back on the floor, placing your arms palms down alongside your body.
● Raise your legs – keeping them straight as you do so – until they are vertical to the floor.
● Extend your legs slightly over and beyond your head.
● Lower them slowly to the floor, and repeat the exercise.
● If you find it difficult to do this exercise with straight legs, bend your knees as you lift your thighs and let your lower legs hang down.
● Lift as far as feels comfortable, and then return your legs to the floor. With practice, you'll soon achieve the straight leg lift.

### 3. The Head Bow and Raise

This stimulates the throat and heart energy centres, and improves the neck muscles.

● Kneel upright on the floor.
● Place your hands on the back of your thighs and lean forward as far as you can without falling over.
● Lower your chin to your chest.
● Lean backwards as far as possible without falling over.
● Bring your head and body upright to the starting position, and repeat the exercise.

### 4. The Bridge

To speed up the energy production in your sexual organs, and strengthen the hips, abdominals and shoulders.

- Sit with your knees bent at 90° and your feet flat on the floor.
- Place your hands palm down on the floor, with your arms straight, and your chin on your chest.
- Now: lift your hips upwards until your body is in a straight line forming a bridge position.
- Allow your head to fall gently backwards.
- Relax and return your hips to the floor, your chin to your chest, and begin again.

### 5. The Arch

This stimulates your core energy centres and invigorates the complete body system.

- Lie face down on the floor, with your body straight and hands placed on the floor, arms bent in line with your shoulders.
- Now arch your back by pushing upwards with your arms whilst keeping your hips on the floor.
- From this position, lift your hips upwards as high as possible.
- Your head should be down and forward, with your legs stretched backwards trying to push your heels down to the floor.
- Slowly lower your hips back to the floor whilst keeping your arms straight and lifting your head.

## Honey and coconut skin reviver

Warm 1/2 cup canned coconut milk in the microwave for 30 seconds. Stir in two tablespoons honey. Massage into skin and leave on for ten minutes. Rinse with warm water. Coconut milk contains lactic acid that renews your skin, while honey hydrates it.

## Invigorate your body with a slice of pineapple

Peel one fresh pineapple and cut into four wedges. While showering, massage wedges into skin, starting at shoulders and working down to feet. Finish by cleansing with a light shower gel and rinse thoroughly.

## End tired-looking skin with this home-made scrub

Mix 1/2 teaspoon baby oil with enough baking soda to make a paste. Massage over skin and rinse with lukewarm water. This scrub will stimulate tired skin and leave it looking glowing.

## Let Cleopatra's 'love shake' get your partner in the mood

Cleopatra's reputed aphrodisiac was said to be a 'love shake' consisting of spices, ground almonds, honey and yoghurt. Each ingredient is said to boost the desire for sex.

- Almonds, for example, are said to contain properties that can revive flagging desire.
- The Chinese have used ginger as a stimulant for 3,000 years.
- Other Eastern cultures use ginseng power and cinnamon for the same reason.

To get your partner in the mood, sprinkle these into your cooking.

## Want a bigger penis? Trim your pubic hair

If you're overweight or have very thick pubic hair, this can sometimes make your penis appear smaller than it is. Another thing to remember is that your penis may look shorter than it is because you're looking down at it. A simple optical illusion.

## How to arouse your partner in just a few seconds

No doubt you have been told the importance of holding your partner's hand – even if you have been married for 30 years. But hands are also a highly responsive erogenous zone that you can appreciate in other ways too – to great effect. Ask your partner to close their eyes and try this tonight.

- Lightly scratch small circles into your partner's open palm using one or two fingernails.
- Then gradually widen the circles so you are delicately tracing the outer edges of the palms, too.
- This little trick will literally send shivers down their spine.

# BETTING INSIDER
## The bets the bookies fear!
## Discover the only ways to make real money... including the bet that never loses!

# 31 straightforward strategies & systems proven to put the odds in your favour

How many times have you heard someone say "Gambling is a mug's game…The bookmaker always wins in the end…You can't beat the system"…?

But as any honest bookmaker will tell you when they cash up at the end of the week, the truth is very different. A small number of sports fans repeatedly win. But these professionals don't rely on 'hot tips' or luck. Sometimes, they don't even have to choose the winner to make a clear tax-free profit!

Now, complex analysis of the UK's leading betting systems has revealed 31 strategies you can apply – quickly, and with no in-depth sporting or mathematical knowledge whatsoever. These straightforward procedures actually work to put the odds in your favour  giving you the statistical edge you need to win money, just like a professional

## How a terrible tipster and a losing horse can win you money

At www.betfair.com, you can play bookie – and quote odds for other punters to back, just like a traditional bookmaker. This means you can now make money from losing in a horse race. Simply find out which newspaper tipster is currently the worst, and take bets on his tips! Here's how.

- Go to www.racingpost.co.uk. You will need to register with the site, but it's free.
- Click on 'Tipsters', then on 'Naps Table'.
- Take a good hard look at the table showing this season's performance of over 60 newspaper tipsters – best at the top, worst at the bottom.
- See which horses the three worst-performing tipsters are recommending today (also shown in the table).

- Go to www.betfair.com and offer odds for the worst tipsters' latest tips "To Win".
- When the horse loses, you will keep all the money bet by other punters foolish enough to follow the tipster's advice!

## Horse fans! Three reasons why picking two-year old winners is easy

Two is the youngest age at which horses can race competitively in Britain. And there are three very good reasons why you should take an interest in these 'youngsters'.

1. Two-year olds mainly race against each other, making their form easier to assess and compare.

2. Most races are over short distances of five to seven furlongs. Tactics play little part in these races and in most instances the fastest horse wins.

3. These young horses are full of zest, and try their hardest to win – so finding winners in these races is easier.

So, identifying a 2-year-old winner can prove easier than other horse races. Plus, sixty-six per cent of all two-year-old races are won by a horse that won or was placed last time out. Here's how to turn this information to your advantage.

- Look in any daily newspaper's horse-racing news.
- Find horses with a 1 or 2 at the end of the numbers and letters on the race card directly before their name.
- Then narrow down your selection to any horses that are first or second in the newspaper's betting forecast.
- Finally, eliminate any horses that last ran more than 30 days ago (the number of days since a horse's last run is shown by a figure after the horse's name). A young horse with a long break is rarely at its peak.

## Professional punter's form guide tip

The secret of deciphering speed figures, and pinpointing a winning horse, is simple. Look in the Racing Post (or visit www.racingpost.co.uk) and find the form pages for today's races. For each horse, under the performance table, you'll see all its previous races listed – the most recent at the top.

At the top right of each race will be a figure like this: Time 1m 12.98s (fst 0.22s). The first figure is the horse's time for that race, but the crucial figure is the one in brackets. This shows the number of seconds by which the horse was faster (fst) or slower (slw) than the average time for the course. Always pick the horse that has achieved the best speed figures previously.

## The best time of year to bet on two-year old horses

The flat racing season starts in March and runs through to November. However, the early season is not recommended for betting, as few two-year olds in a race will have run before, making form almost impossible to assess.

The summer months, from June to early September, are the peak time for betters – horses will have some previous form, plus the going will usually be good, meaning the top horses can perform at their best. From mid-September onwards, forget it – the weather deteriorates and the young horses begin to tire at the end of their first season.

## 5 simple steps to backing the next winner on Big Brother

Do the winners of reality-voting TV shows like Big Brother, Fame Academy and Pop Idol seem random to you? The facts prove otherwise. In fact, you can build yourself a Money Machine every time the nation chooses its favourite 'ordinary' person.

### 1. Back a male contestant

Since the first Big Brother show, there have been eleven reality TV shows with only one female winner. Why? Because 72% of 'reality' voters are women, and they vote for the men they like.

### 2. Choose a bloke under 25

The average 'reality' voter is under twenty-five years old. They will vote for someone similar in age. Of course, to keep the programme balanced, Channel Four always has a number of contestants aged 30+ on the show. But they're unlikely to win. Big Brother's 2003 winner, Cameron, got lucky. His younger male competitors' bad habits put the voters off.

### 3. Pick the teen-girls' heart-throb

Any contestant with the student/school kids on his side will benefit enormously from multiple voting. The all-important teenaged girl voters vote by text message 10, 20 even 30 times! Voting just once by phone is what thirty-somethings do. And they don't pick the winner, remember.

### 4. What turns them off?

Bad hygiene is a big 'no-no'. It cost good-looking Spencer, odds-on favourite for the 2002 Big Brother, a strong winning chance. Swearing is a vote killer too. Just ask Bubble!

### 5. And the winning strategy is...

- Put your personal preferences to the back of your mind.
- The ideal candidate is a young, clean, non-swearing bloke, who appeals to the younger of the female voters.
- Only if such a contestant is not to be found is it worthwhile considering the others.
- Check out the bookies' odds and if you can back all of those who fit this profile, and still show a profit whichever of them wins, you have a great winning strategy.

## Betting on Yankees? This simple staking plan doubles your chance of win

A Yankee bet is really 11 bets in one. It covers four horses in six doubles, four trebles and a four-fold. The pay-out potential is massive. But your odds of winning are tiny.

In fact, following the average punter's staking plan of £1 per line means your £11 outlay is wasted as soon as you've completed the slip. Mathematically, it is far better to stake more money on the bets most likely to succeed.

To boost the return you enjoy on your money, get one of those Yankee betting slips from a High Street bookmaker, and write down your four selections (horse name plus time/venue of race) followed by these instructions:

6 x £1 win doubles

4 x 50p trebles

1 x 25p each-way four-fold

This costs £8.50 (a 25p each-way bet costs 50p). That is £2.50 less than a standard £1 Yankee. And this method ensures most of your money is staked on the most likely  outcomes – the doubles. If you have a loser, you lose only the small stakes first. And if you find just two winners at any reasonable odds, you should be in profit.

## How professional horse-racing fans study the race card

- Back horses with good recent form. You can read a horse's recent form from the  string of letters and numbers in front of its name on the card. For instance, 4032. The most recent race is at the right, so the horse came second last time out.
- Avoid backing horses which haven't run for 30 days or more. They may not be in peak condition. The figure for days since last run is shown immediately after the horse's name.
- Stick to backing horses which are in the top five in the betting forecast. Over 80% of all winners come from there.

# Bets that never lose!

## Claim free money using your computer and a pocket calculator

Backing both tennis players in a match can make you an easy profit – guaranteed. The thousands of different bookmakers on the internet offer such a variety of odds, it is perfectly possible. Simply back both players at the best available price. If the maths adds up, you're sure to win.

This desirable situation is known as an arbitrage, or arb for short. To calculate an arb effortlessly, follow this easy-to-use guide.

**1. Find the very best odds available** using a bet-checking website such as www.betbrain.com.

**2. Convert odds into percentages.** Divide the right-hand side of the odds by the sum of both sides, and multiply by 100. So the percentage odds for 5/4, for instance, are:

$4 \div (4 + 5) \times 100 = 44.44\%.$

**3. Repeat this simple calculation** for the other player too.

**4. Now add up both percentages.** If the total is less than 100, you can profit by backing both players. For example, imagine Gustavo Kuerten is playing David Nalbandian. Kuerten is best-priced 5/4 (or 44.44%), and Nalbandian at 6/4 (40.00%). The total percentage here is 84.44%, well under 100. You have found your arb, and free money beckons.

## The No.1 reason arbitrage gamblers lose money

If you're looking to take free money off the bookmakers by hunting out arbitrage opportunities, don't fall into the trap of placing equal stakes on each wager. Use this secret staking strategy to ensure success instead.

To make your risk-free profit, simply match each bet's percentage odds with your stake. For instance, if one side of a two-bet arb is at 5/4, that's a 44.44% chance of winning. Put £44.44 on it to win. If the other side is 6/4, that's 40.00%, so put down £40. Whichever side wins, it will return £100. And whatever happens in the event, your total outlay of £84.44 guarantees a return of 18% tax-free.

Now that's arbitrage!

## Arb-hunters! Are you making this amateur's mistake?

Make sure your arbitrage profits stay in your pocket. Avoid bookies with hidden  charges. To place arb bets you will need to open online accounts with many different bookmakers. Then all you need to do is deposit some money in your account, and you're in business.

Sounds straightforward enough with familiar names such as Ladbrokes and William Hill. But some overseas online bookmakers make a charge for accepting credit/debit card deposits, or currency conversion charges. If you need to use such a bookmaker to complete your arb, use a cheque or money order to maximise your returns.

## How to find dead-cert betting profits at the click of a mouse

Searching dozens of online bookmakers for best prices can be time-consuming and tedious. But you don't have to. Odds comparison websites can check and compare the odds from tons of bookmakers and display the best prices on offer – free of charge. Both www.oddschecker.co.uk and www.tip-ex.com offer a good service. But the daddy of them all is undoubtedly www.betbrain.com.

This service lists and compares odds for dozens of sports and events, from football to boxing, motor racing to golf. It even displays arbitrage opportunities in a special box on the homepage headed SureBets.

## What the bookies don't want you to know about the 'Round Robin' horse-betting system

The Round Robin is a little-known way of backing three horses in ten profit-packed multiple bets. It can give you a big return for a small investment and, properly applied, will still give you your money back – or even a small profit – if you find only one winner. No specialist knowledge is required.

All bookies know about Round Robins. But unsurprisingly, they don't advertise them! A Round Robin is a bet covering just three horses running in different races. Place £10 on the Round Robin, and each separate bet within it has a £1 stake. Simply identify your 3 chosen horses, and then write out your slip as follows:
Horses A and B, Double = 1 bet
Horses A and C, Double = 1 bet
Horses B and C, Double = 1 bet
Horses A, B and C, Treble = 1 bet
Horses A&B, Single Stakes About = 2 bets
Horses A&C, Single Stakes About = 2 bets
Horses B&C, Single Stakes About = 2 bets

If you don't understand the terms here, don't worry. Your bookmaker will, and the special "Single Stakes About" bet in particular adds great gambling power to your bet.

Round Robin is best used with horses priced between 4/1 and 6/1. If all three horses in the bet are returned at 5/1, your winnings will then be as follows:
● Just one horse wins, you get your £10 back.
● Two horses win, you get £68
● All three win, you collect £390.

Use the racing pages of any newspaper, the daily Racing Post, or www.racingpost.co.uk to help pick your runners. Study the betting forecast for each race (printed under the list of runners and riders) and note horses whose predicted starting prices are between 4/1 and 6/1. Give preference to horses which are quoted as first, second or third favourite and which have the best recent form.

## Doubles, trebles and fourfolds made simple

A straightforward "win or lose" bet is known as a single. You bet on one outcome in one event. But you can enjoy much greater winnings if you tie two or more bets together on a double or treble.

- In a double, your winnings from the first horse are staked on the second runner. A winning £1 double on two horses both at 5/1, would give you £36 (£1 on the first horse at 5/1 returns £6, £6 on the second horse at 5/1 returns £36).
- In a treble, the proceeds of a winning double are invested on a third horse. If this wins, your winnings are multiplied yet again.

Then there are four-folds, five-folds and so on. But take care! If your first bet loses, your entire bet is scuppered. Doubles, trebles and fourfolds increase your potential winnings. But the chances of achieving your win are much reduced.

## This secret bet doubles your stake risk-free

All High Street bookies offer "Single Stakes About". But they'd rather you didn't know about this magical bet. It offers similar advantages to a double, but with none of the risk.

A "Single Stakes About" is actually two bets covering two events. If one of your bets wins, the original stake is taken from your winnings and invested on the other horse. So if you put £10 each on horses A and B, and Horse A wins, £10 of the winnings is added to the original stake on Horse B. This doubles your stake on Horse B to £20. But if Horse A fails to win, your original stake on Horse B still goes ahead, unlike with a standard double or treble.

## What 99% of sports fans don't know about making money from rugby league...

Under 1% of punters ever bet on rugby league. Yet this traditional winter sport, recently reinvented as a summer sport-fest on Sky TV, offers some gilt-edged opportunities for you to make money at the bookies' expense.

All the information you need is in your daily paper. You don't even need to understand the rules.

### 1. Handicap betting

For individual matches, bookies do not offer fixed odds on either team winning (as in the case of football). Rather, they set a handicap, giving one side a head start according to the bookies' assessment of the teams' relative chances. So if the league leaders are up against a team of strugglers, the latter may be given a 'start' of 20 points.

### 2. Common odds

Common practice is for both teams to be quoted at 5/6 on the handicap (i.e. just under evens). In the above example, if you backed the underdogs, and they lost by a margin of less than 20 points, you would win the bet. By contrast, if you backed the favourites, they would need to win by more than 20. This type of betting takes some getting used to. But even blatant mismatches can provide some excellent betting opportunities.

### 3. Assess each team's ability

Turn to the league tables in the sports section of the main national dailies on Saturdays and Sundays, or consult them at any time on the rugby football league website at www.rfl.uk.com. Then follow this simple procedure to calculate your bet:

● First, take away from the total points won by a team in the league the total points lost. This will give a plus or minus figure.
● Divide this by the number of games played to give a rating, which again may be plus or minus.
● Now assess the outcome of any game by comparing the two teams' ratings and calculate the difference between them. Add two points to the rating of the team playing at home to allow for 'home advantage'. For example, if a team has a rating of plus 8, this will become plus 10 when they are playing at home. If their opponents on the day have a rating of minus 5, the net difference between them is 15.
● Finally, compare your net difference with the bookies' handicap. If there is a difference of more than three points between the two figures, a bet is indicated – and the bigger the points difference, the more confident you should be.

In the above example, if the bookies' quote required the home team to win by 10, you would want to bet on them, as your calculation indicates that they should win by 15. Conversely, if the bookies set the handicap at 20, your figures indicate that the home team has been given too much to do, so a bet on the visitors would be favourite.

## Hit the bookies for six betting on county cricket

The nucleus of a good county cricket side continues from year to year. And the winner of the Championship usually comes from amongst the teams that performed well the previous season. So backing the top teams from last season is a canny gamble. When the bookies publish their prices at the start of the new season, back the top 3 to repeat their success. Odds are, you will come out ahead when one of your 3 selections picks up the trophy as the summer ends.

## How to win money betting on final football league positions

Long-term spread bets – such as the total points achieved by a football team in a season – can offer you good money-making opportunities. A run of tough matches, and the bookmakers' quote for that team is likely to fall... no matter what their likely total when the season ends.

To exploit this situation, simply look at the fixture list for this season's strongest middle-rank teams. Do any of them face the top three teams in their division one after the other? If so, expect the bookies to misread the situation, and cut their quote dramatically. Buy that team as the spread falls, and sell to lock in your profit as they return to winning form against weaker teams.

## Using the fixed odds coupon? These three simple systems turn £21 into £1,344

Fixed odds football betting involves betting on the result of one or more football matches at pre-set odds such as 2/1. The easiest way to profit from fixed odds is to bet on the correct scores of football matches.

Fixed odds coupons for midweek and weekend matches are available from all betting shops. They look like pools coupons, but are actually divided into four main sections – the long list, the trebles list, the handicap list and (your all-important) correct scores. Three systems harness the amazing power of permutations to generate big wins for you.

## System 1: The Winning Double

Select two matches you think will produce narrow home wins. Write out your bet like this:
"Match 1: 0-0, 1-0, 1-1, 2-0, 2-1
"Match 2: 0-0, 1-0, 1-1, 2-0, 2-1
"Perm five results, for each match for a correct score double = 25 bets"

Replace 'Match 1' with 'Chelsea vs. Aston Villa' (or whatever) as appropriate. If you use a £1 unit stake and pay tax, the cost of the bet will be £25.

The odds for a 1-0 result (statistically, the most common score) are usually around 7/1. If both matches end 1-0, you'll receive £64 (£1 at 7/1 returns £8). And that £8 re-invested at 7/1 returns £64.

The odds for a 2-0 or a 2-1 result are normally about 12/1. If both matches end 2-0 or 2-1, you'll receive £169 (£1 at 12/1 returns £13). And that £13 re-invested at 12/1 returns £169.

## System 2: The Treble Profit

This is a riskier system that will win less often. But when it wins, the profits can be spectacular. Cover three matches with the three most common home win results, 1-0, 2-0 and 2-1. Write out your bet as follows:
"Match 1: 1-0, 2-0, 2-1
"Match 2: 1-0, 2-0, 2-1
"Perm three results from each match for a winning treble = 27 bets"

Using a £1 unit stake, this bet costs £27. If all three matches end with the same one of these scorelines, you'll be in line for a big payout. With three 1-0 wins at 7/1, your winnings for a £1 unit stake will be £502 (the winning double returns £64, and this money staked on the third match at 7/1 generates a £502 return). Or with 2-0 or 2-1 scores and odds of 12/1, you'd receive £2,197. With returns like these, you can make a tidy profit even if you only win once in every ten bets!

## System 3: The Lucky 21

This system covers seven matches for just one result – but you need only two to be correct to collect a profit. More than two correct scores can produce stunning returns. Write out your bet like this:

"Match 1: 1-0

"Match 2: 1-0

"Match 3: 1-0

"Match 4: 1-0

"Match 5: 1-0

"Match 6: 1-0

"Match 7: 1-0

"Any two correct scores from seven for a winning double = 21 bets."

Using £1 unit stakes and paying tax, this bet costs £21. If any two of these matches finish as 1-0 home wins at 7/1, your return on this double will be £64. But if three matches end this way, you'll have three winning doubles on your coupon (1, 3, 4 combine as 1 and 3, 1 and 4 and 3 and 4). This gives you £192 (£64 x 3). And four correct scores gives six winning doubles and £384... five produces ten doubles and £640... six generates 15 doubles and £960... and all seven correct scores lands you 'Lucky 21' doubles and a £1,344 return!

## The secret of betting percentages revealed... and how you can beat the bookies' rigged game

All bookmakers build a guaranteed profit margin (or 'over-round') into every race. They set the odds so that, whichever horse or dog wins, they still make a profit overall.

For example, imagine a race with five horses, and prices set at 6/4, 3/1, 4/1, 6/1 and 10/1 respectively. To calculate the bookies' profit percentage, perform this simple calculation:

1. Add one point to each price.

2. Divide it into 100.

3. Add the totals together.

In our example, this works out at:

6/4 + 1 = 2.5. Then 100 / 2.5 = 40

3/1 + 1 = 4. Then 100 / 4 = 25

4/1 + 1 = 5. Then 100 / 5 = 20

6/1 + 1 = 7. Then 100 / 7 = 14.28

10/1 + 1 = 11. Then 100 / 11 = 9.09
Add them up, to get 40 + 25 + 20 + 14.28 + 9.09 = 108.37%.

Anything over 100% means the bookie is guaranteed a profit. Below 100%, and they've made a loss. And to improve your profits over the long run, attack the bookmakers on their lowest profit events. The closer their percentage is to 100%, the greater your pay-out if you pick the winner.

## Little-known tip for playing 'spot the ball'

To increase your chances of winning a newspaper's spot-the-ball competition, always put all of your crosses in one of two places on the photograph.

● Imagine the photograph is divided in two with a vertical line across the centre.
● Then divide it into eight, with four horizontal lines down the photograph.
● Number the boxes from 1 to 4 across the top row, and from 5 to 8 across the bottom. Research shows the majority of wins come from the middle of boxes numbered 2 and 3.
● Ignore players' eyelines and body language. They all react at different speeds.

## The secret of winning money from 'Asian Handicap' betting

Predicting whether a football match will result in a home win, draw, or away win can prove tricky. Those three possible outcomes create too many random results. But 'Asian Handicap' betting makes life much easier. It reduces the number of possible outcomes for any football game from three, down to just two.

In Asian odds, the favourite always has a minus handicap, the underdog a plus. A minus figure shows the 'start' a team gives its opponents, while a plus figure is the advantage a team begins with. When calculating the outcome of an Asian Handicap bet, you need to add (in the case of the underdog) or subtract (if backing the favourite) the handicap figure from your team's goal total.

So if you back Fulham at −1.00 and they win 3-1, after Fulham's handicap of one goal is deducted the net result is 2-1. Your bet wins. But if

Fulham only win by 2-1, after their one-goal handicap is subtracted the net score is 1-1. This is a draw, so your stake will simply be returned.

This handicap system means you can win money from the underdog, even if your team loses. A big handicap of +2 will still pay out, even if your team loses 1-0.

## To start making money from Asian Handicaps quickly, simply gather these 4 simple nuggets of data.

1. Goals scored by home team at home

2. Goals conceded by home team at home

3. Goals scored by away team away from home

4. Goals conceded by away team away from home.

Take the number of goals scored by the home team at home and subtract the number of goals conceded at home. This will give you a goal difference figure (GDF) for the home team. Do the same for the away side, taking the number of goals scored away from home, and subtracting the number conceded.

Comparing the teams' GDFs will give a good indication of the likely outcome. Say Spurs are playing Southampton at home. Spurs have scored 29 goals at home and conceded 22, giving them a GDF of 7. Southampton have scored 14 goals away but conceded 21, giving them a GDF of –7. The difference is 14 in Spurs' favour, clearly indicating a probable win for the home side.

Where the difference in GDFs is less than 6, a draw is the likeliest result. If the difference is 6 to 12, bet on a single-goal victory for the team with the better GDF. With a difference of 13 or more, back the side with the higher GDF if they have a handicap of –1.5 or better.

## Three tips for profitable spread betting on football

● Goals supremacy – the goal difference between the winning and losing teams. This is fairly predictable, and bookies usually price matches accurately. So look for matches between badly mismatched teams.

Why? There is often value to be found in selling winning margins here. Winning teams normally ease up to conserve energy when they play lesser opponents.

● Total goals. This occasionally produces profit-making opportunities. But beware! Many people assume that a game between two high-scoring teams will result in many goals. But this is not always so. Instead, look at the average number of goals conceded by the away side. If this is low, a low-scoring game often results.

● Corners. Betting on the total number of corners during a match offers more  opportunities for success. When two good teams play, there are usually fewer corners, as defenders are more adept at preventing them. However, in bad weather, corner counts nearly always rise. So look for opportunities to buy corners in the mid-winter months. Plus, the smaller the ground, the higher the corner count. Expect more corners in tight, compact grounds such as Arsenal's Highbury Stadium.

## 10-step staking plan for low-risk, steadily growing horse-racing wins

Dutching is a system of backing two horses in a single race to guarantee a set target profit if either horse wins. Because, in any race, you will have two good horses on your side, a high success rate is assured and long losing runs are all but unheard of.

Of course, if you are backing two horses to win, one will always lose – but if you follow the clever staking plan revealed here, you'll always make a net profit.

**1. Buy a daily paper with racing coverage.** The Daily Mail is perfect for this system.

**2. Eliminate all amateur races,** ladies' races, apprentice races, selling races and any race with 'novice' in the title. All something of a lottery.

**3. Eliminate all races where the forecast favourite is 10/11** or shorter odds. (You will find the betting forecast under the list of runners in each race.) There is not enough profit in such short-priced runners to make this system viable.

**4. For all qualifying races, find the highest-rated horse.** The ratings figures are at the far right of the race card. The highest-rated horse in each race is highlighted in the Daily Mail by a black circle.

**5. Select the race in which the highest-rated horse ran most recently.** The number of days since a horse last ran, is shown by a number directly after the horse's name (e.g. Red Marauder, 16). Now, you're comparing all the highest-rated horses and seeking the one with the lowest figure for days since last run. This horse is the most likely to be in peak condition.

**6. If two or more races tie** because the top-rated horses previously ran on the same day, give preference to the race with the highest-priced forecast favourite.

**7. Once you have selected a race,** the horses to bet on are the highest rated and the forecast favourite. If these are one and the same, the horses to bet on are the highest rated and the horse named second in the betting forecast.

**8. Set your stakes according to the forecast** price of each horse. Convert the odds for both selections to percentages, by dividing the right-hand figure in the odds by the sum of both figures. Then multiply by 100.

**9. Add these percentages up** and subtract from 100. This gives you your profit margin on your bet.

**10. To win £50 (or any other amount) per race,** divide your target profit amount by the profit margin and multiply this by the percentage odds for each horse – this will give you the stakes required.

## Why British bookmakers always get it wrong on American ice hockey

American ice hockey is a top sport for anyone wanting to make money from betting. Detailed statistics are available free, yet UK bookies regularly slip up in setting prices for NHL.

- Go to www.espn.com or buy USA Today, an American newspaper with a European edition.
- Compile ' Offensive Ratings'. These show how effective a team is in attack. Click on Team Statistics from the ESPN website's main NHL page and find the column headed SOG. This shows each teams average

number of Shots On Goal per match.

- To the left of this, find the column headed GFA. This stands for Goals For Average and shows the average number of goals a team scores per game.
- To produce your 'Offensive Rating', divide the team's SOG figure by their GFA figure. This will show you how many shots a team makes on average before they score a goal. It provides an effective measure of their attacking prowess.
- Now do the same for your 'Defensive Ratings', to discover how good a team is at shutting out opponents. Click on Team Statistics as before, and this time find the column headed SOGA (Shots On Goal Against). Divide the SOGA by the figure in the column headed GAA (Goals Against Average).
- The resulting figure indicates the number of shots an opposing team has to make before they score a goal and provides a good guide to the team's overall defensive abilities.

Look for a strong offensive team playing a weak defensive. And don't forget to check for stories about injuries to a team's top players too. If your ratings show the two teams are at least evenly matched, back that team's next opponents before the UK bookies catch up and shorten their odds.

## Football fans! One crucial statistic can turn a £10 closed-season bet into £640

The British summer can be a dull time for football fans. But the Australian league offers a great opportunity for you to clean up while you're waiting for August. Bet throughout the closed British season with this foolproof Aussie strategy.

In Australia almost as many games end in victory for the visitors (38%) as they do for the home side (41%). Perhaps because the sport is mainly amateur and crowds are small, home advantage does not count for very much. Yet bookmakers frequently price up Australian games as though they were English league matches, with prices more generous than they should be for away wins.

Go through the Aussie Fixed Odds Coupon (from your bookmaker's cashier) to predict those profitable away wins. Starting with the home team, note the total number of goals they've scored and conceded in their home games. For example, in a match between Lalor United and Fitzroy, you might find that the home team, Lalor United, has had 10 goals for and 14 against in home matches, giving them a net figure of –4.

Repeat this with the away team, this time using only goals scored and conceded in away matches. You might discover that Fitzroy have scored 12 and conceded 9 goals, giving them a net score of +3. So Fitzroy has a superiority of 7 and is your pick to win this game. Here's your strategy:

1. When the away team has a superiority of five goals or more, they're worth backing for a win.

2. Only place bets during those weeks when between 3 to 6 matches offer this superiority.

3 If there are more than six, choose the six games offering the biggest superiority to the visiting team.

4 Use the 'Long List' of around 45 matches (on the left-hand side of the coupon).

5. Against each chosen match, mark a '2' in the first column, and place your bet. If you have four to six matches, mark them with '2', and in the column headed 'Perms' write 'Perm any treble'.

6. Your bet will then include every possible combination of three matches from the total shown.

7. With average odds of 3/1 for an away win, a winning treble will return a massive £640 to a £10 stake.

## This 7-step baseball strategy can win you £580 next summer

Baseball is widely misunderstood by UK bookies and the betting public. Yet there is no need to be a baseball expert to cash in on the opportunities it offers. All you need do is check and compare some simple statistics available for free on the internet. If you want to watch the games, they are shown on Sky Sports and Channel Five.

1. Visit http://sports.espn.go.com/mlb/statistics.

2. Call up stats for the MLB pitchers – by far the most important men on the field.

3. Look for the pitcher's 'Earned Runs Average' (ERA) straight away. This figure shows the average number of runs he concedes through poor pitching during a game, averaged for the season so far.

4. Compare these stats. If you are weighing up a game and team A's pitcher has an ERA of 2.5 and team B's has an ERA of 5.6, for example, you will see straight away that team A should have an enormous advantage.

5. Go one step beyond the British bookmakers. Calculate the pitcher's Total Runs Average (TRA). This shows the total average number of runs a team concedes when a particular pitcher is playing for them.

6. Now calculate the pitcher's TRA yourself. Find the total number of runs scored against the pitcher (shown under the heading R), multiply this by nine (the number of innings in a game) and then divide by the number of innings he has played throughout the season.

7. Compare the TRAs of the two teams playing. If one of them has a lower TRA worth 2 runs or more, back them.

Typical odds are 10/11, so if you bet £11 each time and get 20% wrong, over 100 matches you could well be looking at a net profit of £580.

## How to turn one £20 note into two £20 bets... neither of which can lose... and still have the original £20 safe in your pocket

There's no catch. Anyone can do it, thanks to the incredible world of bookie-free bet exchanges. Very few people realise just what goldmines these websites really are.

A bet exchange is a website where any member of the public can bet in total anonymity against other members of the public. You can back a horse, a player or team to win an event, or you can accept bets on those same horses, players or teams, just like a bookmaker.

The tactic is very simple. Accept bets at a shorter price as a 'bookie' than you take as a 'backer'. Here's how.

**1. Find prices,** quoted by the traditional High Street bookmakers, for an event not due to take place within the next few weeks. The Premier League winner or next year's Wimbledon Men's Single winner for instance, is perfect.

**2. Spot odds** for a team or player you think is certain to do better than the bookies believe. In betting terms, these odds are likely to shorten.

**3. Go to a bet-exchange website.** Accept the longest odds on offer, and place a 'win' bet as a punter.

**4. Bide your time,** and check the bet exchange website regularly. When your prediction starts to come true... and other punters push the price of your selection down by backing it... you're ready to strike.

**5. Go back to the bet exchange.** This time, play bookie instead. Offer odds for other sports fans to back. Make sure your odds are a) lower than the price you first accepted as a punter, but b) slightly better than the current price generally available with the traditional High Street bookmakers. Eager fans will bite your hand off.

## Your overall position is enviable...

- If your selection wins, you will win more money as a punter than you have to pay out as a bookie.
- If it loses, you will recoup your loss with the money you keep from your bet-exchange customer.
- Best of all, the bet exchange software will know you cannot lose overall. So it puts your original stake back in your account!

How does this work in action? Take Australia vs. England, First Test in Brisbane, winter 2002. The Australians are by far the best side in the world. So when British bookies offered the Aussies at 6/4, a £20 bet wouldn't have been amiss. That price was also available at www.betfair.com, the biggest and best bet exchange website.

Before too long, Australia's odds had shortened dramatically to 1/6. That's when you could have turned that £20 into a can't-lose investment. Play bookie, and offer other Betfair customers the chance to back Australia at 1/5. Much less than you'd accepted originally, but greater than the High Street bookies' quote of 1/6.

- If Australia won, you'd pick up £30 profit as a punter (£20 at 6/4). But you'd have to pay £4 to your Betfair customer (£20 at 1/5). Total winnings: £26.
- If Australia lost, you'd lose your £20 bet… but keep the £20 stake you took as a bookmaker. Net result? No loss.

# EASY MONEY
## Simple ways to make anything up to £5,000 a month in your spare time

# Twenty-six simple ideas to make £160 a day... £650 a week... even £5,000 per month running your own part-time business

If you've ever dreamed of escaping the 9-to-5...increasing your weekly income without working two full-time jobs...or simply earning extra money to give your family a better standard of living...then the 26 ideas revealed in the following pages are perfect for you.

Each one has been road-tested and proven by its author. These are everyday people with the everyday aim of boosting their income. The only difference? They have stopped dreaming, and started doing something about it instead.

## Plus! 72 proven secrets for making up to £250 in just 2 hours next Sunday, trading popular antiques and collectibles

Making money can be as simple as emptying your attic, and selling your old 'junk' at a car boot sale. In the pages that follow, professional antique and collectible traders share their top money-making secrets with you.

## Did you read comics as a kid? You could have £24,000 sitting in your attic...

Comics and comic-books have risen sharply in value since the stock market crash. Now they are sought after by serious investors.

- The Golden Era (1930s and 1940s) are most valuable. This period saw the first editions of US comics like Superman, and British comics like The Dandy.
- The Silver Era (1950s and 1960s) is dominated by US-publishers DC Comics and Marvel. They launched SpiderMan, the X-Men and the Incredible Hulk.
- Even comics dating back to only 1995 have been known to sell for £1,000. Look out for the Dark Knight Returns (the new version of

Batman, launched in 1987) and the Watchmen.
- Spend at least half a day at a collector's fair or at a comic shop, and look at back issues of The Comic Journal.
- Torn, marked or well-thumbed comics still hold value. But pristine, mint-condition copies fetch the highest prices.
- Look for editions where famous characters make their first or last appearance. The first-ever Spiderman comic from 1963 is worth up to $32,000 in mint condition. That's around £24,000.

## What the rich have always known about investing in wine…

Provided you have the willpower not to drink your investment, investing in wine offers you a serious profit over 10-20 years. Some wines can deliver good returns after just 5 years.

- Tax-free investment possible.
- Either buy shares in a particular wine producer, vineyard or region.
- Or buy the actual wine. You can then store it at home, or keep it in a bonded warehouse for protection, insurance and professional care.
- Private client and institutional brokers now offer professional expertise and general support to the less-experienced wine investor.
- Start with a 'blue chip' like Bordeaux. It has a track record for quality and improves with age.

## 5 tips for making money from vintage cars

- Sports racing cars driven at famous events are highly valued.
- Classic and post-war cars are a great investment.
- With older cars you will need to be willing to put in the effort and cost of restoration.
- Start with research. Join clubs, read magazines and attend shows.
- A good place to buy is at an auction. You can see many cars at once, and judge the best investment.

## Why do the rich and famous risk so much money investing in racehorses?

Some racehorses become financial stars earning millions in their prime, and selling for sometimes even more at the end of their career.

But more often than not, it's simply a fun – and expensive – hobby.

Don't expect to make your fortune out of owning a race horse.

- Join a syndicate that will look out for your best interests.
- If you get a partner, take care over what form ownership takes.
- This is a highly speculative investment.
- If you have the money, buy a horse already in training. Invest in the best trainer you can afford. You need trustworthy and talented advisors.

## Let Agatha Christie, John Grisham and Catherine Cookson pay for your next luxury break

Here are the insider secrets you need to become a book dealer in your spare time and earn some extra money.

- Get a stall at an antiques fair, car boot sale or even your local market.
- Charge £2 for a paperback in good condition (down to 50p for a tatty copy), and around £5 for a hardback.
- Arrange your books into different subjects (crime, general fiction, DIY etc).
- Get some boxes from your local supermarket to make transport easier.
- Price everything with light pencil markings. If you write too heavily, people who are looking for gifts won't buy them.
- Local libraries often sell off their old books cheaply (50p for hardbacks!). Pop in and see what's on offer.
- Simply erase their prices and triple your profits easily.
- Buy more books by placing an ad in your local newspaper. Offer to buy paperbacks.
- Your local auction house may have great deals too, sometimes selling over 100 books for only £5.
- Sell unpopular titles by having a bargain 25p box. You'll be surprised at what people will buy simply because it's a bargain. It's a great way of moving hard-to-sell stock without giving away your profits.

## Book dealers! Boost the value of your secondhand stock by 40%... 100%... 200% or more

Buy second-hand copies of books by popular modern authors. Nick Hornby, Maeve Binchy, Ruth Rendell... as long as they're still alive, you can add at least 40% to the value of their earlier works. Just keep an eye out for book signings in your local bookshop.

The author will be promoting their new book. But ask instead for them to sign an old novel. You've instantly added money to the resell value. Remember not to get it dedicated to anyone though. This can make it harder to sell. Simply ask the author just to sign it 'Best wishes' and their name.

## How to spot fake celebrity autographs a mile off... and become a successful collector and dealer instead

The celebrity autograph industry is fraught with unscrupulous dealers who pass on fake signatures as genuine. If you're buying from a dealer, do a little investigating if the dealer is selling at a particularly low price.

- Call other long-standing dealers and get their advice. It is quite a close network and so legitimate dealers will know who the fake dealers are.
- If you have a celebrity autograph, take it along to a dealer and have it valued. You never know. It may be worth something.
- If you're lucky enough to have an autograph of Marilyn Monroe or Charlie Chaplin in your collection, you are better off taking it to Sotheby's.
- Watch out for pre-printed photographs. These signatures have been printed onto the photograph and look very convincing.
- The rubber stamp method is popular too. The celebrity's signature is etched onto a stamp and then marked onto the photograph.
- Secretarial signatures can prove convincing. The celebrity legally authorises a nominated agent to autograph items on their behalf.
- Always take care when buying signatures off the internet. Many are fakes and so-called 'certificates of authenticity' (COA) mean nothing. Always check the Universal Autograph Collectors Club members list for registered dealers before buying. Visit www.uacc.org. Also look at:
  - www.autographstore.co.uk
  - www.icollectit.co.uk
  - www.autographica.co.uk

## Collecting celebrity autographs? Spot the 'bad signers' and boost the value of your collection

- Marlon Brando's signature is worth a fortune. He's famous for always refusing to sign photos or publicity material for his fans.
- Gary Lineker signs anything put in front if him. Little or no resale value.

- David Jason has stopped signing except for charity auctions. Now his signature is worth around £100.
- A signature of Michael Caine can vary between £25 and £125.
- David Beckham's signature on an England shirt is worth more than his signature on a Manchester United top.

## How to earn £5,000 or more a month visiting the world's most exotic destinations

Less than 20% of companies around the world export their products. As an import-export agent, you could earn up to £5,000 a month helping the other 80% realise their potential. Commission of between 2.5% and 15%!

**1. Keep a sharp eye on your local shops to determine the latest fads, trends and hot sellers.**

**2. Use your holidays to go looking for products and manufacturers to help you introduce great new products back here.**

**3. Don't forget Britain's increasingly multi-cultural society.** It can offer you plenty more great opportunities. Find out what your local Turkish, Indian or Nigerian neighbours miss most from back home. See if there's a way you could get it into the local shops.

**4. Turkey offers a brilliant opportunity right now.**
- Scour local markets and shops for first-class rugs, leather goods and craft silverware that Turkey is renowned for.
- Get chatting to local retailers and ask for introductions to manufacturers of the items that interest you.
- Buy samples and assure your new contacts you will be in touch following your return home.

**5. Malaysia and Indonesia are great for high-quality wicker furniture.**
- Keep your eyes peeled for unusual items that would appeal to UK consumers.
- Contact local manufacturers, introducing yourself as an agent.
- Give them your contact details, get theirs and photograph items of interest to you.

**6. Italy still represents untapped potential.** While there are plenty of French foodstuffs on the market, Italy is surprisingly unrepresented.

- Find out local specialities while on holiday.
- Try them out and, if you like them, talk to the food producers concerned.
- You should easily find buyers at local delis or health food shops back home.

# This secret Blackjack system could make you over £500 a week, even if you've never played cards before...

If you can count to ten, a secret but perfectly legal system could make you at least £70 a day simply from Blackjack, or 21 as it's sometimes known. Even if you've never set foot in a casino before, you can still rake the money in. This simple technique is  designed to give you a massive edge over the Blackjack dealer.

### The game
- A dealer gives you two cards. You add up their value, scoring picture cards as 10 points and Aces as 1 or eleven points. The object is to beat the dealer by drawing a total greater than his, but not greater than 21.
- You either say 'Stick' if you think you're close enough to 21 already, or 'hit' to be given another card and push your total score upwards.
- If you end up with more than 21, you're 'bust'.
- If the dealer has a total exceeding 16, he must stand with that total.

### The trick
Card counting is based on a simple statistical premise. The more low cards that are removed from the deck, the greater your chances of winning. If the high cards are removed, the dealer has the better chance. So just keep a tally on which cards have been dealt. Then you can decide whether to bet your money or hold back.

### Your strategy
You can't take out a notepad and pen though. The casino won't like it. Card counting requires using your memory to keep track of which cards have been dealt from the pack in previous hands. It can give you a 1.5% winning edge over the house.

# Love shopping? Five steps to making £150 a day as a 'mystery shopper'

Imagine being paid to go shopping – and enjoying a free lunch too! There is a great demand for mystery shoppers. Companies want honest feedback on their products and services.

But traditional market research surveys rarely give them the full picture. You don't need specialist training to be a mystery shopper, but experience of the service industries or acting are big advantages. It can prove quite hard work, and you must be reliable with good observation skills, prepared to provide high quality accurate research.

### 1. Make up to £150 on your first assignment

You'll be given a very specific assignment to collect information – anything from investigating a shop's returns or complaints procedures to checking window displays and staff knowledge about their products. It could take just five minutes, or over an hour. You'll be paid according to how complex the assignment is.

### 2. Don't take notes while you are in the store

Go somewhere else to write down your notes immediately after your visit. When writing up your report, make sure it's neat and on time. You won't be paid for late reports and a badly presented report will mean you won't get hired again.

### 3. Get paid to go shopping without leaving home

You can even become an online mystery shopper. Many websites need to ensure their ordering and delivery systems are working. Each assignment typically takes a couple of hours, for which you will be paid around £12.

### 4. Become a consumer consultant

When new products are being developed and tested, companies are always looking for 'real' consumers to test them on. Sign up on www.globaltestmarket.com and you'll be invited to give your feedback and opinion on new product ideas – or to test products at home before they are launched elsewhere.

### 5. Contact details:

www.channelstrategy.co.uk

www.segreto.co.uk
www.ternconsultancy.co.uk
www.macphersonmysteryshopping.org.uk/beamysteryshopper.htm
www.smbs.co.uk/shopper_1.htm

## How a sack of soil and 15 old yoghurt pots could make you an easy £30

Many people simply leave it too late in the year to start planting seeds and end up forking out far more cash for seedlings or mature plants. If you have too many  seedlings to plant out in your garden this year – try selling them instead.

All you need is some good potting compost and a collection of old yoghurt pots with holes poked in the bottom. Fill the pots with the compost and simply transfer your spare seedlings into them. Grow them for a couple more weeks in the pots until they have reached a good size. Sell them at local church fairs or boot sales and charge between 50p and £2.

## Make an easy 50% profit using your flower-arranging skills

Selling hanging baskets is a great way to make a bit of extra money – especially if you have an eye for design or flower arranging.

**1. Use peat or a peat-based compost.** This will make handling the baskets easier and safer.

**2. Start by planting around the base of the basket first.** Trailing lobelia, nepeta or antirrhinums are excellent plants for this – about six plants around the basket.

**3. Then plant the top.** Popular plants include:
* ivy leaf geraniums
* helichrysum silver or gold leaf
* petunias

**4. Sell your baskets for £15-£20 each at boot fairs.** This should be around 50-100% more than what they cost you.

## How you can turn Charlie Dimmock's success into your own garden consultancy business

You may not be Charlie Dimmock or Alan Titchmarsh. But you may have plenty of creative gardening ideas. If so, you could turn your know-how and enthusiasm into a new business venture.

1. Advertise your services by placing notices in your local newsagents and garden centres.

2. When you visit a garden to discuss a potential job, spend plenty of time with your client asking them about their needs:
- Do they have children?
- Do they want a cottage garden?
- Are they interested in growing vegetables and herbs?
- Do they prefer a low maintenance patio-style garden?

3. Type up your suggestions and make a detailed plan showing where you think things should go.

4. Include a list of suggested plants and give an estimated cost for any major purchases such as buying patio slabs, or turf for large areas.

5. You can charge upwards of £70 for this kind of service, depending on your level of expertise and the size of the gardens.

## Like gardening? You could earn £15 an hour pottering around in your neighbours' flowerbeds

People are happy to pay between £5 and £15 an hour for a cleaner. It's physical work they feel needs to be done. But they don't have the time or energy to perform these tasks themselves. Many people feel the same about their gardens. They love the idea of a garden and then find that they do not have enough spare time to do it justice.

Gardens can quickly become overgrown and feel like an oppressive responsibility to their owners. This is a perfect opportunity if you have plenty of spare time and enjoy gardening.

- Offer to mow lawns, trim hedges, do some weeding and generally keep gardens tidy and manageable.

- Charge from £7 an hour for a basic tidy-up, through to £15 for more creative maintenance.
- Advertise in local neighbourhoods with a lot of owner-occupied properties.
- Give business cards to your satisfied customers – so they can pass them on to their neighbours.

## These 17 tips could make you £54.25 tonight running a classic British B&B

Opening a B&B could prove very good fun for you. It could also supply you with an extra income of up to £54.25 per night.

You can either operate as a business B&B all year round, or focus on holidaying families and foreign tourists in the summer. The choice is yours. And don't worry if you have no experience of the tourism or hospitality industries. Eighty per cent of people setting up a tourist business have no previous experience.

1. Advertise your B&B easily and cheaply. Place a card in local shop windows for as little as 20p a week. Tell local shops, pubs, restaurants and taxi firms about your B&B – they often get asked about accommodation by travellers and tourists.

2. Customers don't like answering machines. Get your home phone diverted to your mobile when you're out. And carry a copy of your reservations book with you at all times.

3. Tell the Council. It's a simple procedure. But you need to register your change of use with your local Council.

4. 100% cotton sheets are best. Use plain colours. Change weekly and for each new guest.

5. Beware duck-down duvets or pillows. Asthma sufferers could suffer a serious allergic reaction.

6. All mattresses must have sprung interior, foam or similar quality. Modern and comfortable with mattress protectors and/or under blankets.

7. If you can't offer a guest lounge, make provision. Put a comfortable

chair in the bedrooms. Drawers should run freely and should be lined or have an easily wiped surface. Wire coat hangers are not acceptable.

8. Rooms must have at least one window with clear natural light, plus adequate ventilation. You should always provide a curtain or a blind. If a room is on the ground floor you will need to provide additional privacy in the form of a net curtain or blind as well as curtains.

9. Overall lighting must be 160 watts for a single room and 220 watts for a double room. A bedroom light needs to be controlled from the door, and you need to supply a means of controlling a light from each bed.

10. If your floors don't have carpet, you'll need to provide slip-resistant rugs or mats by the bedside.

11. Go for robust furniture and fittings that will stand heavy use. Bright, clean rooms will attract higher-paying guests too.

12. Refurbish your guest room every two years.

13. At least one bathroom and toilet between six people. The WC should be separate from the bath or shower room, unless you have a B&B with four or fewer bed spaces.

14. Just serve breakfast, and you won't have to register for a food hygiene certificate. Full English fry-ups are best.

15. Write to publishers of travel guides too. Many will list your B&B for free (especially if you offer the editor a complimentary night's stay!)

16. Get your outlay back from the taxman. Tell your local Inland Revenue Office you're starting a B&B, and you could claim your extra expenses back against tax.

17. For further information, contact:
English Tourism Council
www.englishtourism.org.uk for a free
information pack contact 020 8563 3000.

## Nine easy steps to make financial spread betting simple

Clever chaps that they are, bookmakers have gone far beyond just quoting odds for the gee-gees. Today, you can take a punt on the value of the stock market, without buying any shares. The rewards can be dramatic. But financial spread betting is a high-risk venture too. Here's how to approach it.

### 1. The Gamble

You bet on the FTSE rising or falling. You stake a certain amount of money on each point of the index. So the more right you are, the more you win.

### 2. The Spread

Bookmakers quote a 'spread' around the current value. So if the FTSE is at, say 4200, the bookies may quote 4180-4220. If you think the FTSE will rise from 4200, you have to 'buy' the spread at 4220. If you think it will fall, you 'sell' at 4180. As you can see, the bookmaker has already set the odds against you.

### 3. The Contract

Each contract (as a bet is known) is for one 3-month period of the year. It is titled with the month when it will end – March, June, Sept and Dec. You can 'close out' your contracts at any time in between though. Your winnings (or losses) are determined by the amount of your stake multiplied by the difference between your bet and the price you close out at.

### 4. Closing Out

Imagine you bought at 4220 (when the real FTSE stood at 4200), and you want to get out when the index hits 4300. The bookies will now quote a spread of, say 4280-4320. To get out, you 'sell' this new spread at 4280. The difference between your 'buy' and 'sell' bets is 4280 – 4220 = 60. If you bet £1 per point, you've made £60.

### 5. The Catch

Note that whilst the FTSE actually rose 100 points, you can only claim winnings on 60 points. As we saw earlier, the bookies set the spread to limit your winnings.

### 6. The Risk

Imagine your 'buy' bet goes wrong, and the FTSE falls 100 points to 4100. Then bookies now quote 4080-4120. You have to 'sell' at the lower price to close out… meaning a difference of 4220-4080 = 140 points. If you were betting in tenners, that's a loss of £1,400. Ouch!

### 7. Your Strategy

Paper trade until you're ready to bet with real money. Simply place imaginary bets and follow them. Access live spread quotes from the big 4 internet spread betting bookies at:

- www.finspreads.com
- www.igindex.com
- www.cityindex.com
- www.cantorindex.com

### 8. The Opportunities

It's not just the FTSE 100 index you can bet on though. Individual shares, the price of gold, oil, currencies and metals, interest rates… a huge range of markets.

### 9. How to Protect Yourself

Use small unit stakes to start with. You can trade to as little as 1p a point, so a bad bet won't bankrupt you. And as your stakes get larger, set a stop loss limit with your bookmaker. It will cost a little more, but as soon as your bet hits the agreed level, he will close you out. This strictly limits losses to avoid losing your shirt.

## Make £500-£650 a week spinning PR stories from home

Public relations is the art of getting free advertising through newspaper articles, radio shows and TV programmes. Swanky agencies charge thousands for doing what you can do cheaper, better and more profitably from home.

**1. Every company needs PR but medium-sized businesses are your best clients.** Target clients in your immediate area. It's easy to get free exposure for local companies from your local newspapers, for instance. They're crying out for stories to fill their pages.

**2. Agree a new PR 'story' with your client every Monday morning. The best stories:**
- A new product or new lower price
- Charity donation
- New member of staff

- Your client's take on an important local or national story
- 'How to' information leading to a recommendation for your client's services

### 3. Now write that story up into a press release.
- Use the firm's stationery.
- Write News Release in capitals across the centre of the top of the page.
- Place the words Release Date a few lines below this, and state the date.
- Lead with people, names, local interest, exciting headlines and newsworthy angles.
- Make sure the Press Release includes full contact details for your client's business.
- End with your contact details in case the journalist wants more information.

**4. Mail, fax or email every newspaper, magazine, TV and radio station you can think of.** Wednesday and Thursday are good days. Journalists are often desperate for space fillers at the end of the week.

**5. Bill your client.** A short paragraph or 20 seconds of airtime can literally be worth £500-£5,000 free advertising to your client. So, even as a newcomer, you should charge £100-£130 for writing one press release. Build a stable of five regular clients and you'll earn £500-£650 each week from part-time home PR.

## Earn £12-£20 per hour just by reading your favourite books

Every non-literary book needs an index. If you have an eye for detail and a love of reading, it's easy to become a freelance indexer. Invest in the Writers' & Artists' Yearbook from your local bookshop. Write to publishers listed in it and introduce yourself. Nine out of ten publishers outsource indexing, so it's no hard sell. When you receive the page proofs you'll be working from, read each page and note the topics covered and relevant page number on an index card. Then, sort the cards into alphabetical order and type up the entries to create your index.

- You need flexibility to work unsociable hours.
- You need patience – you may have to read a book that bores you.
- You need the ability to interlink concepts and construct a system. It's not just about listing words.

Freelance indexers earn around £16-£30 an hour. Indexing a 200-page non-fiction book typically takes around 18 hours, so could earn you £540, while a 700-page technical reference book might take you 70 hours and earn you £2,100. If you have small children or a lot of time on your hands this could certainly prove to be a worthwhile small business.

For more information, contact:
The Society of Indexers
www.socind.demon.co.uk

## Mills & Boon insider reveals 7 secrets to get your book published

### 1. Go to a literary agent

Most fiction publishers don't accept unsolicited manuscripts. Aspiring authors should get hold of an up-to-date copy of Writers' & Artists' Yearbook, and find a literary agent they want to work with. This will help you get a foot in the door.

### 2. Your crucial first three chapters

Don't write the whole book before consulting an agent or a publisher. You'll need to submit a synopsis of the plot and the first three chapters. This stage is all about style, tone, structure and plotting. Capture the reader's attention right away and engage them in your story.

### 3. Don't despair if your book is rejected

J.K. Rowling was turned down 8 times before Harry Potter was assigned to a publisher. That's why it's good to have an agent. They will try to direct the book to the right person at the right publishing house. Try and try again.

### 4. The No.1 mistake of unpublished authors

Don't simply try to imitate what has been done before. If it's a literary book you're writing, you'll need to have a very individual style. On the more commercial front, narrative drive is important, plus good plotting. Your words and story need to be compelling and unique, as publishers are looking for new, fresh, individual voices.

### 5. Throw away your CV

Publishers aren't specifically looking for journalists or published short-story writers. It doesn't matter what your background is, if you've a talent for writing, then this is all that matters.

### 6. Know your facts inside out

Realism is crucial in any work of fiction. For instance, if someone suffers a heart attack in your story, research what it feels like and what happens at hospital. Don't rely on what you think you've learned from TV health dramas.

### 7. Write from the heart

Publishers are always looking for a new trend and the next bestseller. Passion is the key to hitting the right buttons. You never know, you could eventually be £175,000 better off. So what are you waiting for? Get writing.

## How to find the Harry Potter in you!

Booming demand for children's literature is set to continue. Here's how you can cash in with your own bestseller.

### 1. Understand the market

Read as many different big-name sellers as you can, not so you can rip them off, but so you know what has already been done and what works. Visit your local library, and see what's missing from the children's shelves – these are the most popular books.

### 2. Target your age group

0-3 years: animal stories only, with full-page illustrations

3-7: notoriously difficult. Publishers have strict guidelines. Mostly written by teachers or child psychologists.

7-11: children begin reading by themselves, so there's more scope for intricate stories and complex characters. Subjects these kids will understand and relate to include starting school, going on family holidays, and keeping pets.

### 3. Get the length right

0-7: Books for reading alone are about 3,500 words long

8-10: around 10-20,000 words long.

Pre-teens: 30-50,000 words long.

### 4. Outline your story using the three Cs

The older your readership, the more you can develop:

- Character (from simple heroes and villains to greater psychological depth)
- Contrast (light and shade, tears and happiness, anger and love, rich and poor)
- Conflict (parents against children, questions of guilt or conscience, conflicting loyalties).

### 5. Create characters kids will love

Your central figure should be as close as possible in age to your target reader, or just slightly older. Describe them to your reader, remembering to show, not just tell. Don't simply say a character is 'pretty' or 'selfish' or 'generous'. Let them display these qualities through their words and actions. Your characters should also develop throughout your story. Show how their experiences change them.

### 6. Keep your readers hooked

Create a plot which is more than just a sequence of events. Think of it as a chain of cause and effect. For children's stories, your plot should build up through a series of mini-climaxes before the final showdown at the end. But avoid an overlong ending that explains too many loose ends. These should have been resolved as your plot moves forward.

## These 5 simple steps could turn your 'how to' skills into publishing profits

The biggest best-selling books, year in, year out, are 'how to' books. If you can show other people how they can achieve something worthwhile, then you've got a potentially profitable book on your hands. Here's how to write, market and fulfil your own 'how to' book from home.

### 1. Decide your subject

Choose whatever it is you know most about. If you're a teacher at your local college, a how to book relating to study skills will be easy for you to write well.

### 2. Narrow it down

Visit your local library, bookshops and Amazon.com. Find out what topics in your field have already been covered in depth. What gaps are there? Which audiences have yet to be addressed? What topics could be hot news this time next year?

### 3. Plan your project

A 'how to' book will normally comprise 35,000-50,000 words. Expect to write about 2,000 words (the equivalent of seven A4 sides) per day. Total? Just 17-25 days' work.

### 4. Structure your book

Break your book down into eight or more easy-to-digest chapters. Use explanatory diagrams, flow charts, bullet-point checklists, chapter summaries whenever possible.

### 5. Find the right publisher

Use the Writers' & Artists' Yearbook to identify publishers in your chosen field. Find the name of the commissioning editor at that publisher. Call her, and start hustling to get your book published.

## Five insider's tips for making £160 a day as a TV extra

The vast majority of extras on TV and film sets are ordinary people. You could join them, commanding daily fees of £80 to £160 just for being in the background. The trick to securing this great income is to skip auditions, and act professionally when you get your first job.

**1. Simply look in The Stage newspaper** for contact details of agencies. Or visit www.ukscreen.co.uk and search for Extras and Walk-On agencies in your area.

**2. Put yourself forward.**

**3. Have some professional-quality black and white photographs** to send in, along with a description of your physical characteristics and availability.

**4. Avoid agencies asking for a huge fee to put you on their books.** No reputable agent will charge you, although a fee of up to £100 is sometimes payable if you want to go in their glossy directory.

**5. How to avoid looking like a total beginner...**
- Make sure you know where you are going and have your journey planned.
- Take warm clothes with you, even in the middle of summer. You don't know how long shooting will go on.

- You'll get free food when on location, but have to pay for canteen fare if you are working in a studio.
- Make sure none of your clothes have large logos, bright colours, whites or reds. You are not meant to stand out!

## Earn £150 an hour running your own history & crime tour guides

Profit from your local knowledge and expertise. Start guiding tourists and day trippers around your town or city.

1. Start small and profit fast. Offer simple town or city centre tours.

2. Take ten people around on foot for one hour, charging £15 per person.

3. Prepare a timetable giving arrival and departure times at key stops.

4. Devise a basic script containing main points to ensure everything is covered properly.

5. Offer little-known stories and amusing anecdotes.

6. Hand out brief notes about interesting features of the tour.

7. Encourage word-of-mouth recommendations. Include your contact details on all your new business stationery.

8. Eliminate your competition, by running 'behind-the-scenes' tours to lesser-known sites. Celebrities' former homes, so-called haunted houses, scenes of old, gruesome crimes. Leave the major tourist attractions to the big tour operators.

9. Get free publicity. Tell local newspapers, radio and TV stations what you're doing. Invite local journalists to come along free of charge.

10. Ensure you can answer clients' questions, by constantly adding to your knowledge.

# Casino owner reveals how to beat the system at roulette

Roulette is a fun game, easy to play. And with this clever system to help you, you can turn ordinary luck into a profitable night at the casino.

- A European roulette wheel has 37 slots, numbered 1 to 36 (coloured red or black) plus zero (coloured green).
- A US wheel has 38 slots, with an additional double zero (00) slot.
- In the game, you can bet on a single number (high odds, biggest payouts) or on pairs or groups of numbers (lower odds, lower payouts). Bet by simply placing your chips across the relevant numbers.
- The most popular bets and their respective payouts are:

  | Name | Numbers covered | Payout |
  | --- | --- | --- |
  | Single | 1 | 35-1 |
  | Pair | 2 | 17-1 |
  | Row/street | 3 | 11-1 |
  | Square | 4 | 8-1 |
  | Block | 6 | 5-1 |
  | Column | 12 | 2-1 |
  | Section | 12 | 2-1 |
  | Red/black | 18 | Evens |
  | Odd/even | 18 | Evens |
  | High/low | 18 | Evens |

- Mathematically, even-money bets offer the best chances of success. The in-built house advantage is lowest with these bets – just 1.35% in European roulette, compared with 2.7% for all other bets. This house advantage is among the lowest in all forms of gambling, including the pools, horse racing and the Lottery. Your prospects for winning are good.
- Bet successfully using 'The Pyramid System'. Imagine you're betting in tenners. Each time you lose, add £10 to your next bet. Every time you win, subtract £10. One exception! If you lose first time, simply bet £10 again.
- Use this system with any even-money bet (red/black, odd/even, high/low). The great advantage is, every win is worth £10 more than the previous lost bet. Given any average sequence of win/lose bets, this system should guarantee regular profits.
- Even with more losing bets than winners, the distribution of results still gives you a good chance of coming out ahead.
- Don't stay at the table too long though. The laws of chance dictate you'll eventually hit a long losing run, and wipe out your profits.

# Roulette players! Avoid 'The Martingale' system

This system is only for big-time, high-risk gamblers. You place an even-money bet (for example, betting on red or black) each time. If you win, you've doubled your money. But if you lose, you double your stake and keep playing until a win is achieved. In theory, this method cannot fail to produce a profit. But in practice, just a short run of 7 losing spins starting with a £10 bet will result in a stake of £1,280.

# What casino owners don't want you to know

Don't drink too much alcohol if you're winning at a casino. You'll be plied with free drinks by the management. But it's not to help you celebrate. They simply hope these free drinks will loosen you up, so you bet recklessly. Better to set a reasonable profit target, use your system to achieve this, and then stop gambling to enjoy your profits.

# Earn up to £20 an hour sharing your skills in adult education

A young mother may not be working formally at this time, but her involvement with the parent teacher association at her children's school may have developed brainstorming, speech-making, letter-writing and additional communication skills – all valuable to a further education college looking for new courses to run. If you have life skills picked up at work or in civil societies, you too could earn up to £20 an hour sharing your experience with students in further and adult education.

- **Draft a timetable for your proposed course**
  Show you can organize and run your own course. Get the most recent prospectus from your nearest adult education centre or college. Check the length and contents of various, similar courses. Then fit what you want to teach about your subject into that framework.

- **Make your course 'student-centred'**
  Chinese motto: 'I hear and I forget. I see and I remember. I do and I understand'. Today's adult education is built on this principle of practical workshops and discussion groups using the information you teach, rather than simply learning it off-by-heart.

- **Meet the principal of your local college**
  Say this meeting is to ask advice about becoming a freelance tutor,

rather than to actively seek employment. They're more likely to agree this way.

● **Clinch the deal**
Offer to do a free, short talk or workshop on someone else's course first, as a demonstration of your ability.

# Professional wedding photographer's money-making secrets revealed

If you've a good camera and enjoy taking photographs, you could earn a useful second income as a home-based, wedding photographer. These are the professional tricks of the trade:

### 1. Take as many photographs of your friends' weddings as you can
They will provide you with an all-important portfolio for selling your services. Choose the best 30 to 35 photographs you've taken, and have them processed as 7" by 5" prints. Put them into the smartest album you can afford. Include:
● the bride, bridesmaids and the bride's parents at home
● church arrivals and interiors
● formal groups, especially bride and groom shots.
● mix in photographs from as many weddings as possible to suggest you are already popular.

### 2. Have some business cards printed
And hand them to everyone you know. Word of mouth is the easiest way to get enquiries. Have some leaflets printed outlining your services. Find out what kind of packages to offer by contacting professional photographers in your area and pretending to be a potential customer.

### 3. Use soft-sell to bag your first job
Getting bookings is often the hardest part of the job. But it's easy if you adopt a personal approach. Remember you're selling dreams, not products and services. Don't treat your customers too businesslike. Suggest a free, no-obligation visit to show them your portfolio.

### 4. Meet the bride & groom
Suggest that the bride's parents are present. They're probably paying the bill. Describe your most expensive service first. If the couple show an interest in a particular style of photo from your portfolio, make a note to

take a similar one on the big day. And ask about extended family. The more you know, the better your photos will be.

### 5. On the big day...

- Check you can take photos inside the church and during the service with the vicar.
- Go to the bride's home if she wishes. Take shots of everyone getting ready, and especially her getting into the car.
- Don't forget throughout the day – keep snapping the parents of the bride. They're probably paying! But don't overlook the groom's parents.
- Photograph the church arrivals.
- Straight after the ceremony, photograph formal groups in the churchyard. Note! If a registry wedding, you'll need to locate and suggest an outdoor venue for these crucial pictures.

## Earn up to £150 an hour as a voiceover artist

Next time you are at the cinema or watching TV, listen carefully to the voices doing the voice-overs. Sure, some of them have a deep, booming tone. But many of the voices are quite ordinary. Voice agents need a range of voices and accents on their books. And while they predominantly recruit trained actors, there are plenty of opportunities for you

### ● Record a demo tape

Write down advertising voice-overs when you hear them. And practise saying them yourself until you are satisfied with your 'performance'. Then tape them on to a good quality tape or mini-disc. Make lots of copies and send them off to agents and production companies.

### ● Get the right agent

Many specialise in certain areas – foreign production, corporate videos, advertising, movie trailers and so on. To find agents in your local area, go to www.ukscreen.com and search under Voiceover.

### ● Relax

Being anxious at auditions tenses your abdominal muscles. This will interfere with your breathing, and make your voice sound forced and high pitched – not a good effect. Relax by saying a simple sentence over and over again until your voice is naturally resonant. Consider taking classes from a voice coach. She can train you in breathing properly, pronunciation and the elementary acting skills you may need.

### ● Look for foreign opportunities

As English becomes spoken more and more around the world, the demand for native English voice-overs also increases. Tourist videos are especially good sources of work. And training videos for new staff often have little competition for voice-over work.

## Cheap as chips! 72 proven secrets for making up to £250 in just 2 hours trading popular antiques and collectibles

## The 21 secrets of profitable antiques investment

David Dickinson, author and presenter of BBC TV's Bargain Hunt, has been a successful collector and buyer for over 25 years. His biggest tip is to look for quality. But how do you start assessing it?

1. Start by visiting flea markets, car boot sales, local antique shops and auctions.

2. Local auction houses will sell less expensive items. And advice is nearly always free!

3. Established fairs such as Olympia are carefully vetted. What you are told by a dealer is guaranteed.

4. Bigger fairs are great for learning. Plus, you have more chance of finding an antique worth investing in.

5. Choose your subject and bone up on it. Furniture or china? Regency or Edwardian? Focus your time, and read the history.

6. Sniff out quality. Even if a little scruffy, don't overlook the fact something could still be worth money.

7. Look to see whether a satisfactory restoration is possible.

8. Touch items, ask questions, talk to the dealer, open the drawers. Any dealer will explain in detail what you are looking at if you ask.

9. Let the dealer know you are not experienced. It will be obvious to the

dealer anyway.

10. Steer clear of controversial items like anything made of animal skin.

11. Avoid coffee tables – often cut down from normal tables or a table with a brand-new top or base.

12. Examining a marble table? Look at the legs. Are they old stone or modern cement?

13. Spot worthless stainless steel pretending to be platinum. Simply check the weight in your hands. Platinum is very heavy.

14. Only buy what you like.

15. Never spend more than you can afford.

16. Always ask for the best price. Dealers expect to negotiate.

17. Ask for full written receipts.

18. Remember VAT will be added at an auction.

19. Always consider the price of transporting your item home. It can prove quite costly.

20. When you're selling an antique, you may want to start by offering the item back to the shop you bought it from, or exchange it for an item you like better.

21. At auction, always read the catalogue carefully. If unsure, ask questions.

## How to buy antiques and collectibles for profit online

- You cannot actually see or touch what you are bidding for. So watch you don't misinterpret the description.
- Make sure you check out the authenticity of the seller, too, especially if it's a private seller. Get a definite postal address, and look at comments on the website from other buyers.
- Never pay cash unless it's on delivery. Always pay by credit card

instead.

## Nine 'in the trade' discount tips for buying at antiques fairs

1. If you're buying at an antiques centre or a fair, look at the label. If it says something like "T 5" beside the price, it means the dealer will give you a £5 discount if you're in the trade.

2. But don't just offer £5 less – or even worse, hand over £5 less. Depending on what kind of day the dealer is having, they might knock off even more.

3. Spot a bargain by judging the fair. If the dealers have had a bad day or a very good day (which doesn't make sense, but it's true), they may well be in the mood to offer discounts. Or just want to get rid of a bit of old stock or something large/bulky.

4. Got your own transport? Look out for large and bulky items the dealer might not want to cart all the way back home again. Make an offer.

5. Never say "I'll give you £££" straight away. That's bound to annoy the dealer. You might not get a discount at all.

6. Be realistic. When a dealer gives you his best price, that's your lot. But judge every dealer when you meet him. Can they afford to give a bit more, or is there enough profit left for you in their best price? If not, walk away.

7. Remember, if you're buying at an antiques centre, there's no point demanding more money off from the people serving you. Usually, it's not their stock. They only have a 10% discretion if the dealer hasn't marked the discount already.

8. If you really want the goods but aren't prepared to pay the discounted price, ask them to ring the dealer – you might get a bigger discount that way.

9. Don't bother haggling aggressively for items under £20. Most dealers won't have time for that. If the discount doesn't suit you, walk away.

## Three dealers' secrets for buying antiques at auction

- Stick to your pre-decided maximum price. With the added buyers' premium (generally 10% + VAT) you might pay more than it's worth just to beat someone else.
- Look everywhere, even in cupboards. That's where some auction houses store  excess lots or where sneaky dealers hide the better pieces.
- Don't always believe the catalogue. If everything listed as Victorian really were from that era, she'd still be alive today!

## Why you should ignore expensive 'price guide' books

Always ignore book price guides. They become out of date so fast nowadays. Instead, use these tips to find out what your items could be worth:

- Visit http://www.bbc.co.uk/antiques/ to search the Antiques Roadshow database of over 5,000 items valued by experts.
- Sign up for free with http://www.atg-online.com/ to access price guides for 16,000 items.
- Ask your local dealers. Valuations by auctioneers and other professionals can be free if you show you're genuinely interested in selling.

### Contact:

www.bonhams.com, tel: 020 7393 3900
www.sothebys.com, tel: 020 7493 8080
www.christies.com, tel: 020 7839 9060

## Car boot professional reveals her top 5 money-making finds

- Beatrix Potter goods, especially by Royal Doulton china. People throw them out when their children grow up. But recently a Peter Rabbit moneybox for £1 was worth £20. A figural plaster shop sign of Peter Rabbit for £5 sold for £60.
- Carlton Ware cruets. A split apple cruet for £3 sold for £25 a week later. A £6.50 Carlton Ware eggcup was actually worth £60, because of its Alice in Wonderland connection.
- Midwinter crockery (simply look for the name underneath).
- Old Steiff teddy bears and toys (look for the button in the ear).
- 1960s clothes – Biba is best. Buy for under £3 a piece and sell on the

internet or to a specialist dealer for £200+.

## Four hard-won secrets of successful car boot trading

- Arrive early, and join the professional dealers in hunting out genuine antiques and valuable collectibles amongst the household tat and rubbish.
- Always look in boxes and go through piles. You never know what the other dealers have missed, no matter what time you arrive.
- Be prepared for friendly haggling. The bigger your smile, the bigger the discount.
- Cheap is not always good. Some things are £1 because that's all they're worth.

## Let the internet turn your car boot finds into hard cash

When you get home from a car boot sale or antiques fair, quickly take some photographs of your finds with a digital camera. Make sure they're in focus. Take pictures of the marks (backstamps) under the china etc. Then upload those photos straight onto the internet.

- Go to www.ebay.co.uk, the biggest and best online auction.
- Click on 'sells internationally' to increase the number of potential buyers
- Set up a week or 10-day auction.
- When sending the item to your final buyer, charge them for the postage and ask if they want insurance added.
- Save any spare boxes for packing up future sales.

## Got more than 30 collectible or antique items to sell? Forget eBay...

If you have 30 or more collectible or antique items to sell, take out a stall at your local fair. You'll get lower profits than selling at www.ebay.co.uk, but a faster turnover. And local fairs or antique centres are the best places to attract professional dealers.

# 16 hot tips for making £250 in just two hours this Sunday morning

Almost five and a half million people attend car boot sales during the summer months alone. Well-advertised car boot sales attract large number of eager buyers. You can make easy money, selling unwanted items for low prices.

**1. Check your local papers** for listings of upcoming events.

**2. People will buy anything,** even if it's broken or has holes – just price accordingly.

**3. Check with the organisers** as to their rules regarding 'sellable quality'. And contact them in advance to get an allocated pitch. It costs £8-10.

**4. Request a pitch** near the entrance for maximum visibility.

**5. Clean all of your goods** before setting out, and label the prices clearly.

**6. If you want £1, price it higher.** Put 50p to £1 on top of what you want, so you can play the haggling game.

**7. Price books or sheet music in pencil –** you'll decrease their value and lose buyers if you don't.

**8. Take a float.** Save your change before you go and take plenty of 10p, 50p, £1 coins and £5 notes. If you don't want to deal with fiddly 5p pieces, then price accordingly. No 25p or 75p items for you. Take plenty of spare change. Bound to be someone who pays for a 40p item with a £5 or £10 note.

**9. Never leave your handbag or wallet in your car.** It will get stolen. Use a bum-bag to keep your money safe or wear clothes with extra deep pockets.

**10. Arrive early, two hours before the official opening time.** This way you've got plenty of time to set up.

**11. Display your goods on a wallpaper-paste table.** Ample space, and easy to transport.

**12. Cover with a good clean cloth.** It not only looks better, but you can store other items under it too.

**13. Take your time –** don't be pushed into anything before you're ready. Dealers will pounce on you before you've even parked. Tell them to wait until you've set up your tables before they can buy. Don't let them unpack for you.

**14. Never agree to put things aside** for people before they've seen them. People might ask you to save all of your crockery, for example, but then not buy. They're just trying to stop other people from seeing them. Refuse, and sell them to the first person who sees them.

**15. Don't forget to pack your own food and drink.** Car booting is thirsty work. But be careful not to drink too much liquid. The toilets are often filthy.

**16. Don't be duped into buying fake or defective goods.** Missing parts, badly damaged goods, faulty labels on so-called designer gear. Avoid at all costs.

## Can you spot the car-boot virgins? They offer you real bargain buys

It's normally easy to spot first-time traders at a car boot sale.

- Their stalls display poorly arranged items that aren't priced.
- They just want to make some fast money, and leave early.
- It's easy to haggle and bring their prices down.

How to turn their desire to make easy money to your advantage? If you think you've identified a car-boot virgin, use these four tips to bag yourself a bargain.

**1. If they have labelled their goods,** don't pay the price given.

**2. Ask for a discount of 10-20% instead.** If an item is priced at £10, for instance, offer £7 and expect to pay £8.

**3. Negotiate further discounts for bulk buys** – on boxes of collectable items for  instance.

**4. Remember,** traders prefer cash to cheques.

## Three top tips for making money via the internet

- Think internationally. Learn what appeals to foreign buyers – in particular those  from North America, as they dominate the internet trading scene.
- Specialise in one area. You'll be better able to spot bargains, and your expertise will show through in your marketing and customer support.
- Keep it simple. The last thing you need is a big idea. The simpler you keep your business, the easier it will be to make money.

# YOUR NEAREST & DEAREST

## Guarantee your family's future wealth, health and happiness with these canny tips

# 79 tips and insights to protect your family's home, future, stability and wealth

The British family has been under attack for more than 50 years now. From the loss of married couples' tax relief to our failing schools…from soaring divorce rates to teenage crime…the government and the media have conspired to destroy the traditional family unit and all it holds dear.

But there are ways you can fight back, using tried and tested strategies for better parenting, more honest and open relationships, and stronger family finances. The tips and insights shared here by fellow parents, partners and professional counsellors will help your nearest and dearest thrive as part of a loving family unit – come what may.

## Nine documents you should never throw away – ever

It's tempting to spring-clean all your official papers, but be warned. Being too enthusiastic to chuck everything away could end up costing you money.

**1. Your birth certificate:** You'll need your birth certificate if you lose your passport.

**2. Share certificates:** Never throw these away, and make sure that you keep them in a safe or secure place. Most people now hold their shares in electronic form, to reduce the risk of damage by fire, flood or theft. If you've still got paper certificates, consider transferring them to an account with a low-cost stockbroker for safekeeping.

**3. Pay slips:** You should keep these for a couple of months, except for your P60 end-of-year tax slip, which you should keep for six years in case the Inland Revenue wants to look at it.

**4. Anything to do with tax:** If you are self-employed this is particularly important and you can be fined if you fail to keep proper records. If in doubt, ask an accountant.

**5. Personal bank statements:** It's best to keep these for three years, as you'll need proof of your income and expenditure to show to a potential mortgage lender. If you need to ask your bank to dig out copies of your old statements because you have lost them, they may decide to charge you. The same goes for mortgage statements.

**6. Receipts:** Whenever you buy anything of value, keep the receipts for at least three years in case you need to show proof of purchase to your insurance company after a flood, fire or burglary. If you have any items of high value, for example jewellery, which you are planning to keep for many years, you need to hold onto the receipts indefinitely.

**7. Details of buy-to-let or business property:** Keep these for six years, as the Inland Revenue can request them at any time. If you run your own business you'll probably need the assistance of an accountant, who can advise you on how to keep proper records.

**8. Financial gifts:** If you're passing on gifts of money or assets to relatives or children, you need to keep a record of these disposals for at least seven years.

**9. Your marriage certificate:** Your solicitor will want a copy of your marriage certificate if you bought a house with your partner before your wedding and are now selling it as a couple.

## Turn your kids into millionaires... without upping their pocket money

With the average student now £15,000 in debt, you need to start teaching your children how to look after their own money today. Don't expect the government or schools to do it for you. Use these simple lessons taught to children across the USA to help your kids grow up money savvy, cash rich.

### 1. Save all cash gifts in a new account
This is like teaching your child to save before they're even born! Any cheques you receive as gifts when you're expecting your child, bank them.

Then, show them how much extra has magically appeared (thanks to bank interest and further deposits) as they grow older.

### 2. Don't pay tax

You'll be the trustee until your child is seven years old. Then, they're allowed to run it themselves. If they have an income of less than £4,615 a year, then they don't pay tax (2003-04). But you must register them to receive tax-free interest on their savings. Your building society or bank can give you Inland Revenue Form R85.

### 3. Get top interest rates

Don't settle for less than the best. Go to http://www.thisismoney.com/saving.html and find the best account for your child's needs. And no need for short notice periods on withdrawals. You can stump up any cash your child needs in the short term. Remember to check the age limit of the accounts though.

### 4. Set savings goals with your kids

For example, when they've saved £20 they can buy the toy they've been plaguing you for since Christmas. Or you might agree to 'top up' their account every three months if they save well.

### 5. Give them coins, not notes

Instead of giving them a £5 note, make sure they have five £1 coins. This way, it's easier for them to decide what to save and what to spend – and they will understand that a fiver is not the smallest unit of currency we have!

### 6. Make them work for their money

Don't simply give your kids pocket money. Give them an income instead. Exchange cash for housework – washing up, cleaning the car, tidying away their toys, vacuuming. You'll be teaching good work habits for later life.

### 7. Teach the value of money

Teach your kids to have a healthy relationship with money. Encourage price comparison when they go shopping. And help them work out the dilemma of choosing between one toy and another. Just like an adult, they can't have everything they want. They need to learn to choose.

## Discover the hidden benefit in giving your grandchildren a pension today

Any UK citizen can have a stakeholder pension. Even new-born babies can start saving for their retirement today. Plus, there's a lovely inheritance tax twist available too.

For an annual pension contribution of £3,600, you only need hand over £2,808… just less than the annual limit for Inheritance Tax on gifts. You and your children will have no potential Inheritance Tax liability.

Also, your kids don't have to wait until they are 50 before taking money out of the stakeholder you build for them today. If they work, say, in a family firm, they might be able to convert this pension into more useful plans, such as a self-administered scheme, from age 18.

## How to escape Britain's failing schools without spending £8,500 a year on independent fees

Choosing the right school for your children is a serious parental headache. Unless you've got £8,500 to spare a year on independent fees, you have little choice. But today, over 100,000 British families are fighting back – by educating their children at home. Particularly successful with kids who find school boring (often the brighter ones!), those with other special needs, and victims of bullying. You don't need to be a qualified teacher, or have a comprehensive education yourself. All you need is a desire to discover new things yourself.

### 1. Exercise your rights
Under UK law, it's your duty to ensure your child is educated whether at school or otherwise. Your Local Education Authority can ask to assess how well you're doing, but it must make an appointment first, and you can choose to have a friend with you during the inspection.

### 2. Give your kids the education you want
You can take what you want from the National Curriculum (see www.nc.uk.net and www.ngfl.gov.uk for government resources). Or you can follow your instincts and create your own programme.

### 3. Keep the benefits of a regular timetable
If your child has already started a traditional school or is just about to

begin, it's a good idea to follow the curriculum, and establish a 'schoolday' timetable to ease them into the new learning environment.

### 4. Get the best resources

Your local bookshop will have textbooks, software and revision plans to help your child succeed. The various examination boards can advise on each syllabus. Your key aim is to develop basic skills – literacy, numeracy, physical and social interaction – in ways that interest and stimulate your child. And you'll know better than anyone else how your child is responding to each lesson.

### 5. Turn new experiences into instant lessons

Any new experience can be used to develop your child's basic skills. Different children need different learning experiences – and home-educated children are generally ahead of their peers. Professional teachers know this. In fact, they make up over 30% of home educators!

### 6. Develop your child's social life

Without the risk of bullying or negative peer pressure. Enroll them in extra-curricular activities such as Brownies, Scouts, Woodcraft Folk, or specialised interest clubs. And home-educating families often share responsibilities and child-minding. For support and local contacts, visit www.heas.org.uk or www.education-otherwise.org.

## Warning! Why gifting your home could bankrupt you and your family...

Older people who 'gift' their home to their family to avoid a forced sale to pay for residential care costs are being bankrupted by local authorities pursuing funds. This scenario can be avoided if major gifts are made at least six months before going into residential care. Beware though. The time limit varies from one council to another – so check before taking this course of action.

## The truth about independent schools in Britain today

To get an accurate impression of an independent school, ask one of the pupils to show you round. Most teachers and headmasters will take you through the showpiece areas only. They will only provide stock answers to your questions too.

Hand-picked pupil guides will do the same. You'll only find out what the school wants you to know. Instead, approach a pupil loitering about, and ask for their assistance. Clear this with a teacher as soon as the pupil's agreed, of course.

The student's response will tell you much about the general attitude of the school and its pupils. Also, they will probably not know where they should take you and what they should say. Result? A revealing tour and a more realistic assessment of the school.

## Top university insider reveals how to get the place you want at college

What happens if you miss out on the A level grades you need to get into your chosen university? Here's how to secure your place in Higher Education on a course that suits you:

### 1. Ask your first choice again

You might still get in. Call the admissions department immediately to find out. You might have to phone several times. About 60,000 young people will still be looking in August. But do keep trying. All UK colleges are now set up to cope with all your enquiries.

### 2. Don't get sidetracked

Only your firm and insurance choices can contact you at this stage. And your insurance choice can only get in touch after you've been formerly rejected from your firm choice.

### 3. How to get through 'Clearing'

If you can't confirm a place at your Firm or Insurance choice, concentrate all your time on identifying and researching as many other possibilities as you can. You'll automatically receive a Clearing Entry Form from UCAS along with your clearing Entry Number. This is your passport to gain a place.

### 4. Start your research at www.ucas.ac.uk

Full lists of vacancies also appear in the Daily Mirror, The Independent, and The Independent on Sunday.

### 5. Act fast

As soon as you find a place you like, contact the university by telephone, fax, or email. Make sure you give your full address, a contact telephone number, and your A level and GCSE qualifications. Tell them the name of the course you'd like to discuss.

### 6. Don't miss out

If have to leave your house for any reason, make sure someone who knows your situation is able to take any calls for you. Carry your mobile phone with you at all times.

### 7. Secure your place

Once you've been offered a place and you've agreed to go, you must send your UCAS clearing form to the institution to confirm everything. You can only send your form to one place at a time – the university which you're sure you want to attend.

## The 'Mickey Mouse' scandal affecting young students today

It's a fact that the more students a college or university has, the more money it receives. And many smaller institutions now offer popular new courses simply to get "bums on seats". These courses are not recognised by potential employers as worthwhile or valid. Beware! The best route to picking a valuable course is to read the recruitment advertisements for the type of job you want, and see what skills, qualifications and training are required.

## Is your family owed a fortune by the government?

Discover unclaimed premium bond prizes easily and quickly. Simply go online at www.nsandi.com. Go to "Have you won", and enter your premium bonds' holder number. Any unclaimed prizes will be revealed. To check your holder number if you can't find your bonds, write to National Savings, Blackpool, Lancashire FY3 9YP.

## Nine simple steps to beat the taxman from beyond the grave

Think you don't have to worry about inheritance tax? Think again. House prices have risen a phenomenal 60% in the past 5 years. But the portion of your estate exempt from inheritance tax has only increased 16%.

This means today 1.4 million British taxpayers are at risk of having

IHT eat up 40% of the money they leave to their family. You can leave your heirs just £255,000 before the Government begins taxing your estate. But these nine simple steps mean they won't actually need to pay any IHT at all.

### 1. Reduce the value of your estate

Your heirs must pay tax at a rate of 40% on the value of your estate over £255,000. But you can give away up to £255,000 during the seven years before you die. Of course, you don't know when you have only seven years left – so be proactive and start gifting your money to them today.

### 2. Check the wording of your will

Make sure your will refers to the 'current nil-rate band', rather than quoting a sum. The amount you can give away tax-free is subject to change in the Chancellor's annual Budget, so unless you refer to the 'current nil-rate band' you could be short-changing yourself.

### 3. Invest in AIM/Ofex shares

Shares in smaller companies are exempt of IHT if you have held them for two years or more. The shares cannot be included in the value of your estate when you die. But be careful, shares in smaller companies tend to be riskier investments.

### 4. Celebrate by giving generously

Weddings are a great time to make the most of the government's tax-free gift rules. And they don't just apply to family weddings. You can give wedding gifts of up to £5,000 to each of your children or the person your child is marrying, and up to £2,500 to each grandchild or the person your grandchild is marrying. And you can also give up to £1,000 to anyone else you know who is getting married.

### 5. Give your money to a good cause

Gifts to charity are exempt of IHT. So leaving money to your favourite cause in your will won't eat up any of that valuable £255,000 limit. You can also gift to political parties (if they have at least either two MPs at Westminster, or one MP and 150,000 votes in the last General Election), and museums, universities and organizations like the National Trust.

### 6. Gift your cash properly

If you're giving away an asset whilst still alive, make sure you give it away entirely. Don't continue to benefit from it. For example, you are not actually giving away your home if you continue to live in it and you are not giving away an investment if you continue to receive interest on the investment. If you still benefit, the 'gift' will be treated as part of your estate. Beware!

### 7. Make your life assurance tax-free

Have any life assurance policies written in trust for your next of kin. This puts them outside your estate for IHT purposes. Simply ask for a form from your life insurer, and complete it easily by following the step-by-step instructions. Any pay-outs will also be made sooner without having to wait for probate too.

### 8. Leave your estate to a trust

With the help of a specialist, leave your estate to a 'nil rate band discretionary will trust' instead of to your intended beneficiary. This takes the assets out of your estate. And your beneficiary can request a 'loan' from the trust, only payable to them after your death. Trusts can be used by married couples, unmarried couples and even single people.

### 9. Change your home ownership

Change the way you and your spouse own your property. Become 'tenants in common' rather than joint tenants. Also set up a 'nil rate band discretionary will trust'. You can then 'sell' your home to the trust. The trust, not having any money yet (because you haven't died), will give you an IOU. But now you've 'sold' the home to the trust, it's not part of your estate and won't be included when figuring out your IHT liability.

## The 5 best ways to defend your home and family from the trauma of burglary

Three British homes are burgled every minute today. But by using the know-how here, you can rest assured you are doing your best to defend your home and family from attack. Make sure yours is the last house a burglar would break in to:

1. Fit all ground floor and basement windows with locks.

2. Make sure all doors are locked and windows shut when going out, even for a short time.

3. Never leave door keys under the mat or under a plant pot outside. Instead, give a spare set of keys to a neighbour or friend in case of emergencies.

4. Fit a trellis on top of fences in your garden – this makes it more difficult for burglars to climb into your garden.

5. Install lighting on the outside of your property and put gravel on your drive.

## Cut £750 off the cost of divorce and stay married to your money

The average UK divorce now costs £750 in solicitor's fees alone. Contentious divorce can cost a whole lot more. But you can cut the lawyers out of the equation completely.

1. First, agree to divorce amicably with your spouse. It's best to wait until you've been separated for some time, so emotions have cooled.

2. Sit down and make a list of all your assets. Work out how to maintain any children. You will have to do this anyway, and involving lawyers will only make it harder.

3. Now check your Yellow Pages, and find out the nearest county court that deals with divorce. Not all of them do.

4. Go and collect form D8 and – if you have kids – form D8A. Complete the forms, and send them back to the court together with the £180 fee. Include 3 copies of D8. If you can't find your Marriage Licence, call the General Register Office on 0151 471 4200.

5. Next, the court will send copies to your spouse. Provided they stick to the deal, and don't oppose it, your divorce will move onto the final stages in 9 months' time.

6. Complete form D84 from the court, your 'application for directions for trial'.

7. The District Judge will review your papers. She will be especially concerned about arrangements for your children. It is essential you and

your spouse are in full agreement here.

8. Once the judge has confirmed she is satisfied, you spend a further £30 on a decree absolute.

## Camcorder users! Protect your cherished memories from the ravages of time

Video and camcorder tapes last only 10 to 15 years before they start to deteriorate. It starts with "static" lines running across the image – much like a video that is not tracking properly. But it cannot be solved with your tracking control, and pretty soon you can't see anything at all.

To slow and delay deterioration, make sure you look after your videos properly:
- Temperature range should be from 59 to 77°F.
- Humidity should be kept at 40% to 60%.
- Fast forward and rewind tapes at least once every three years. That should keep the polyurethane binder from sticking to the adjacent layers of a tightly wound tape.
- Before storing your tapes, rewind them from end to end, in one complete uninterrupted procedure to make sure the tape is wound evenly and uniformly
- Buy only the highest quality tapes. They are coated more evenly and last longer.
- Seal the tapes in plastic bags to protect them from dust, smoke and moisture.
- Store them vertically, with the tape wound onto the bottom spool.
- Keep tapes away from strong electromagnetic fields such as speakers and television sets.

## Don't let care home fees steal your inheritance

Selling your parents' home to pay their carehome fees can seem like your only option if cash is tight and they don't qualify for State support. But there is a way you can defer this decision for up to 12 months.

- Make certain the property remains 'available' for the return of your parents.
- This allows residential or nursing home residents to have 'temporary' status for twelve months.

- If the property remains available and residents have temporary status, the property's value is ignored in calculating who will pay the fees.
- This gives you valuable time to arrange a more complex strategy based on your specific circumstances.

# Could you be heir to a fortune?

State-of-the-art software and hundreds of great websites can now help you uncover your family's history, locate long-lost relatives overseas – and maybe discover that you're heir to a fortune! Here's how to get started quickly:

### 1. Ask your parents and grandparents

You already have a lot of the information you need. Start with your own personal reminiscences, and then ask other members of your family. Take notes on basic questions like dates of births, deaths and marriages. It's also a good idea to include dates of any major upheaval – if your family emigrated for example, became bankrupt, or was involved in a feud.

### 2. Now use professional tools

Town records, genealogy societies, and the internet offer easy cheap tools to trace your roots. But don't jump online just yet:

- Scour your family records to see what you already know.
- Check Bibles, baby books, old letters, photo albums and scrapbooks.
- Make sure you've interviewed all your relatives about their memories.
- Make a list of what you don't know (and of contradictory information).
- Where are you most likely to find the answers? Visit churches and public records offices in areas where your family lived for a long time.

The central Family Records Centre can be contacted on 020 8392 5300.

- Check out libraries and genealogical and historical societies for details of migration patterns into these areas to help you understand why your ancestors might have arrived (or left) when they did.
- Next, compile a list of what you still don't know and prioritise its importance to your search.

### 3. Make your research simple

Use your computer to record, store and compare your information. And now you have a new list of questions, visit the websites dedicated to helping you. A good starting place is www.genuki.org.uk, an award-winning, non-commercial site run by the Federation of Family History. For serious investigation, visit www.genealogical.co.uk, the UK-based publisher of Genealogical Services 2000 Directory.

## Stop temper tantrums with simple sign language

Is your baby crying and you don't know why? It was realised in the late 1970s that hearing babies of deaf parents could communicate their needs at a much earlier age than those with hearing parents.

Teach your baby the 3 most important signs from 6 months old, and you will also increase bonding and boost their future IQ. Here's how:

**Milk** – mimic the action of squeezing a bottle

**Pain** – push her two index fingers together

**Tired** – make the sign for a bed by resting her hands besides her face

Make sure that you sign close to your eyes as your child looks directly towards you. Then mimic this sign again motioning your child's hands in exactly the same way. Make sure it's turned into a game and reward your children's attempts to sign with you.

## Baby due for jabs? Use tea to ease their pain

If your baby's skin looks sore after an inoculation jab at the doctors, dab with a cool wet teabag. The tannin will soothe the pain.

## Six simple tips to help your child through hospital

### 1. Talk about what's going to happen

This way, your child won't be so frightened of the unknown. Too often, children don't understand what's happening and pick up snippets of adult conversation that terrify them. Find out what you need to know from your GP, and explain it to your child in language they can understand.

### 2. Ask them what worries them

Identify your child's specific concerns, and you can resolve them more easily. Their worries may seem trivial to you, but they're not to your child.

### 3. Arrange a pre-admission tour

Many hospitals will arrange this, if requested. Walk through the wards, see other children, and show your child where they might sleep. Show them the playroom especially. Beware showing them the operating theatre though. Some children will respond well, but others will hate it.

### 4. Tell the staff about your child

Ask the nurse to write these details on your child's notes: food likes and dislikes, allergies, personal habits, names for body parts and toilet functions.

### 5. Take in toys to comfort them

A favourite cuddly toy or game, for example. And don't forget the most comforting presence of all – you. Be there as much as you can. Research proves it makes being in hospital much easier on young children.

### 6. Ask their friends to visit too

Most children perk up when a playmate calls in. It makes the whole experience feel more normal.

## Beat travel sickness by shutting your eyes

Motion sickness is caused by conflicting messages being received by your eyes and inner ears. Your eyes know you're going in one direction, whilst your ears think you're going in the opposite direction. Shutting your eyes resolves this conflict and remedies sickness for many people, children included.

## How to raise a well-behaved child with good manners

Adopt a 'once-only' approach to every instruction you give your young children. Get close to them, make clear eye-contact, and say what you want them to do in simple terms. If the child does not respond within 10 seconds, take them by the hand and guide them to do the task. This puts over the clear message that you expect them to do whatever it is now, rather than when it suits them. Beware repeated requests. They just encourage the child to ignore you.

## Parents! Why you must have aloe vera in your kitchen

The aloe vera plant is hardy, attractive and requires very little daily care. And it can help prevent scarring from sunburn, grazes, minor cuts and more serious burns before going to hospital. Simply rip off a stalk, split it open and squeeze out its cooling gel onto the damaged skin. It will soothe and encourage healing.

## Parents! This simple trick reduces your baby's risk of ear infections by 30%

Wean children from dummies early to reduce the chances of them developing painful and distressing ear infections. A Finnish study shows that children who stop using dummies regularly after 6 months of age have 30% fewer ear infections than those who continue. The effect may lie in pressure changes in the ear cavity, caused by prolonged sucking. Dummy use also contributes to increased oral fungal infection and tooth decay. And doctors advise that dummies can spread germs if children share them.

## Reduce a child's asthma wheezing by 30%

Children suffering with asthma should eat oranges or kiwi fruit 5-7 times a week. Research by the Regional Health Authority in Rome shows these great sources of vitamin C can help reduce coughing and wheezing by up to 30%.

## Parents! Beware what your doctor tells you about painkillers

Never give your child paracetamol and ibuprofen at the same time, no matter what your doctor tells you. Mixing over-the-counter drugs can have dangerous side effects. Yet research at University Hospital in Mineola, New York, USA, shows that almost 50% of doctors interviewed told parents of feverish children to give both acetaminophen and ibuprofen in alternating doses. But using both drugs together could result in liver damage and even death.

## Mystery rash? Quick test for meningitis could save your child's life

Find out if a rash is linked to deadly meningitis quickly. Press the side of a clear glass tumbler against the rash. If it does not change colour, call a doctor immediately.

A meningitis rash is caused by blood leaks from blood vessels under the skin. This condition is unaffected by pressure. If the rash fades and loses some colour or the skin turns white when pressed, then you can relax. The illness is unlikely to be meningitis. But test hourly. The rash may change.

## Doubts about your spouse's honesty? These five questions could save your marriage

Marriage and relationship counsellors have often noted how one partner's fear of being cheated on actually signals their own desire to find love elsewhere.

If you have felt insecure about your long-term relationship recently, use this checklist to ensure it's not you that's about to cheat on your partner.

1. Would you use the word 'bored' to describe your feelings towards your partner or your relationship?

2. Do you often argue about crucial aspects of your life together, such as children, schedules, extended family and spending?

3. Have any of your friends commented how you spend all your time criticising your partner?

4. Have you developed strong feelings for someone other than your partner lately?

5. Do you spend more time than previously out of the house and away from your partner?

## Is your partner cheating on you? The 11 classic signs of a secret love affair uncovered

Many marriages suffer communication problems and a lack of intimacy from time to time. But if your partner suddenly seems very distant, even weirdly calm, and you feel concerned they're cheating on you, check for these 11 classic signs.

1. Your home phone starts receiving a lot of hang-ups and wrong number calls.

2. New odours and fragrances on clothes – such as colognes, cigarette smoke or sweat.

3. Do you share a car? Then sit in the passenger seat to check whether it's been moved.

4. You discover your partner's secretly opened a new bank account.

5. He or she visits a tanning salon, beauty parlour or fitness gym for the first time during your relationship – without mentioning it to you first.

6. Sudden and unexplained change in the style of clothes they wear.

7. Your wife tells you she's visiting a friend who is sick – a classic rouse.

8. Your husband mentions a new female colleague at work, but says she's plain-looking. When you meet her, you discover she's stunning.

9. Your partner regularly starts coming home later than usual, but without explaining why to your satisfaction.

10. When you feel like being romantic, your partner suddenly turns very cold, even angry.

11. Your partner suddenly starts talking about subjects and topics you never knew they were interested in before.

## Save up to £59 or more by writing your own will

Be careful here. Solicitors make more money from sorting out the problems created by DIY wills than they do from drawing up original wills. It's important to get things right.

- Avoid the preprinted forms available in bookshops. By trying too hard to make the wording fit the framework of the form, it can be easy to make a mistake.
- Far better to write out in simple terms what assets you have and who you want to receive them as beneficiaries.
- Explain who you are and clearly name your executors.
- Then describe what you want to happen with your estate.

- Sign and date the will in the presence of witnesses – this makes your will complete and legal.
- Finally, make sure someone, maybe your executor, knows where to find your will in the event of your death.

## Five plain facts for making your will

1. If you want to change your will, you should draw up a new one, rather than alter the old one.

2. Make a new will after you get married, remarried or divorced.

3. Make sure your latest will clearly states it revokes all others

4. A will is the only document that legally requires two other people to witness your signature.

5. Anyone who will benefit from your will can't be a witness.

# TRADE SECRETS

**Make your home and garden
beautiful by using vinegar,
Bovril and bubblewrap..?
Dozens of amazing secrets
revealed inside**

# 165 tips to make your everyday life easier at home, in the garden, fixing your car and in case of emergency

## Did you know that…

- Toothpaste can be used to polish bathroom taps, clean ceramic tiles, and remove lipstick stains from shirt collars…?
- Egg white makes a great shoe polish…?
- Some professional breeders use tomato ketchup to shampoo their dogs…?

Our readers have sent us thousands of crazy-sounding tips like these over the last 7 years. The home remedies and quick fixes they recommend often prove much more effective than big-name branded products!

Here, we've selected our favourites. Guaranteed to make the routine tasks of everyday life easier, they will save you time, money and – most importantly – hassle. Whether at home, in the garden, fixing your car, or in case of common accidents requiring simple first aid, these are our top 165 all-time great 'trade secrets'.

# THE SECRET WEAPONS IN YOUR KITCHEN CUPBOARD

## White vinegar's secret use as an air freshener

White wine vinegar makes an excellent air freshener. Pour some into a spray gun, and spray neat into the air to kill cigarette, cooking or paint odours. Alternatively, put a bowl of white vinegar in your living room overnight to soak up any such smells.

## Real coffee lover? Don't throw away your used grounds…

The leftover grounds of coffee from a cafetiere or espresso machine make a brilliant air freshening tool. Leave the damp grounds in a bowl to soak up unpleaseant odours. And smokers! Place the grounds from your morning coffee into your ashtray to clean up the lingering smell of your cigarette smoke.

## Asthma sufferers! What to do if stuck without your inhaler

Two cans of Coca Cola, drunk quickly at the first sign of an asthma attack, can provide enough caffeine to ward off danger.

## Nosebleed won't stop? Trickle this liquid into your nose…

To halt a nosebleed, wrap some ice cubes in a clean tea towel, and apply to the bridge of the nose. If that doesn't work, add a couple of tablespoons of cider vinegar to a glass of warm water, and trickle a little at a time through each nostril. It can be uncomfortable, but it is very effective.

## Mayonnaise and vinegar kill head lice in just one wash

Unlike chemical treatments from your doctor or pharmacy, this natural head lice shampoo works in just one wash. There is no need to repeat this treatment in 7 days as is normally required.

● First, smother your hair with mayonnaise.
● Work the mayonnaise into the hair roots until they're extremely greasy.
● Then wrap your hair as tightly as possible inside a shower cap.
● Leave for two hours to guarantee 100% effectiveness.
● Now wash your hair with your regular shampoo.
● Rinse with white vinegar to remove the lice, and rinse with water until clean.

## The hangover cure you take before you start drinking

Anyone who wants to avoid a hangover after over-indulging in alcohol should eat plenty of toast and honey before they start drinking. The carbohydrate in this snack will prevent the sharp drop in your body's blood sugar levels that normally occurs whilst you're drinking. It is these low levels of blood sugar that make you feel weak.

## How tea can cure your toothache in just 15 minutes

Research proves you can use tea bags to relieve the pain of toothache quickly. The tannins in the tea can help draw toxins out of the roof of your gum. If you have a sore tooth or gum – drink a cup of black tea. Or moisten a camomile tea bag and place it on the painful area for 15 minutes. The herb will help to draw out the toxins and relieve the pain. Do this once a day for up to three days.

## When to rub onions, leeks and lemon juice on your skin

All bites can be soothed by lavender oil, fresh garlic or neat aloe vera gel. But you can also use a leek or onion – which are both anti-bacterial – to ease the pain, by rubbing them into the affected skin. For mosquito or gnat bites, rub lemon juice over the area or use slices of cucumber or tomato.

## Treat bruises, black eyes and sprained joints naturally with a potato

Potatoes are high in potassium and other substances that have healing properties. Speed the healing of bruises, black eyes or sprains by applying grated raw white potato to the affected area. Grated potato will also soothe burns.

## A natural cure for headaches

Next time you have a headache, eat a dozen almonds (unless allergic to nuts). They're full of salicin and other active pain-relieving ingredients. Equally effective as aspirin, but far less likely to upset your stomach.

## Cure headaches with half a lime

Simply rub it on your forehead to ease the throbbing.

## Impromptu BBQ? Don't waste time looking for firelighters

An old empty sugar packet or the paper butter is sold in can all be rolled up and used as kindling for your barbecue. They will burn slowly enough to light the charcoal.

### Why squash players should rub a wet bar of soap over their heels

Squash players often find that the heels of their feet develop black rings – this is caused by pivoting repeatedly on them during play. Solution: before playing, rub a wet bar of soap over your heels. And: reduce hard skin on heels by rubbing in moisturising cream on a daily basis, and use a footfile once a fortnight after a bath when the skin is at its softest.

### Fend off gnats and mosquitoes with this pleasant natural repellant

To ward off pesky gnats and mosquitoes, mix one tablespoon of vanilla extract with one cup of water and apply to skin. Works a treat. It's safe for babies and around eyes.

### Why you should clean your teaspoons with Bovril

How to eliminate stubborn stains on teaspoons effortlessly? The quickest method is to rub them (whilst dry) with Bovril. Leave a few seconds, rinse, and wipe off the residue. Sparkling!

# HOUSEHOLD TIPS

### Simple tip to keep your kitchen appliances in mint condition

Use car wax to repair scratches and marks on your fridges and washing machine. Those small scratches will disappear.

### Sparkling bathroom tiles tip

Keep your bathroom tiles looking shiny and new for as long as possible. Treat them with some lemon oil. It will help prevent water stains from building up.

### The little-known household use of nail polish remover

To remove scuff marks on linoleum, rub the marks with nail polish remover on a cotton-wool ball. The solvent in the polish remover will bring the mark up easily and quickly.

## Use fabric softener to clean burnt pots and pans

If you have something stuck to the bottom, and you can't remove it, pour half an inch of fabric softener into the pan. Leave to soak overnight, and it will clean up easily the next day.

## Denture tablets aren't just for teeth...

Transform your net curtains by putting a denture-cleaning tablet into water and soaking the curtains. They'll come out looking newer than new!

## Is your carpet looking a little faded?

Just sprinkle over a mix of tea-leaves and salt, then vacuum. Those colours will come alive!

## Scrub your pans with baking soda

Next time you burn a pan, sprinkle 1/4 cup of baking soda in the dampened pan. Let it sit for five minutes and scrub it clean.

## White bread is not just for sandwiches

To remove finger marks from your wallpaper, rub them gently with plain white bread.

## Lemons are great for cleaning copper or brass

Simply mix the juice with a little salt in a bowl and then dab in a cloth. Then rub as you would with cleaner. Lemon juice is also good for removing food odours from your hands or cutting boards.

## How to get rid of grease spots from wallpaper

Hold several white paper towels over the spot. Then press with a warm iron until the grease is absorbed.

## How salt can cut down the dust in your home

Remove dust from silk flower arrangements by sprinkling ordinary salt over them. Shake off the salt and the dust goes with it.

## Use toothpaste to polish your taps

Simply rub it on with your hands and rinse well.

## This clever little trick avoids hammer marks damaging your walls

Turn your hammer into a no-mark mallet by popping a rubber furniture boot over the hammerhead. The boots, normally slipped onto the end of furniture legs to stop them scraping the floor, are available at hardware shops and home centers. A one and 1/8 inch boot fits a 16-oz. hammer. A one and 1/2 inch boot fits a 20-oz. hammer.

## Clear up broken glass safely and thoroughly

Use a lint roller (the kind you can buy to pick up fluff and hair from your clothing) to clean up small shards of broken glass. After picking up the large pieces by hand, roll the tacky tape of the lint roller around to pick up the smaller ones. It just might save you from a painful glass splinter in the bottom of your foot.

## Dissolve limescale with ordinary salt

Unlike conventional anti-limescale products, salt isn't dangerous if inhaled. Nor is it harmful if splashed on the skin, and neither does it corrode surfaces. Simple apply to the affected area with a damp cloth, leave to work for a few minutes, and then rub  briskly and firmly with a clean cloth before rinsing.

## Remove stubborn marks from your bath, ceramic or plastic

Put a small lump of toothpaste on to your finger and rub the mark gently with it. Wipe clean with a damp cloth. You'll be amazed what you can clean up with a bit of toothpaste!

## Get white marks from deodorant off your shirt or dress easily

Wipe it with the foam pad that some clothes hangers come with. It will save you from embarrassment!

## Keep glass-topped tables, TV screens and stereo lids clean for longer

Use a little fabric conditioner in warm water, then rub dry. This will prevent dust settling on the surface.

## Remove the smell of smoke from your clothes

Add a cup of vinegar to a bathtub of hot water, and hang the clothes above the steam.

## Shine patent leather shoes and handbags easily

Simply rub with unbeaten egg white. Allow it to dry, then polish with a soft cloth. Alternatively, rub with the inside of a banana skin.

## Don't let red wine stains ruin your favourite clothes

Saturate them with white wine. No matter how old, the stain will disappear.

## Rust stains are easy to get rid of

Put lemon juice and salt on the spot, then place in the sun to dry. After a few hours, the rust mark will disappear.

## Vinegar – nature's secret stain-remover

Sweat, fruit and grass stains can be removed by soaking in vinegar before washing.

## Get rid of stubborn sticky label residue

Can't shift the sticky glue left behind by price labels and stickers? Wipe the problem area with a little eucalyptus oil on a piece of cotton wool.

## How to beat the ugly curse of chewing gum

If you get stuck with chewing gum on your clothes, place the garment in the freezer to harden the gum. Then simply scrape it off.

## Remove wax from upholstered furniture easily

Freeze the spill with ice cubes or a packet of frozen peas and take off with a blunt knife. Apply dry cleaning liquid and wait a few minutes before working the waxy residue out of the fabric.

## Clean awkward vases easily with a plastic bag

Trying to clean a vase with an awkward-shaped neck? Place a clear plastic bag in the vase, fill it with water & then insert the flowers. When you empty the vase you simply need to rinse it.

## Smokers! The little-known use of milk and raw potatoes

Remove a cigarette stain from your carpet. Pour a little milk on the stain and leave to soak in. Then rub the stain with a raw potato and wash as normal.

## The safest, most effective way to clean paint off your skin

Cooking oil will remove most paint from your skin without the side effects of some commercial products. You can also use butter or margarine. Also, you can rub petroleum jelly on the back of your hands and face before painting. It will make washing up easier.

## How to make ink stains disappear

Horror! You've discovered an ink stain on the sofa. No problem. Just spray it with hairspray before cleaning.

## Keep your vegetables fresher for longer

When you bring your vegetables home from the greengrocers, be sure to poke holes in the plastic supermarket bags.

## Ripen a delicious avocado overnight

Put it in a brown paper bag with an over-ripe banana, and leave overnight. Come morning, it will be ripe and ready to eat.

## Don't let fresh strawberries spoil too quickly

Kill the bacteria that produces mould. Remove the leaves and stem of the berries. Wash and place them in a colander, then pour boiling water over. Place the strawberries in a plastic container in the fridge. They will last twice as long.

## A quick remedy for heartburn

Mix a teaspoon of cider vinegar in half a glass of water and sip with a meal.

## A Chinese remedy for dizziness

Drink fresh celery juice mixed with honey.

## Keep potatoes fresh for up to 8 weeks

Put an apple in the bag with them. This will prevent them sprouting and wrinkling.

## Tired, wilted vegetables in your fridge?

Here is a good way to freshen vegetables using vinegar. Soak wilted vegetables in a mug of water and one tablespoon of vinegar.

## Silence a dripping tap with a piece of string

Obviously, if you have a leaky tap, you should fix it as soon as possible. But in the real world, it can take a while to get round to dealing with such chores. If a drippy tap is keeping you awake at night, tie a piece of string to the end of the tap and let it hang down to the sink. The drips will quietly run down the piece of string until you have a chance to fix the problem.

## How to prevent Delhi Belly ruining your holiday

If you are travelling to places where you believe the food may be contaminated or there could be parasites in the water, take an acidophilus supplement before and during the trip. Acidophilus is found in live yoghurt and helps good bacteria grow in your stomach. Eating yoghurt is a pleasant way of getting the culture.

## How to maintain the nutrition in fresh milk

Buy your milk in cartons rather than plastic bottles. Milk that's exposed to light (through plastic packaging) loses 90% of its vitamin A within 24 hours. Alternatively, don't keep milk for more than 24 hours.

## Ripen pears quickly

Place the unripe fruit in a paper bag along with a banana. Fold the bag closed and check regularly for the next day or two. The fruit will soon be ripe and ready to eat!

## Two proven tricks mean no more tears cutting onions

Simply place them in your freezer for 15 minutes before cutting or slicing. Another trick for tearless cutting is to light a candle and place it next to the cutting board.

## Peel garlic easily and quickly

Zap it in your microwave for 15 seconds, and the skins will slip right off.

## Sterilise your toothbrush in the washing up

Clean your toothbrushes in the dishwasher along with the rest of your dishes once a month. The hot water will sterilise them.

## Beat body odour without toxic antiperspirants

Sweating is your body's way of keeping your temperature constant, and while most of the liquid you perspire evaporates immediately, some of it remains on your skin. Bacteria just love this warm, moist environment – and they cause unpleasant body odours. For safe natural deodorants (which don't contain deadly chemicals such as aluminium) dab on a mixture of baking soda and cornflour with a powder puff in the morning. Essential oils such as lavender and geranium can be applied first if you wish as they have antibacterial qualities as well as a pleasant perfume.

## Empty a can of beans effortlessly with this handy cook's tip

To get all of the baked beans out of a can with none left stuck to the sides and  bottom, store the cans upside down and turn them up the right way for opening.

## Let rhubarb put the sparkle back into burnt pots and pans

Pick some rhubarb leaves and boil them in a little water in the pan that needs cleaning. Wash thoroughly and your pots are clean again. Rhubarb leaves contain oxalic acid that acts as a cleaning agent.

## Top chef's tip for the perfect bacon butty

Plunge bacon in ice cold water for five seconds before patting dry with a kitchen towel and frying. This prevents it from curling around the edges and results in lovely, evenly crisped bacon.

## The secret to easy-to-peel hardboiled eggs

According to the American Egg Board, fresh eggs can be hard to peel when hard-boiled. If you store the eggs for a week to ten days before cooking, peeling will be easier. The AEB also suggests you cool hard-cooked eggs immediately after cooking. Place them in iced water or under cold running water. For easiest peeling, roll the eggs on a flat surface to crack them and then roll the egg between your hands to loosen the shell. Start peeling from the large end.

## Move a washing machine effortlesly with this handy tip

Move a washing machine more easily by squirting a little washing-up liquid beneath the rubber feet. It will then slide out smoothly. Use the same trick for fridges and freezers.

## Low-cost and effective body scrub tip

Add some salt to your shower gel while it is in your palm. Massage in and rinse well.

## Make your own bubble bath

Add half a cup of baking soda to your bath. Watch it fizz – this will neutralize the acid and sweat on your skin and leave you feeling refreshed.

## How to always have smooth hands

Rub a small amount of butter and a spoonful of sugar onto your palms and wash away.

## Why you should pack baking soda if you go camping this summer

Baking soda can be the best friend for campers! It is a dish washer, pot scrubber, hand cleanser, deodorant, toothpaste, fire extinguisher, and a first aid treatment for insect bites and sunburn.

## Make hairline cracks on crockery disappear easily

Simply put the item in a saucepan of milk and boil for 45 minutes. The cracks should disappear!

## Eliminate warts with the peel of a banana

Tape the inside peel of a banana to them, and leave overnight. Mucilage (found inside banana peel) helps remove warts. Repeat nightly until all signs of the wart have gone.

## Clean dirty glassware with denture tablets

Fill a glass with warm water, add an effervescent denture-cleaning tablet and shake. The fizzing removes the residue. Let it stand for a while before rinsing – to get maximum sparkle.

## Tackle athlete's foot successfully with baking soda

Apply a baking soda paste to the afflicted area if you suffer from athlete's foot. This changes the pH balance, killing the fungi. Mix one tablespoon of baking powder with enough lukewarm water to form a paste. Rub onto the foot, leave for one hour, wash and dry thoroughly.

## Opening a window over a sink has never been so easy

If you have a bad back or are disabled then the best way to open a kitchen window if it's over a sink is to use a long pair of BBQ tongs to twist and push the handle.

## Get rid of felt-tip pen stains easily

Rub felt-tip stains and marks with soap and a toothbrush. Lemon juice will also help.

## Beautiful dried flowers, instantly

Dry flowers quickly and effectively by heating them in a microwave. Within three minutes they'll be ready to put into an attractive arrangement.

## Cut your heating bills and save energy today

Call the Energy Efficiency Advice hotline for free and impartial advice. Whether you are concerned about energy costs at home, or in your business, call freephone 0800 512012 today.

## Why you should lag the cold water pipe on your tank

Save money on heating your water – insulate the pipe that carries cold water into the hot-water heater, as well as the tank itself. The heat from your water heater travels back into the cold water pipe, losing heat and costing you money. Insulating this pipe minimises the energy waste.

## How painting your radiators black will cut your heating bills 10%

Make your radiators work for your money, by painting them black. White is the worst colour for conducting heat. Paint your radiators black or dark green, and you will improve their efficiency by 10%. And avoid radiator covers which promise to warm your house. Instead, get some Thermos reflective foam board and slip it behind your radiators.

## What the NASA space programme revealed about the secret power of magic plants

Twenty years ago, NASA scientists discovered certain plants remove common household toxins such as formaldehyde, benzene, trichoroethylene and ammonia. To sort out your domestic environment, grow lady palm, rubber plant, spider plant, ivy and areca palm. And place a cactus near your TV to absorb some of the electromagnetic emissions. Other magic plants include:

- The spider plant absorbs smoke fumes and gases.
- The eau de cologne plant releases vapours that keep away flies and other insects.
- Ferns helps to moisturise dry air caused by central heating systems.
- Cacti neutralise the emissions from computers, printers and photocopiers, as do banana plants, Chinese evergreens and coconut palms.
- The Herb of Jupiter's leaf sap eases burns and stops cuts bleeding.
- The camomile plant's scent can help send you to sleep.
- Plus, the areca palm, the lady palm, the bamboo palm, the Dracaena Janet Gray and the English ivy and the rubber plant are effective at removing air toxins and releasing moisture into the atmosphere. They're also the easiest to grow and maintain, and are resistant to insect infestation.

## A professional trick for spotting draught problems

Discover whether you have a draught problem easily with an incense stick. Check your windows to see if you need to weatherproof them by running a "smoke test". DIY shops will sell special smoke rods for this purpose, but professionals use a lit cigarette or a stick of incense. They work just as well, and are much cheaper.

- Firstly close all doors and windows in the room you are testing.
- If you have a fireplace, close the flue.
- Turn on any fans that ventilate to the outside – such as in the bathroom or the exhaust fan over your stove. This will lower the air pressure in the house just enough for you to test for leaks.
- Check your windows and doors with the smoke. Any draught will cause the smoke to flicker.
- Check the cellar, too, and the trapdoor to your attic.

## Make your piano shine again

If your piano has a varnish or lacquer finish, polish it with a non-silicone furniture polish or wax. Never use wax or furniture polish on a piano with a high-gloss polyester epoxy finish. This will ruin it. Instead just clean and buff with a chamois cloth.

## Brighten ivory keys on your piano

Rub them with fine sandpaper. Make sure the sandpaper you use is very fine (400 or 600) and carefully rub it along the length of each key. Take care not to go against the grain. Buff with a soft cloth. Do not try this on plastic keys as it will mar them. If you need to remove any stains first, just apply a little baking soda.

## Draught-proof your house with just a daily paper

Fill in the gaps under skirting boards and between floorboards with newspaper, papier maché or sealant. This will cost next to nothing and will save you energy costs of £10-£15 a year by beating draughts.

## Find the edge of the Sellotape first time

Simply affix a small button underneath the end. Don't forget to stick it back again afterwards!

## Clear clogged drains in 5 minutes, guaranteed

Pour a little baking soda down the drain with some vinegar, let it sit for five minutes and wash down with warm water.

# GARDENERS' TIPS

## This clever trick lets you mow your grass taller

Adjust your mower height to the highest setting to help your lawn grow deeper roots to match the increased leaf growth. A taller lawn will be a better competitor against creeping weeds and weed seedlings. Your lawn will also be better able to withstand hot dry weather.

## Why every gardener should keep bubble wrap in his shed

Extra insulation for a potted tree's root system is essential for keeping the roots free from frost in the winter. Roots are the most cold-sensitive part of a plant. They die at below-freezing temperatures. To protect them, construct a loose cylinder of chicken wire around the pot and fill it with chopped leaves or bubble wrap. And remember to water your container plants on a warm, non-freezing day.

## Little-known tip for watering your hanging baskets

Use ice cubes to water your hanging baskets. This will release the moisture slowly and evenly, without disturbing the soil. But take care not to let the cubes touch the plants themselves.

## When should you water your lawn?

When your steps leave footprints on your lawn, it could use some water. Water long enough for your soil to get moisture down deep. Lawns need about one inch of water a week from rainfall or watering.

## Don't let your grass starve

Provide proper nutrition by fertilising. One or two feedings a year make a marked improvement. However, the big difference between a so-so lawn and a truly beautiful one is four or five feedings a year. Follow the schedule on the fertiliser package to keep your lawn problem- free.

## How to stop cats destroying your flowerbeds

Put plastic bottles half-full of water in the places where local cats go to urinate. This can be an effective deterrent against them ruining your prized flowerbeds.

## Escape the noise of motorway traffic... without moving home

Here's a simple way to reduce noise and interruptions from your neighbourhood in your home.

- Collect a few flat stones from a beach or garden shop.

- Go to your local DIY shop and buy a large stone bowl with a two-inch-high rim.
- Buy an inexpensive garden pump (the smallest you can find) and a foot of clear tubing.
- Now put together a rock fountain. It is fun and relatively cheap.

Water features have been shown to be a great way of offsetting neighbourhood noise, like motorway traffic or loud stereo systems – very valuable when it comes to selling your home.

## Sore knees from gardening?

Put an old cushion or pillow into a double layer of carrier bags. It makes a cheap and easy-to-carry garden kneeler.

## Beat whitefly this summer

Keep whitefly off your tomato plants by planting a strong-smelling variety of French marigolds.

## How to stop rabbits digging up your vegetable patch

Try keeping rabbits away from a vegetable patch by putting onions around the perimeter.

## Soap stops rabbits eating your trees

To stop rabbits chewing your trees, rub carbolic soap onto the bark.

## Invite these pretty birds to defend your garden

Get rid of caterpillars by attracting tits into your garden – one nest of tits can devour 500 caterpillars a day. Plant teazles to attract tits. They love them.

## Avoid injuring your back with this simple tip

Always remember to put an empty wheelbarrow down facing the way you want to go when it's full. An empty barrow is easy to turn around. A full one isn't.

## How to avoid getting dirt under your fingernails

Before you set outside, scrape your fingers on a bar of soap. It really does prevent soil from building up beneath your nails.

## Protect your barbecue from the changing seasons

Late September is the time to put your barbecue away for the winter. Clean it thoroughly and cover it to avoid premature rusting. With a gas grill, make sure you boil the lava-rocks for about 25 minutes in a large pot of water and a little dishwasher detergent. Rinse and dry completely. This will remove any grease build-up on the rocks that may have occurred over the summer.

## How to limit snow damage to small conifers

When it's forecast snow, tie the branches to the trunk with string. Do not leave them tied for more than a day or two.

## How to avoid burn marks on your lawn

Maintain your lawn's appearance by moving your lawnmower onto concrete before switching it off. This way, the heat from the engine won't damage your lawn.

## Do you suffer from sore hands when gardening?

If you find your gardening tools make your hands sore or uncomfortable – buy a foam bicycle handlebar grip. Use washing up liquid to slip the grips on. You can also try pipe-insulating foam.

## Clear your garden of leaves effortlessly this autumn

Invest in some bird netting. Picking up leaves from low-growing landscape plants or fish ponds can be a real drag. So instead, cover these features with bird netting and then, after all the leaves have fallen, simply haul the net wherever you want to deposit them.

# CLOTHES & SHOES

## Stop new shoes from rubbing your heel

Put the heel over the arm of a chair, cover with some cardboard and hit them with a hammer.

## Loosen shoes that are slightly too tight

Stuff the toes with potato skins and leave overnight.

## Wear sandals without embarrassment

Fungal infections of the feet and toenails can be treated with tea tree oil. Soak your feet in a hot foot bath with Epsom salts and around ten drops of tea tree oil. Keep your feet clean and dry and make sure they get plenty of air, since moisture contributes to the growth of fungus.

## Get rid of slippery soles on your shoes

Simply sand them slightly with some fine sandpaper.

## Two clever uses for old pillow cases

To stop tights and stockings getting all tangled up with shirt sleeves and trousers in your washing machine, put them inside an old pillow case before washing. Also use an old pillow case as a protector for woollen items when you put them into your spin-drier.

## Do your clothes smell of damp after you've hung them in your wardrobe?

To stop damp making your clothes smell musty, simply tie together two or three sticks of chalk, and hang them inside. This will soak up any moisture in the air, leaving your clothes fresh and dry.

## Men! Is your favourite shirt getting tight around the collar?

If your favourite shirts start to feel a little tight in the collar, don't throw them out. Simply unpick and re-sew the button in a more comfortable place. No one will notice when you're wearing your tie, nor when the top button is undone for a more casual look.

## Tailor's secret for sewing more easily

To grease a needle just enough to make it slip through cloth, simply roll its flat sides against your nose.

## Important meeting, but run out of black shoe polish?

Simply polish your shoes with the inside rind of a freshly peeled orange.

## How to remove grease spots from suede

Dip a cloth in a little vinegar and blot grease stains from suede. Then brush with a suede brush to restore the nap.

## Sick of your shoelaces coming undone?

Stop shoelaces coming undone as you walk. Simply wet them before you tie them.

## Get the sharpest crease in your trousers

Run a line of paper glue all along the inside of the crease, press and allow to dry. But remember to do it on the inside, not the outside!

## Tired of picking up clothes from the bottom of your wardrobe?

Stop clothes from falling off their hangers. Simply wrap a rubber band around each end to prevent them from slipping.

## The cheapest, most effective way to keep trainers 'just-bought' white

Spray white leather trainers with window cleaner, then wipe with a damp cloth. This is better at keeping them clean than expensive, specialist products the shoe shop will try and sell you.

## Remove lipstick stains easily

Rub toothpaste onto the area before washing or even spray a little hairspray onto the stain and then wash!

## Grease or butter stains won't budge?

Pour Coca Cola onto the stain and rub it in a little. Then tip some more on and leave for about 15 minutes. Wash as normal. Alternatively you can sprinkle talcum powder onto the item, leave overnight and then wash in the morning.

## For removing blood stains...

Rub an ice cube over the stain to soak up the blood. Wash as normal. Or you can pour milk over the blood, leave for a while and then wash. Sure enough, this does work!

# PET CARE TIPS

## This herb can save you money on vets' bills

Keep some sage in your pet's medicine cabinet. It is useful for treating gas and gas cramping in cats and dogs. In addition, sage can be used to prevent secondary infections after surgery, and it prevents gingivitis. Cats and dogs can take the herb as an infusion. Steep one cup of dried herbs in one cup of boiling water for 20 minutes. Measure one fluid ounce for every 20 pounds of body weight and add this to drinking water two to three times per day. But don't use sage externally as its essential oils can irritate the skin. And don't give to pregnant pets or new mothers as it can induce abortion and inhibit lactation. It may also interfere with hypoglycaemic or anticonvulsive treatments. Ask your vet for advice.

## Stop a cat scratching wooden furniture

Use lemon scented polish. Cats hate it!

## Stop cats from climbing over a fence

Simply spray the wood with surgical spirit.

## Rid your home of stray pet hairs for good

Buy a box of latex gloves.Wear rubber gloves or keep your hands wet when stroking your furry pet. The hair will stick to the gloves or your hands instead of falling all around your home.

## Keep your pet flea-free forever

If your pet already has fleas, then a prescription from the vet is necessary. But once you have got rid of them, there are two preventative methods you can take in the future to keep them flea-free.

- Give your cat plenty of yeast and garlic in her natural diet – up to half a clove a day.
- Shampoo your pet with a mild soap.

## How to cure your dog's bad breath

If your dog suffers with bad breath, look at his diet. Also look inside his mouth to see the level of tartar build-up on his teeth or to see if there is anything stuck inside. If it is really bad, and brushing alone won't help, then take him to the vet. If the level of tartar is not too bad, it may be your pet's digestive system. Believe it or not, you can try giving your pet garlic in an odourless tablet – this will help purify the digestive system and helps clear bad breath. Sage is also good at keeping gums healthy.

You could either rub the leaves on teeth and gums, or buy herbal toothpaste from your pharmacy.

## Clean pet urine from carpets easily with vinegar

First, blot up what you can with paper towels. Mix one teaspoon mild dishwashing detergent in one cup warm water. Dip a clean towel in the liquid and, working from outside in, dab at the stain. Do not over-wet. Rinse with fresh water and blot dry. Next, add one-third cup white vinegar with two-thirds cup water, and repeat.

If a new cat insists on urinating in the same spot – try moving her food bowl there. She will soon stop!

## Poorly cat? Feed him through his nose

Cats often won't eat if they cannot smell the food. So heat a sick cat's food in your microwave. Warming it releases additional smells. And always give canned meat rather than dry food to a poorly cat. Canned food has a tasty aroma the cat can smell.

## How to talk to your cat

To boost a nervous cat's confidence in you, yawn as you make your approach. In cats' body language, this shows that you don't mean any harm. Also, avoid eye contact. Cats think this aggressive. Try squinting instead. It looks more affectionate. Or even wear sunglasses so they can't see your eyes!

## Buying a puppy? Buy an old-style alarm clock too

Keep a ticking clock near a new puppy during the night. It will help him feel more secure as it will remind him of his mother's heartbeat.

## Ketchup – the ultimate dog shampoo

Wash your dog with tomato ketchup instead of shampoo if he has rolled in something unpleasant. It will kill the odour quickly.

## An easy way to change the cat litter tray

Stack three clean litter trays on top of each other. Fill the top one with litter. When you need to change the litter – simply take the top tray away and fill the new tray. This can cut down on time in the morning.

# CAR TIPS

## The best colour to choose when buying a new car

Some car colours keep their value better than others. Beware special paint finishes, such as metallics. They are popular, but are very difficult to maintain. Go for classic black or solid, bright colours instead. And avoid greys and dark greens – very unpopular.

## The three car maintenance tasks no garage will perform for you

- Repair the nicks in your windscreen twice a year. Seasonal changes in temperature make it vulnerable to minor damage. A new one can set you back hundreds of pounds. But a windscreen repair kit (available from your local garage or Halfords) will set you back just £10.
- Install a screen (from your garage or Halfords) behind the front grille. This will prevent gravel or insects from blocking up your cooling system. Replace this screen annually.
- Small scratches can be fixed by polishing your car with a colour polish. This evens out the paintwork. For deeper scratches, simply buy a can of paint to match your car. When the paint has dried, sand gently with 500-grit sandpaper (or use rubbing compound if it's a newer car).

## How to protect yourself from death-trap secondhand cars

Before you test-drive any secondhand car, make sure the steering is safe and sound. With the engine turned off, pull the steering wheel left and right about 20-30 degrees. It should not feel "free" – and there should not be any knocking noises.

## Why "one careful owner" is a bad sign

Beware secondhand cars sold by old ladies and country vicars. Contrary to popular belief, "one careful owner" is often not a desirable feature. Older people tend to make over-cautious drivers – slipping the clutch and burning the brakes.

## Five questions to ask when buying a used car

1. "How many owners has the car had?" – as a rough guide, you should expect a five-year-old car to have had two owners, including the person who is selling it now.

2. "What's the mileage?" Standard use is 9,000 miles per year. Any more, and the engine may be worn.

3. "How long have you had it?" If the owner replies "Less than six months,", don't buy. There is probably a serious problem.

4. "Can I see all the maintenance records?" If not, use this as a bargaining tool. Do they expect you to pay full price, with no assurance of good maintenance? You can offer them a reduced price – after giving the car a full inspection of course.

5. "What's the interior like?" Are there any cracks or stains on the upholstery? Are any of the fittings missing? These problems are cheap and easy to fix. But they could give you useful bargaining points if you decide to buy.

## Why you should never switch on your car radio before you start the engine

To detect early signs of car engine trouble, get used to the sound of your car when it's running. This way, you'll be able to identify when anything does go wrong. In particular, don't play your car stereo loudly (or at all) when you first start the engine. You won't be able to hear the squeaks or rumbles which signal potential problems.

## Scandal! The great British car mechanic rip-off

British drivers spent £9.5bn on servicing and repairing their vehicles last year. But according to a report by the Office of Fair Trading, much of the work paid for was shoddy or even dangerous!

Yet it's relatively easy to save money on your car costs, and extend the life of your motor significantly. You don't need lots of fancy tools or specialist know-how. Here's how to avoid paying cowboy mechanics to perform basic maintenance starting today:

### Daily checks
- Keep an eye on your fuel gauge. An empty petrol tank can leave you stranded, and will damage your engine.

### Weekly checks
- Ensure tyre pressure is right. They'll last much longer.
- Top up the windscreen washer water bottle.
- Keep windows and lights clean and check your bulbs to maintain your safety.
- Battery level. Top with distilled water if needed.

**Monthly checks**
- Top up oil level if necessary.
- Check the cooling system has enough liquid in it. Add antifreeze all year round. It protects against corrosion as well as ice. And buy your antifreeze in the summer. It's almost always cheaper.

## Five top car dealer's tips for adding £100s to the price of your secondhand car

1. Rid your bumpers' rust spots by rubbing the areas with kitchen foil and Coca Cola.

2. Use a toothbrush to get your car clean in every hard-to-reach place.

3. Never use washing-up liquid – it actually promotes rusting.

4. Replace all non-standard parts and take any stickers out of the car that are not from the AA or RAC.

5. Chrome, trims, windows and lights come up sparkling after being cleaned with a mixture of baking soda (1/4 cup) with warm water (1 cup).

## What car thieves and your insurer would rather you didn't know...

Whenever you park your car, be sure to lock all doors, and put valuables out of sight in the boot. Locked doors will not stop a determined car thief. But damaged locks will make it easier for you to claim on your insurance.

And always leave a few loose £1 coins in your car's ashtray or glove box. If thieves cannot steal your car, this may dissuade them from vandalising it.

## Ex-policeman reveals how to beat costly speeding fines

Most speeding tickets are written during the morning and evening rush hours, when there are more motorists and more police officers on the road. Late night and very early morning are not monitored nearly as carefully.

# How to drive defensively and keep your car running longer

- Use your clutch sensibly to protect your car's gears. Under-use causes the gears to stick, and over-use (called 'riding the clutch') makes them slip. It's potentially dangerous too.
- Take your foot off the brake if you're heading for an unavoidable pothole. Braking on impact will cause more damage.
- After driving through a large puddle, run through an emergency stop. Check first that no-one is behind you. This will make sure your brakes are in good order. It also helps to flush fresh brake fluid through the system.

# BETTER BUSINESS
## Discover the proven ways to get your business up, running and making BIG money

# 97 tips and tactics to make any business more profitable… including 21 top internet sales techniques

Few jobs can match the thrill, excitement or rewards of running your own small business. Seeing your idea succeed – and taking ownership of that success – can make all the hassles and stresses worthwhile.

But with so much red tape to fight through nowadays…and so many clients bent on delaying payment until the very last minute…it's easy to forget why you chose to go it alone in the first place. Simply getting invoices paid can eat up almost all your time and energy.

Use these 97 proven tips and tactics, and you can regain control of your business. They will help you deal with the small stuff quickly and effectively…leaving you free to create and manage your own vision for your company's long-term future success.

## How to persuade your bank manager to give you a business loan

Banks only make money by lending money. So provided your business venture is viable, your lending manager really does want to give you the money you need to get started. Here are the secrets of securing the capital you want:

### 1. Find the right bank
● Are they always advertising?
● Have they just opened new branches near you?
● Have they just merged with another bank?

### 2. Spend 95% of your time on the task
The pursuit of start-up capital is a full-time job.

### 3. Borrow more than you think you need
All projects cost three to five times as much as you initially think.

### 4. Interview financial institutions
- Are they actively looking to lend money?
- Are they an asset-based or cash-flow based lender?
- What industries are they currently lending to?
- What additional services can you expect if you select their bank?

Interview two to three banks per week. Go to your worst prospect first, to practise your skills.

### 5. Ask the magic question
"What is your unsecured and secured lending limit?" When you ask this question you will separate yourself from 99.9% of all others the banker has ever talked to. Then place your initial request just under his limit. If it's £50,000, you ask for £45,000.

## The three secrets of successful business plans revealed

To succeed in getting your business idea off the ground, you need to write out a full, clear plan. It needs to be:
- Attractive: use best-quality, white A4 paper, typed (error-free), with generous margins at the top, sides and bottom. Keep text short, to the point, and in separate, easy-to-read paragraphs.
- Understandable: your business plan should match your reader's know-how. For example, you may be an expert in underwater photography. But your high street bank manager probably isn't. Use clear, simple words, and explain all technical words and phrases.
- Adaptable: You may want to show your plan to your bank manager, work colleagues, potential partners, landlords and suppliers. Make sure your plan can be adapted quickly and easily.

## The three key sections of a well-researched, realistic and well-supported business plan

### 1. The commercial section
Title page: list the plan's title, your name, contact details and date.

Contents page: compile this last so changes don't trigger rewrites.

Introduction: summarise what you want, and what's in it for the other party.

Business: detail its background, location and premises.

Products/Services: Just detail main features like composition, varieties, prices.

Team: include CVs of key staff.

Market: detail customers and competitors.

Objectives: state your aims in the short term (one year), medium term (two to five years) and long term (five years plus).

## 2. The financial section

Your bank will provide you with profit budget and cash flow forecast forms, plus step-by-step guidance. Use them to help you.

Profit budget: details your sales, costs and profits over a six- or twelve-month period.

Cash flow forecast: shows incomings, outgoings and cash balances over a six- or twelve-month period.

Put numbered footnotes beside each line, and include an extra sheet explaining your thinking.

Financial requirements: type of credit needed (loan or overdraft), planned use, planned timings. NB! The more of your own money you can put up, the more likely your lender will have confidence in your commitment.

Repayment schedule: base this on (practical) cash flow forecast figures rather than (theoretical) profit budget. Don't promise to pay back too much too soon. The more you have, the better your prospects.

## 3. All-important appendices

Appendices should back up your earlier statements. For example, partnership agreement, price lists, product photos, Every statement made in the plan should be verifiable in the appendices. The more independent evidence you have, the greater your chances of success. For easy reading, number documents in the order they're referred to in the plan. Put them in a clearly marked separate file, and include a ready-reference contents list. Where possible, include originals rather than photocopies.

## Fourteen proven tips for successful self-employment

**1. Offer a specialised service** no one else provides.

**2. Don't underprice yourself.** Compare prices of your competitors, and make sure you're in the middle band to start with.

**3. But always take the work,** rather than go broke.

**4. Employ your spouse and save tax.** If your spouse isn't working, make a note of the 'work' they do, and pay them by cheque. They can earn up to the limit of their personal income tax allowance and save money for your family.

**5. Claim household expenses** against tax – heating, lighting, telephone.

**6. Keep all receipts,** and make sure you claim for anything work-related – magazines, stamps, pens… everything.

**7. Register to pay VAT**
You're obliged to register for VAT if your annual turnover is £51,000 or more. You add 17.5% VAT to your invoices, and pay the accumulated amount to Customs & Excise each quarter. But you also get to claim back the 17.5% VAT you pay other companies too. Registering if you earn less than £51,000 means your bigger clients can reclaim the VAT, and it makes you look more professional.

**8. Pay less stamp**
You're legally obliged to pay two kinds of National Insurance contributions. Class 2 costs £2.00 per week, and class 4 costs 7% of profits from £4,615 to £30,940, and then 1% above that. But you might still be paying Class 3 as well. To make sure you're on the minimum, call 08459 154655 for further information and apply for exemption.

### 9. Build freelance contacts before going self-employed
Go freelance only when you've five regular customers.

### 10. Set aside one hour a day
Use this time for networking and marketing. The most difficult part of freelancing is finding new work. Schedule time every day to keep making new contacts.

### 11. Invoice immediately
And chase promptly when due. Slow payments are the curse of most freelancers' lives.

### 12. Accept at least one regular contract
Chopping and changing between new jobs sounds more exciting. But reality is, you need a constant and guaranteed source of income to cover any lean or irregular periods.

### 13. Register your company name
If you've spent time developing a good name for your business, contact the Patent Office about having it registered as a trademark. Visit www.patent.gov.uk for further information.

### 14. Become a Limited Company
This will add credibility and impact to your business's reputation. People immediately assume dealing with a Limited Company is safer and more straightforward. Contact www.companieshouse.gov.uk for details.

## Three little-known ways to beat bad debt and keep your firm afloat

One in three new British businesses fails within the first year. Why? The no.1 cause is late payment of debts. British businesses are owed £18bn in overdue bills from customers and other firms. But there are ways you can fight back – and keep your venture afloat using the money you're owed.

### 1. Charge an extra 4% interest on outstanding debts
Under the Late Payment of Commercial Debts Act, you can now charge up to 4% interest above the Bank of England base rate on late payments. But only half of small businesses know about this right. Make sure you state your terms clearly on every invoice you send out.

### 2. Serve a statutory demand for payment

Whether your debtor is a small or large business, you can send them an official statutory demand – pay up, or risk being closed down by a court.

- The debt must be for £750 or more.
- Set a time limit to pay up not less than three weeks after the agreed settlement date.
- Name one or more individuals (with addresses and telephone numbers) that the debtor may contact to settle the debt.
- Sign the demand.
- If the debtor is a company, send your demand to the registered office, not simply their main place of business (details will be included on their stationery).
- Obtain official forms from a legal stationers (see your Yellow Pages).

### 3. What if your debtor goes bust?

Include a retention of title clause in all of your business dealings. If you're selling goods on credit, simply state "all risk in the goods pass to the purchaser on delivery, but title of the goods remain with (your name) until full payment has been made". Insert this clause in the small print of transaction documents (invoices, delivery note, statements). If the purchaser fails to pay, you are legally entitled to retrieve those goods.

## Business owners! Why your bank could chase you for debt long into retirement

Many entrepreneurs now trade as companies to limit their liability to debt. If the business fails, creditors pursue the (insolvent) company rather than the (cash-rich) directors/shareholders.

But in practice, most banks only lend money on condition that directors or shareholders give personal guarantees. If the company goes under, the bank can chase them for settlement… and this can still happen even after you've left!

Anyone leaving a company in these circumstances must always negotiate with their lender to lift the charge on them.

## Selling goods online? How to build a good reputation quickly

To develop a strong reputation amongst the online buying community, be painstakingly honest about conditions.

Remember you're dealing with people, not computers. Be friendly, courteous and efficient – especially important in an international market with different cultures and language barriers. And thanks to bulletin boards, your reputation for honesty and fair dealing will precede you.

## Six tips for better online business

- Be businesslike and realistic about your potential sales and expenses.
- Monitor what it's really costing you, right down to the last penny.
- Ensure you have the cheapest possible access to the web.
- Remember the time spent on admin and packaging.
- Insure your purchases in transit.
- Keep track of your transactions.

## Website designers! How to attract more buyers with perfect pictures

When taking photos of your goods for online promotion, keep the shot simple. Have a plain background, and only allow a small section of the picture to show it. Focus on the item instead, homing in on its details.

## Don't fall for this myth of internet designers

Keep your website's sales pages profitable. Don't let professional internet designers con you into paying for hundreds of pages with thousands of links.

It's a lie that people would rather click on 'Continue' or 'Read More' than keep scrolling down when they're reading a sales letter online. Marketing results at leading publishers prove long letters work better than short, jumpy text. Keep the journey from visiting your site to buying your product simple.

## Top 5 commercial website design features

1. No 'Flash Plug-in' intro page

2. Simple graphics make it fast to download

3. Order page is secure and simple to use

4. Give telephone number and real postal address

5. Send an email to confirm every order

## Internet retailers! Do you understand the risks of taking credit payments online?

Internet fraud cost British businesses £28 million last year, according to the Federation of Small Businesses. This compares with just £3.8 million in 2000. The growth in stolen and copied cards risks upsetting the whole internet revolution.

The main problem stems from misunderstanding the term "authorisation", and the fact that the card holder is not present when the transaction is processed.

When a transaction takes place over the internet, credit card authorisation is not a payment guarantee. It only indicates the card has not been reported lost or stolen, and there are sufficient funds available in the cardholder account.

Plus, the transaction is done remotely. The card holder is not there in person to sign the slip and prove their identity. Under current banking practice, this means that liability for fraud in fact lies with the retailer – not with the bank, as is usual with "in person" transactions.

If you are taking credit card payments over the internet, make sure you understand your rights and liabilities. Check with your merchant account provider for full details.

## 5 tips to protect yourself against fraud at eBay.com

If you're buying or selling goods online at eBay.com, use these tips to protect yourself against fraud and deception.

- Use a well-known and reliable escrow company (www.escrow.com) for transactions over £300. They will hold the money in trust until the seller sends the merchandise to the buyer.
- If you accept personal cheques, wait for them to clear before sending

off the goods.
- The minimum charge for a credit card transaction is $18 (£10).
- Don't buy anything with a no returns policy.
- Ask about warranties and expected delivery times.

## Improve your telephone technique

Tape your telephone calls. Hearing yourself as others do allows you to eliminate your irritating phone habits. Their repeated use can distract from your message and even alienate your listener.

## Work more efficiently

Set aside one hour of uninterrupted work time a day. This is the one uninterrrupted hour you're going to spend on a major task. Group together all the time-consuming interruptors, and complete them at one particular time.

## Impress networking contacts

Always write something on the back of their business cards. Name, description, subject discussed, follow-up requirements. This flatters the other person. And it helps you to remember key facts.

## Write a better sales letter

Add two or three personalised touches. The most effective sales letters appear to have been written for that one, specific person. Letters that aren't personalised are rarely read. Best is a handwritten greeting, handwritten signature and a handwritten PS.

## Exhibit more effectively at trade shows

Follow up all sales leads within three working days. Exhibition enquiries offer the most 'enquiry into order' opportunities during this time. The exhibition is still fresh in visitors' minds. But after that, their interest fades, and they're more open to competitors' advances. Bottom line? Act fast to get the most from your exhibition expenses.

## Manage your time better

Use all your 'on-hold moments' to achieve mundane, repetitive tasks. Those times when you're waiting to do something, like waiting for everyone to arrive at the start of a meeting, can be used to sign letters, count order envelopes, perform simple accounting tasks and so on.

## Seven secrets to advertise anything to anyone, anywhere... without paying a penny

Your local radio station is always looking for interviewees for their shows. You can use this to advertise your business, for free.

### 1. Know your subject inside-out

The presenter isn't likely to be an expert. She will simply adopt the role of an interested and reasonably intelligent member of the public. So write down the types of questions they might ask – and think how you will respond to them.

### 2. Only interview 'off air'

Never admit you want to pre-record because of nerves. The radio station will try to talk you out of it. But a pre-recorded interview gives you greater control.

### 3. Rely on the presenter

The presenter wants to create an entertaining and informative conversation for their listeners. It's easiest to do if you're working together.

### 4. Put your headphones on straight away

You'll be able to hear your own voice, which can be disconcerting if you aren't used to it.

### 5. Use notes

Jot down sound bite expressions on a postcard, short and catchy words and expressions to emphasise what you want to say. Avoid lengthy notes.

### 6. Be natural

Look at the presenter and chat naturally during the interview. It's a one-to-one conversation... only with other people listening in.

### 7. Paint pictures for the listeners

Imagine you're trying to raise £47,000 for your local hospital. Explaining this sum will buy four extra kidney machines and save 15 lives over the next 3 years is much more graphic than simply giving a cash figure.

## Why you should always offer to shake hands first

Extend your hand first when meeting a business contact. It boosts your confidence, and gives you control of the situation. Remember to keep your right hand free whenever you're approaching hand-shaking scenarios.

## How to find out if someone has a 'murky past' – bankruptcy... terrible credit rating... whatever they're hiding...

1. Discover someone's credit history easily and cheaply. See if they have any county court judgements against them. Go to www.registry-trust.org.uk and you can search the Register of County Court Judgements for just £4.50.

2. Have they been declared bankrupt or mismanaged a company into compulsory liquidation? Contact www.insolvency.gov.uk (tel: 0121 698 4000).

3. To check the truth of someone's claims on their CV, you could pay an agency like http://www.ndfassociates.co.uk/crc.htm up to £195. Or you could perform the same tasks yourself for free.
- You must ask the person's permission first. This is to comply with the Data Protection Act.
- Simply call the schools, colleges and employers listed, and ask them to confirm (or deny) the statements made by the applicant.
- To find contact numbers, simply search via www.google.co.uk.

## The deep psychology of closing a sale revealed

### 1. Know your customer's 'pain' and 'pleasure' principles

People are most motivated to buy when they're moving away from pain and towards pleasure. 'Pleasure' covers anything from wanting to look more successful (buying the latest fashions) to being financially secure (buying into investments). 'Pain' represents the problems they currently face... problems which your product may be able to solve.

### 2. Create a 'pull' between their pain and pleasure

People buy when the pull (or motivation) between removing pain and obtaining pleasure is at its strongest. You can develop this 'pull' by forming a 'present picture' (relatively painful) and a 'future picture' (far more pleasurable) in their mind. For example, if you're selling a car, draw attention to the condition of the buyer's current vehicle: "Have you been having mechanical problems with your car?". Then detail the engine features of your model.

### 3. Now use 'reflection' and 'benefit' questions

Draw your customer's attention to their current pain, and pull them towards their potential future pleasure again: "How will you cope when the machine breaks down again?". This encourages the customer to grasp the personal benefits of buying from you today. The quicker your product can move them from pain to pleasure, the easier the sale will be.

### 4. Close that sale

Let the 'pull' do it for you. Simply put the product into the customer's hands by saying "When would be best for us to deliver this to you?". It implies choice for the customer. But the sale is taken-as-read in your question!

## Why you should mimic your customer's language

Next time you make a sales call or follow-up with a customer, listen for key words and phrases they use to describe your product. Using the same words and phrases as your customers creates rapport and boosts sales potential.

Conduct a 'Customer Satisfaction Survey' to gather more evidence. Then sprinkle these key words and phrases throughout your sales literature. The closer you mirror your buyers' language, the more buyers you will have.

## Sick of long, boring meetings? This simple question gets things done – quickly

To control an unruly, directionless meeting, ask questions regularly. You will be seen as authoritative and focused. And leading the conversation will enable you to speed things along and get the meeting's objectives achieved more quickly.

Raise questions especially whenever key points are repeated. This signals it's time to move on to the next subject. In particular, use this killer "agenda driver" to keep the meeting to schedule:

"This wasn't included on the agenda I received. Can we agree to discuss it at a separate meeting?"

## How to soothe an angry customer quickly

Simply say "You seem frustrated, tell me about it" to calm an angry customer. Be prepared for a tirade of complaints and bad feeling. But also expect their anger to subside as they vent it.

Encouraging your customer to vent their feelings is the only way to deal with them. Once they've got their anger out of their system, you can resolve the situation. Shorten the conversation by saying "I'll tell you what we can do" as your customer's anger subsides.

## This simple trick delivers the best customer service – always

Many companies test their staff by employing outsiders to make 'ghost' telephone calls, visits, and enquiries. Callers are vague on personal details (name, account number and so on) but specific on complaints. If you and your business treat everyone as ghost customers, you'll provide the best possible service every time.

## Recruiting new staff? How to get the right person for the job

Prospective employers should always remember recruitment is a two-way process. The mutual aim is a well-matched employer, employee and job.

But many employers talk up a job to attract high-calibre candidates. They gloss over any possible drawbacks to maintain interest. And if the job's oversold, a high calibre employee will become disillusioned and may leave.

If the role your business needs to fill includes routine tasks, say so. The right person for this job will have to be willing to perform and enjoy repetitive work.

## Lacking motivation? Follow the four Ds to get your project finished

'Drive' to get started.

'Desire' to want to accomplish your goals.

'Discipline' to stick with it.

'Determination' to overcome stumbling blocks and difficulties.

## Three simple questions unmask even the cleverest home-working scam

Answer 'yes' to these 3 questions, and you can guarantee the money-making scheme you've been sent through the post is a con. Bin it straight away!

### 1. Is this an offer of work?
If the opportunity you're reviewing looks and sounds like you'll simply be getting a job, throw it away. You should never pay to be given the offer of working for someone else.

### 2. Does it promise easy money, instantly?
No genuine money-making scheme can deliver big returns, for little or no work, within minutes. If the offer you're looking at makes these claims, forget it.

### 3. Do you have to buy the scheme to find out what it involves?
A classic. To find out what the scheme involves, you must send away your cheque first. Kiss goodbye to your money if you do.

## Inventors! Protect your idea from intellectual theft

● **Always keep your ideas strictly to yourself**
If you withhold all the know-how until you're ready to protect it legally, nobody can steal your ideas. Many first-time inventors automatically send details of their new product to relevant manufacturers to attract their interest. Their ideas are rejected... but similar products appear in the shops a year or so later.

● **Save your time and money**

Check to see if you've invented someone else's invention. Many innovations are simply improvements on prior inventions. If these prior inventions are less than 20 years old, they may be protected by patents. Check using the Patent Office's search and advisory service (Tel: 01633 811010, visit: www.patent.gov.uk).

● **Apply for the right patents**

To obtain a patent, your invention must be 'new', 'involve an inventive step', 'be capable of practical application' and not be in an 'excluded category'. And don't just apply for a UK patent. This leaves you open to exploitation by European companies. Take advantage of international conventions and treaties. The Patent Office can advise you.

● **Always follow up any infringements**

It is up to you to police patents. The law will only assist you if you first draw infringements to the attention of the authorities. Read trade publications, surf the net, keep a close eye on competitors' catalogues. But beware. International litigation is very expensive. It may not succeed. Better to contact the other party, and propose a licence agreement. You get paid for use of your idea. They don't get taken to court.

## Seven secrets of inspirational leaders

● Move location. Choose a new venue, according to your business objectives. Make sure all the details are right: the physical setting, the facilities, the hours and break times, the agenda.

● Choreograph. Go all out, and mimic the corporate ceremonies used by big firms when they meet to discuss crucial issues like 5-year plans and mergers. From 9 to 5, attendees experience a carefully choreographed production – much like a stage play – of inspirational speeches, technical presentations, how-to workshops and interactive learning activities.

● Free your mind. Gordon Mackenzie, formerly a "creative genius" at Hallmark Cards and now a lecturer on business creativity, uses Tibetan cymbals and mind exercises to teach "the visualization of letting go".

● Slow brainstorming. People write down their ideas privately and then share them with the group later.

- Brainwriting. Ideas are written on a card, which is then passed around. Each idea gets augmented as it goes.

- Brainwalking. Ideas are put on big sheets of paper tacked to the walls. People walk around and write comments on them.

- Convey your vision – as forcefully and vividly as possible – to every person in the room. You need to have a good idea. And you need to "sell it" to the troops.

## How to inspire anyone in three steps

James O'Rourke, director of the Fanning Center for Business Communication at Notre Dame University in the USA, says selling a big idea starts off by clarifying it.

- What, exactly, is it that you want to accomplish during a particular meeting?

- What, exactly, do you want to get your people to do?

- Are your objectives measurable, observable and rewardable? If not, review and rewrite them until they are.

# YOUR CAREER
## Short, sharp tips to get you a raise, get you promoted and make you indispensable to your boss

# 165 ways to secure your job...boost your income... and get ahead at work

We Britons work longer hours, for less pay, than anyone else in Europe. And for what? Five million of us suffer depression caused by work-related stress. Forty per cent of us have no say whatsoever over the work we do. The growing number of redundant British workers receive on average just one-fifth of the cash payment offered to Spanish employees.

It is no wonder two-thirds of us regret our choice of career. And yet planning and succeeding in a career you find rewarding needn't be a mystery. The secret to finding and keeping a job you love can be as simple as making a note of all your friends' phone numbers today...or even telling your boss what you really think of him! Plus, there are simple tactics you can employ to stay safe from Britain's growing problem of work-related court cases.

## How to protect your job, your income and your career right this second

A life-changing career move won't come from the job section of your newspaper. It will come through the people who know and like you, and want you to succeed. Friends, family, acquaintances and colleagues can all help you find an exciting new job. They are also your best route back from shock redundancy.

Protect your career right now, by making a list of all your friends, colleagues and business associates. Include their postal address, telephone number and email address. And note how each of them could be useful to you when you next look for work. Don't feel uncomfortable about this. You would help them out if they asked you for a favour, wouldn't you?

# How to bullet-proof your job in these uncertain times

With much of the country still in recession, you need to be sure you are doing your utmost to make your job as secure as you can. Surviving and thriving in your career means keeping your boss up to date with all your good work – so copy him in on what you are up to. Openness and communication are vital if you're to see your hard work rewarded, and your job kept safe.

# The secret to boosting your job security by doing fewer hours

Top economists all agree the 'job for life' is finished. Eight out of 10 companies already accept that flexible working arrangements are inevitable. Escape the 9-to-5 rat race today, and you could enjoy a better quality of life… plus greater job security.

Former bosses at Asda, Barclays Bank, Prudential and Marks & Spencer have all swapped their stressful jobs for a portfolio of part-time projects recently. Here's the jargon you need to know:

- Tele-working involves working a minimum of 3 days per week, usually from your home. You communicate with colleagues by fax, phone and email.
- Part-time working involves a regular schedule of less than 40 hours per week. So you can work shorter days, or fewer than 5 days each week, or a combination of these options.
- Job sharing is when you and a colleague each work less than full time – and share the responsibilities of one position.
- Voluntary reduced work time (often called V-time) allows you to voluntarily swap some of your income for time off. It gives you the option of reducing your hours for a number of weeks or months, but keeping the right to return to full time at the end of that period. This time off can be taken daily, weekly, or a block of time off in the year.

# Why quitting work could boost your career

Most of us get roped into a 40-hour working week for more than 40 years of our life. It can feel like a treadmill, grinding you down into retirement. But it is possible to take a break during your working life – and to explore life outside the workplace.

Taking a planned career break will give you the skills and confidence you need to get to the very top. School leavers and young graduates often take a 'gap year' to travel or focus on their own personal development before starting a career. And recruitment statistics show this adventurous spirit can be a valuable career investment. It's not just a privilege of youth though. Taking a year out to travel the world, while you are still physically fit, can be a tremendous experience.

- First, convince your boss it's a good idea by demonstrating you're too good to lose.
- Ask to have 'continuity of service', so all your benefits will continue when you return.
- Then prepare your finances to cope with unpaid leave.
- Stay visible in the office when you are away, by keeping in touch with an email diary.
- On your return, give presentations to your colleagues to share what you have learned.

## Fired unfairly? Seven steps and 21 tips for getting the big cash payment you're owed

As an employee, you're entitled to be treated fairly by your employer. If you're not, you may be able to seek financial compensation and even get your job back via an Employment Tribunal. Here's how:

### 1. Decide if you have a case
- First check your contract to make sure you were an employee and not an independent or short-term contractor.
- Think about why you were sacked. By law, your employer has to have a potentially fair reason to dismiss you. Examples of this are poor conduct (persistent lateness, theft), incapacity (long-term sickness), and redundancy.
- Your employer will have to prove they had one of these reasons. It's not your responsibility to prove they should have kept you on.

### 2. Did your employer follow due process?
Your employer has to follow certain legal procedures, usually laid out in your staff handbook. Typically, this includes three verbal or written warnings first. If your employer didn't follow his own procedure properly, you have a very strong case.

### 3. Gain the respect of the tribunal
- Submit a comprehensive application immediately.

- Although there's a time limit of three months (from dismissal or the date you actually left), an immediate and detailed submission shows your employer that you intend pursuing the matter properly.
- The Originating Application form (IT1) is available from your local Citizen's Advice Bureau. See your Yellow Pages.
- The tribunal will then copy your complaint to the employer. They then have 21 days in which to file a Notice of Appearance (IT3) form, which sets out the grounds on which the application is contested.
- The tribunal may well give directions requiring each side to disclose any relevant documents and prepare written statements of their evidence. Plus, it will set a timetable for this to take place, together with the date for the tribunal hearing.

### 4. Strengthen your case with detailed evidence
- Produce as many notes and supporting statements as you can, covering all the details – quickly!
- Freshly-made notes carry more weight than those compiled several months later.
- Describe what happened before, during and after your dismissal.
- Include supporting statements from colleagues.
- This may persuade your ex-employer to settle out-of-court. The tribunal will aim for this too.

### 5. Ask a lawyer what he considers an appropriate settlement
This could amount to up to one year's salary or more. And if your ex-employer refuses to reinstate you after you've been awarded reinstatement, they could be legally obliged to give you your job back and credit you with all the money you would have earned had you not been fired. If he doesn't, the court will order him to pay additional compensation.

### 6. Win your case at court
- Read the notes the tribunal sends to you about the conduct of the hearing  beforehand.
- Sit in on another tribunal in advance too, to see what goes on.
- Remember, the onus is on your ex-employer to explain why you were fairly dismissed.
- Record everything he says at your hearing, and look for errors and inconsistencies in his testimony. When cross-examining him and his witnesses, ask questions like:
- "Why wasn't I given a formal written warning?"
- "What training was I given to improve?" (but only if you weren't

given any)
- Put your version of events to the witness. Say, "The truth is, I didn't get any, did I?"
- Also prepare a statement in advance and read from it.

### 7. Don't give in to your emotions

This would make you seem less convincing. If you call witnesses, ask open questions starting with "What...", "Why…" and "When…" rather than "Did you…". Simple yes/no answers won't get the information you need from witnesses to win your case.

## Beware! These 7 clear signs warn you could be made redundant in the next 90 days

- Your company's managers can't seem to develop or stick to a clear plan for the future. Their 'big picture' goals change every couple of weeks.
- Temporary and contract staff are not re-hired.
- The Managing Director becomes less and less visible in the office. Ask yourself, "What's he (or she) up to?"
- Your company stops hiring new full-time staff.
- You hear rumours that senior managers have started their own private businesses.
- Bonus schemes and loyalty offers are not honoured.
- Voluntary redundancy is offered to older staff.

## Four steps to dealing with redundancy

Today's economic environment means it's unlikely that you'll be with the same employer throughout your working life. The best way to deal with redundancy is to seize the opportunities it offers by actively seeking it.

But if you're caught off guard by changes in your company, try to get on top of the situation quickly. Here's how to turn redundancy to your advantage.

- What to do: If possible, take voluntary redundancy as soon as it is offered. It almost always precedes compulsory redundancies. Your terms of disengagement are up for negotiation. If you're not happy with the deal offered, walk away... back to your desk while it's still there.
- Get more tax-free cash: By volunteering to go, you are doing your

employers a favour. They avoid negative press about their relations with employees, and also avoid speculation about how badly they may be performing financially. Take into account your level of responsibility, your salary and your years with the company – your loyalty value. With this in mind, look to get a lump sum between 5-10 times what the statutory payment would be.

- Get other great benefits too: Ask about other benefits that come with the job: your pension, your company car and health insurance. Can you extend these benefits beyond the termination of your employment? If so, you can focus on getting a better job with no material discomfort.
- Get paid while you find a new job: If your skills are out of date, or your industry is in decline, ask for vocational training at your employer's expense. Use your usual office and its facilities, including phone, fax, PC and postage, will enable you to look for a job. Your employers must also be flexible about allowing time off to employees threatened with redundancy for you to attend job interviews. Some employers may be happy to provide careers counselling to help you remarket your skills.

## Clever tip for getting a job fast

Don't waste time reading the latest books written for job hunters. Read the latest books being written for recruiters instead. Why? Because the easiest way to get a job is to give employers what they want. And the quickest way to find out what they want is to view the process through their eyes. Recruiters' handbooks and management manuals will provide that information more effectively than job-seeking books.

## Does your CV pass the 15-second test? Nine steps to a stronger resume

Your CV has to sell you and your skills faster than a television advert. Recruiters decide whether to bin your application or invite you to interview within just 15 seconds of opening the envelope. And this window shrinks to 3-5 seconds if you're making an unsolicited application!

## Grab your potential employer's attention right away, by preparing the perfect CV.

- Keep it short. It must fit comfortably onto 2 pages of A4 maximum.

- Keep it focused. Start by writing down every qualification, job, certificate and pastime you've ever had. Now look carefully at the advert you're replying to – and delete all irrelevant part-time jobs and training certificates.
- Don't waste space listing qualifications or achievements you've since surpassed. If you've been through higher education, for example, don't list all of your 'O' levels.
- Show, don't tell. Describe the skills and talents your achievements have taught you. Repeat key words and phrases from the job advert. Quantify your achievements with numbers, volumes and monetary values for greater impact.
- Use action words to describe your achievements. 'Increased', 'achieved', 'succeeded' always beat weak words like 'assisted', 'helped', 'aided', 'participated in', 'involved with', 'handled'.
- Do not use nouns. "Organisation of newspaper PR and promotion of sales" should read "Wrote PR for newspapers to promote new sales".
- Don't write a mini essay under Activities & Interests. Keep to the bullet-point style.
- Don't forget your phone number! Simply give your full name, address, telephone number and email address at the top. Don't include your age – you'd be inviting discrimination.
- Never, ever include a photograph unless applying for work as a model. Few of us photograph as well as we'd like. Plus, it can look pushy.

## Liars! Beware the curse of Friends Reunited

You should never lie on your CV. Employers have many ways of checking your details. If you've joined Friends Reunited, for instance, potential employers can simply log on and check your work history is the same as you claim on your CV. Beware!

## How to boost your CV with simple white lies…

Improve your CV instantly by listing interests that highlight your job suitability. Recruiters read these sections to discover 'the real you'. And including a team-related interest (like committee work or cricket) to show you're a team player could swing you an interview.

If you're older, also list a lively activity to show you're still active. Make your interests sound exciting and focused too. Don't just say 'running'. Say "Aiming to run a half-marathon this summer" instead.

# Illegal but true!

## Why young mums should hide their kids from employers

Women! Don't mention your children (especially school age and younger) on your CV. Although it's illegal, some recruiters believe young parents won't be committed to a new job. They will discriminate against you without even meeting you.

Far better to save mentioning your kids until interview. And even then, be aware that any employer asking if you have school-age children is on very thin ice. The fact you have a family should not prevent you being hired – by law.

## Where the perfect job looks for you...

The internet has revolutionized the recruitment industry. Today, you can post your CV online, ready for potential employers to search and scan. And many leading websites will email you with instant alerts of jobs suited to your skills and experience.

To find online agencies relevant to your profession, go to www.dogpile.com. Or visit these agencies online and see if their vacancies list matches the kind of job you are looking for:

- www.tiptopjob.com
- www.cvtrader.com
- www.fish4jobs.co.uk
- www.JobSniper.com
- www.jobswebsites.co.uk
- www.caterer.com
- www.jobsearch.co.uk
- www.reed.co.uk
- www.jobsite.co.uk
- www.topjobs.co.uk

## The five secrets of successful jobhunters

To find a great employer, turn the tables and interview them before you apply.

- First, find out all you can about the company from its brochure and website.
- Also call their customer services with a fake query.
- Make notes on the service you receive.
- Ring their Human Resources department too, or better yet, the person who is doing the hiring.
- Ask them what type of person they are looking for. What qualifications, degree, training, and experience do they want?

A friendly and reputable company should want to answer your questions. If they're not interested in giving you this information, don't bother applying. If they are helpful, then you are ready to prepare detailed questions to ask them in interview.

## The five most common mistakes job seekers make

**1. Waiting until tomorrow to answer an ad.** If you see an advert for a job you like, apply straight away. Don't leave it until the recruiter has been deluged with hundreds of CVs – later applications will seem dull and repetitive. If you have only just discovered a vacant position that has been advertised for a while, call the company and ask if the post is still open. Explain you've just returned from holiday and would be interested in applying. If they are still looking, get your application in the next day and refer to your telephone conversation in the covering letter.

**2. Branding yourself a 'corporate thief'.** Don't use your current employer's franking machine to send out applications. Always use a first-class stamp instead. Second class can make your application look a little half-hearted. It sends a subliminal message that you are not dead set on this job – and are sending out loads of applications.

**3. Becoming the office joke of the day.** Make sure you spell every personal and company name correctly. Getting names and gender wrong could make you the laughing stock of the recruiter's office. It guarantees your CV goes straight in the bin too.

**4. Sending a generic cover letter.** Give your application a personal touch by writing a new cover letter each time. Using the same stock words and phrases for every application you make really does show. They lack enthusiasm – make sure your application proves how excited you are about the job.

**5. Fizzling out with "Yours sincerely".** Finish the letter with a strong call-to-action. State clearly what you expect the next step to be. Say either:

● "I am available for interview at your convenience and look forward to meeting you," or

● "I will call your office next Monday to arrange a time for us to meet." Being bold proves your conviction that you're the right person for the job.

## Five myths of modern job interviews

### Myth 1: "Once you've sent off your CV, all you can do is wait."

Don't fall into the trap of thinking you can't contact a company you've sent a CV to until they get back to you. Be proactive – do some research on the company to make sure you have identified their needs. One great way of finding out more is to do an internet search for press releases about the company. Simply log on to www.google.com and type in the company's name.

### Myth 2: "Your goal in the interview is to get the job."

Wrong! Your goal in an interview is to be invited for a second interview. Never assume you will only have one interview for a specific job. Many companies are now using a series of interviews to find the people they need to hire.

### Myth 3: "You can't prepare for an interview, as you don't know what questions they will ask."

Every company is different, so there will always be a question or two that will be a surprise. But the vast majority of interview questions are quite predictable. Draw up a list of your achievements, your job progression, personality, strengths, weaknesses and your goals and prepare for those. Preparation will give you confidence too. You'll be less likely to come a cropper on the unexpected questions.

### Myth 4: "Don't ask any questions about the role, as they will think you haven't done your research properly."

Wrong! Asking questions will demonstrate how well you have researched the role. Use everything you know about the company to ask thoughtful questions to show the employer the extent of your knowledge.

### Myth 5: "Once the interview is over, go home and wait to hear."

Wrong again. You must be proactive to keep yourself in the recruiter's mind. Before the interview is over, make sure you find out what the next step is and ask for a timescale by which time you should have heard of their decision. Also write a letter by hand – that day, as soon as you get home – to your interviewer, thanking them for their time.

# Men! Wearing short socks could ruin your career

Dress to win at interview. Stick to a dark suit, navy or dark grey is best. If your suit is pinstriped it needs to be conservative. And wear socks that are a decent length. If you cross your legs during an interview and your socks are shown to be around your ankles with your hairy legs exposed, it will not look very impressive.

## Women! Choose your interview clothes carefully

A plain suit or skirt and blouse is still the best outfit for a job interview. But be careful that the skirt is at least to your knee when you sit down. Don't wear long earrings. And if your hair is long, tie it up. You won't be tempted to play with it – a sure sign of nerves.

## This secret trick shows up lazy job applicants

Beware this common trick played by recruiters in job adverts. They ask interested candidates to send CVs to a person who could be either male or female – for instance, Chris Brown. The employer is testing your initiative. If you start your cover letter "Dear Mr.Brown", you've already lost one point if Chris Brown is in fact a woman. To get it right, find the company's telephone number, ring up and ask. This is a test. Always check first.

## Big interview coming up? Get ready to make small talk…

Impress a would-be interviewer by making good small talk when you first meet. Walking from Reception to the Interview Room, for instance, can invite painful silence, especially if you're nervous. But many jobs today require good chit-chat skills. You must be able to meet clients, suppliers and competitors in a relaxed and productive way. So open short conversation by asking simple ice-breakers like "How long has the company been in this building?" or "How long have you worked here?".

## Job seekers! Beware the Jim'll Fix It cover letter

Too many job applications read like something from Jim'll Fix It. They ask the employer to help the writer by giving them their dream job. "I would be perfect for this role because I have always loved doing this kind of work, and your company sounds really exciting." Focus instead on why you are perfect for the role, and how your skills, talents and experience will help them succeed.

## How to smuggle your CV onto an employer's desk

Many employers today ask for CVs sent by email. Sounds convenient for you… but it usually means they will use a computer programme to scan your CV for keywords. If those words are missing, the employer will reject your CV out-of-hand!

Take special care with recruitment agents advertising on the internet. To beat the system, check job adverts for important words, and rewrite your CV to include them. For example, 'developing', 'leading', 'managing'.

Also, don't simply say you are familiar with, say, desktop publishing packages. State exactly which programmes you are skilled in using. The more specific you are, the more likely you are to pass the computerized scanning test.

## Four secrets for getting a job before you have an interview

Competition for jobs is getting tougher. In order to select the best candidates for interview, more employers and employment agencies are now cold-calling job hunters to quiz them on their CV. Here's how to impress them when they do.

**1. Be confident.** Clearly, you have already sparked your prospective employer's curiosity. They simply want some more information, and to check the details on your CV.

**2. Stay in control.** Always ask to call back at another time. This will give you more time to prepare and make sure you'll be free from distractions.

**3. Make a good impression** – stand up and smile! Your confidence will come through in your voice.

**4. Impress the caller with three simple sentences.** Prepare for your phone interview by writing down your biggest and most relevant achievements.

1) What you did and who you did it for
2) Three steps you went through to achieve it
3) What was the result – try and talk in numbers if possible, e.g. sales increased by 25%.

## Interview going badly? Turn it around – fast

If a job interview is going badly, stop the interview and say:
"Look, I just didn't get started right. I don't think this is indicative of my background. Could we start again? I have a lot of good information I want to pass on to you. And I am extremely interested in your company."

Many interviewers will be impressed by your desire to fix the problem so assertively.

## Why doing everything wrong will impress your interviewer

It's well known that you must prepare thoroughly for a job interview. But don't let your preparation trap you into a scripted performance on the big day. Employers want quick, perceptive employees, people who can size things up deftly and see what is happening around them. They're looking for the ability to think on your feet.

Reveal this by showing you're thinking during the interview. Don't stick to a prepared text and give out pat answers – that's what the other interviewees are doing. And be sure to interrupt your interviewer mid-question. It will show you are confident and assertive. Do it gracefully and with good humour. But make sure you do it. And resist being interrupted or sidetracked yourself. Let the interviewer interrupt you, and then say "I see your point, and it's a good one. Now let me return for a moment to..."

## Job seekers! Are you prepared for this killer interview question?

"What are your weaknesses?" may sound an easy question to answer. But it leaves ill-prepared and less confident interviewees speechless. To shine, write down what your weak points are right now. Edit them to make sure you don't sound lazy or stupid. But don't fall for the myth that you should present them as a strength.

For instance, saying "I'm a bit too keen on computers. I'm always on the net looking for new marketing ideas." This won't impress your interviewer. It will simply prove you've been told to turn the killer question into an answer about your strengths. Result? You look smarmy and dishonest. Instead, state your weaknesses, and say what you are doing (or have done) to improve them.

## How to stay in control of a job interview by phone

If you're applying for lots of jobs, beware the telephone interview. A potential employer might call you to discuss your application, leaving you on the backfoot.

To beat this trick, say you're tied up, and arrange a good time to call them back. This way, you can find the advert you replied to, and your copy of your application, before returning the call.

If you're still in work right now, and don't want your boss to know you want to leave, never put your work phone number, work email or mobile number on your CV. Better to set up a separate email address from home, and take phone messages you can return when convenient.

## Do you have a copy of your CV by the telephone?

More and more employers are carrying out initial telephone interviews. If you can't remember who you are talking to and what company they are from, you won't get the job. Questions at this stage will be informal. But keep a copy of your CV and a list of the firms you have applied to next to the phone at all times.

## Over 40? Six top tips for interview success

If you're seeking work after 40, it's all too easy to suffer low morale. You have a greater need for a job than younger people. Don't let this urgency put you off your best performance at interview.

**1. Have a positive attitude.** You have life experiences and wisdom other candidates cannot offer. Plus, you have many years of energy and enthusiasm ahead of you too. Be proud of your work history, and excited about your future.

**2. Speak slowly and clearly.** Most of us speed up when we're under pressure. Pauses are fine and much less noticeable to the interviewer than you think.

**3. Make the most of your assets.** If asked why they should give the job to you, talk up your reliability, proven track record, awareness and knowledge.

**4. Use confident body language.** Stand up tall as if there is a string attached to the top of your head, pulling you erect. Even when sitting, keep as upright as you can to indicate interest, energy and involvement.

**5. Get your image working for you.** Invest in a new navy blue or dark grey suit to ensure you are looking current. Geometric designs in ties work better than swirls or random patterns. For maximum authority, swap bright white shirts for off-white or ivory ones unless you have very strong natural colouring.

**6. Convert your nerves into valuable energy.** Take three deep breaths before entering the interview, and again if you lose your thread. Remember to smile at the start and the end of the interview. Everybody feels nervous, so drive on through your anxiety – you have an important message to convey about the contribution you could make.

## Why you should think in threes at interview…

For every question you're asked at interview, answer in three parts. This response will show balance and structure, suggesting maturity and confidence.

For instance, to the question "Why do you want this job?" you could respond by discussing your skills, your experience and your personality. "Describe a difficulty you have faced" could be answered by saying which experience comes to mind, explaining how you overcame the difficulty, and what lessons you learned from it.

Introduce each answer with a quick preview of the points you are going to make, and conclude with a summary.

## The one question proven to boost interview success

Don't ask interviewers to describe the perfect candidate for the job. Skilful interviewers will usually side-step that question. Instead, ask what factors are most important for success in the position.

Your interviewer will be impressed by the communication skills this approach demonstrates. And now you can show how those crucial areas are precisely your greatest strengths. Use specific examples to illustrate your points.

## How to sneak past a secretary and speak to the top dog himself...

- Find out the secretary's name from the receptionist. Try to establish a rapport with the secretary by repeating at least twice his or her name.
- If you want to guarantee being put through to the manager then you need to say that the call is personal. Chances are that because the manager won't have heard your name before they'll assume they're being head-hunted.
- Call at 8.30am or 6.30pm when you think that the secretary will have gone home for the evening.

## These four questions can get you any job you want

Have the edge over every other candidate applying for a job by answering these four simple questions. They are the key points every interviewer wants answered. If you're prepared and ready to talk about them, you should breeze even the most difficult interview.

1) Do you understand the job that needs to be done?

2) Can you do this job?

3) Can you do the job the way the employer wants it done?

4) Can you do the job profitably for the company?

Before the interview, make it your business to find out all you need to answer "yes" to these questions. Then it will be impossible for your interviewer to say "no" to giving you the job!

## How to succeed in a panel interview

During a panel interview, you'll normally find it is controlled by a chairperson with one or two other interviewers. But don't be fooled into automatically thinking the most talkative person is the most influential. He or she may be there just to put you at ease – a variation of the famous police technique of "Good cop, bad cop".

So don't simply target your replies to just one person. Give equal amounts of eye contact to all the interviewers whilst still keeping focussed on the person who asked the question. The other interviewers may be assessing your body language and mannerisms.

## "Tell me a little about yourself…"

To answer this question successfully, remember you are trying to give a positive, friendly and responsible impression. So always include outside interests and don't just focus on your work history.

It may not be wise to include any extreme sport hobbies you have though. An employer may worry about you having time off for broken limbs or accidents.

## Three top tips for interview success

- Remember to smile.
- Sit back in your chair with your arms by your side.
- Try to make sure your eyes meet your interviewer's up to 70% of the time you're talking.

## Watch out for these tricky 'icebreaker' questions

At the start or towards the end of an interview, interviewers will often use an icebreaker question that can leave you on the spot and flustered to find a suitable answer.

- Who is your role model?
- Can you tell me a joke?

- If you had to go into the Big Brother house, who would you like to take in with you?
- What is your most embarrassing moment?

Be prepared for this kind of 'wacky' question. Even though you can't prepare an answer, because you don't know what they're going to ask, just be ready to think on your feet.

## Award-winning questions for you to ask at interview

Never leave an interview without asking questions yourself.

- If I got offered this job, why should I take it?
- What are the main problems currently facing the company?
- What are you doing to tackle them?
- How would you see this role progressing over the next 2-5 years?

## Don't be afraid of silence in interviews

A well-thought-out reply is better than a load of waffle. Never reply with just a 'yes' or 'no'. If you're prepared with answers to the key questions regarding the job, taking a little time to think of your best answer will work in your interest.

## Job seekers! Why you should reject the first job offer you receive

When you have spent months searching through the appointments pages and applying for jobs, it can prove very difficult to reject the first job offer you receive. But accepting the wrong job simply because you feel you can't say 'no' could prove very costly.

**1. Steer clear of vague promises.** If a prospective employer says "We will review your salary and position soon", don't accept. Ask them if they will put the date and amount of the raise in writing instead. At the very least, ask for a written guarantee your performance review will take place in so many months. You have every reason to doubt the good intentions of a company that will do neither.

**2. Beware 'broken jobs'.** Ask lots of questions in the interview. If the specifics of the job are not made clear, don't accept. You may be headed towards a "broken job", where the company only wants you for a short-term project or, even worse, to fill a head count.

**3. Don't stop looking when you receive an offer.** Job hunting can be very taxing on your physical and mental energy. You will feel relieved when that first offer comes in. But is it really for the job you want? Don't cancel any other interviews just yet. There is no law to say your first day at a job can't be your last. Keep your options open.

**4. Write a formal rejection letter.** Should you decide to turn down a job offer, make sure you inform the employer with a formal letter – even if you have previously spoken with them and told them you don't want to accept it. In the letter, thank them for their time and make it clear it was not an easy decision. You may get called back for interview for a more suitable position.

## Why your past success doesn't matter anymore

Show a potential employer you can make money for their company. This is the most important consideration in any job interview, whatever business the company is in.

Don't get side-tracked into talking about your past glories. Your interviewer wants to know the difference you'll make to his company. So spell it out. Be specific about numbers, ideas, strategies and skills you would employ. Detail how you will increase their profits. For example, give ideas for cost savings or improved sales.

## Warning! Why writing a good reference could land you in court

A job reference seems easy to write. A 'good' person is praised and a 'bad' one is not. But these days, you are inviting trouble if you say anything more than the date someone started working for you, and the date they finished work.

Why? Because if their next employer has problems with them, and you failed to disclose similar problems in your reference, it will be deemed inaccurate or negligent. The popular use of a disclaimer – "No responsibility can be accepted in respect of this reference", for example – is not an adequate defence.

And beware! A bad reference, stating that someone was regularly late or disruptive could also land you in court. The person you're writing about could try to sue you. So stick to the basic, indisputable facts only – dates and job titles.

## Two expert sales tricks for successful phone calls

You probably have a "phone voice", the one you use at work or when calling your bank manager. But do you have a "phone personality" too? Assertive and confident, make sure you use it during important calls.

- Stand up when speaking. You'll instantly sound more assertive and commanding. Your voice will naturally be steadier and more resonant.
- Smile – people can hear it on the phone. People who work in call centres and in telephone selling are taught this trick on their first day in the job.

## Managers! Three tips for giving bad news effectively

If you have management responsibility, giving bad news is part of your job. Missed sales targets, cancelled bonuses, failed promotions, even redundancies… they are all inescapable in today's business environment. And the best way of delivering such bad news is to do it in a matter-of-fact way.

- Always choose a quiet, private location. In the middle of an open-plan office won't do. Speak in a straightforward manner.
- Don't fluster and mumble.
- Most importantly, avoid making it sound negotiable. If someone's being dismissed, for instance, it isn't negotiable. It's a fact.

## Learn to love your job in 5 easy steps

If you love the job you do, you're far more likely to succeed in it and climb up the career ladder. But what if you hate your current job?

**1. Value your skills and achievements.** Look to uncover transferable skills in your experience you can take from job to job. For instance, even if your only work experience to date is working in a burger bar, you have the proven ability to work under pressure, follow instructions, work independently but in a team atmosphere. All while dealing with the general public. Valuable to any employer.

**2. Learn to commit.** Without commitment, job security soon becomes your greatest insecurity. The symptoms of not being truly committed will destroy your career – arriving late, taking the odd day off as a 'sickie', missing deadlines. If you're passionate about your work, it becomes enjoyable.

**3. Adapt to change.** Only one thing is certain in today's job market – uncertainty. Management styles, technology, the economy, everything is changing. Learn to respond positively to change, by understanding why change is necessary. For your business to stay competitive, it needs to ride the front of that wave of change.

**4. Invest in becoming a 'general specialist'** – someone who sees the big picture, expert in a number of its parts, and always abreast of new developments. Beware over-specialising. It leaves you nowhere to go when (and not if, you'll note) the company or economy shifts. If you work a 40-hour week, invest two hours in continued learning. Read trade journals, practise a present skill, or study for the latest qualifications.

**5. Think ahead – far ahead.** For example, an assembly-line worker may be relatively well-paid. But a lower-paid sales assistant in the same firm gains experience of dealing with computers, pricing, stock control, handling customers. This wealth of transferable skills could prove more valuable in the future, despite the short-term cut in pay.

## The little-known reason you should stop doing what your boss expects

The secret of 'Value Innovation' is now used by many leading employers to boost productivity and profits. Here's how you can apply Value Innovation to get yourself a pay rise too:

**1. Analyse your job.** Look at everything you do, and start analysing how valuable each task really is. Look for areas of work significantly different to what other employees offer. Mark each task out of five – 5 being crucial, 0 being utterly worthless to your company's profit sheet.

**2. Target your energy.** Drop any task scoring 1 or 0. Don't spend too long on any task you marked 2 or 3. Concentrate on the jobs you scored as

4 or 5, those tasks delivering maximum value to your company. You may worry you will look like you're not pulling your weight if you drop the dross from your schedule. But provided you are performing well overall, your employer won't question how you handle the details.

**3. Offer a service or expertise nobody else does.** Don't waste time and energy doing tasks simply because you're worried you'll stand out for not doing them. And don't rely on your boss to prioritise your workload. Be innovative instead. Think of a service that no one offers in your company and carve yourself a niche.

Don't get bogged down simply doing what's expected of you. Talk to your boss about positive changes you think could be made to your role today. You'll soon develop the reputation of a valuable problem solver.

## Five simple tricks for better 'networking'

There's no mystery to networking successfully with business contacts or new acquaintances. To get the very most from your business contacts, simply:
- Decide what you want to achieve with their help before every meeting you have with them.
- Be clear in your own mind about your goals, or your network won't deliver.
- Then, when you meet, remember that networking is a 'give and get' relationship. Balance the tips, advice and new contacts you receive by returning the favour.
- Look at your list of contacts, and see who could benefit from being put in touch with each other.
- Keep the conversation as informal and friendly as your relationship already is.

## The easy way to maximise your career prospects

The easiest way to impress an existing or prospective employer is to gain new skills and qualifications in your spare time. Here are your top tips:

**1. Choose a course that will advance your career.** Concentrate on tomorrow's key skills – IT skills, languages, management skills, basic accountancy.

**2. Find the night course.** Try your local adult education centre. Most offer a wide and diverse range of part-time and evening courses starting from late September.

**3. Use these clever A-grade tricks.**
- Talk to the tutor before signing up, to make sure he/she is enthusiastic and well experienced in your industry.
- Attend every session.
- If you have to miss one, ask for missed material.
- Sit at the front of the class, so you don't miss anything.
- Take notes – lots of notes.

And don't forget! Any educational course you study to advance your career can be offset against tax. Ask your local Inland Revenue to confirm your course qualifies. You can also get good loan rates from banks and building societies to help pay your fees.

## Can your colleagues read faster than you?

Almost all jobs today involve reading detailed information, and understanding instructions quickly. You can boost your productivity easily, making your job more secure and your potential paypacket much greater.

Here's how:

1. Measure your reading speed. Simply take a report, magazine articles, or a chapter of a book. Count out around 3,000 words (by multiplying the number of words-per-line by the number of lines).

2. Time yourself as you read. Then calculate your current words-per-minute (wpm). Divide the words by the minutes taken.

3. The average person reads around 200wpm. You should work towards at least 400-500wpm.

4. Improve your understanding by always asking Who-What-When-Where-Why-How? Skim over the material to search for this information. Ignore any information you don't need to know.

5. Concentrate on keeping your eyes still as you read. Look at sentences as blocks of words, with blocks of meaning. Use a pencil to guide your

eye. Avoid using a piece of card. It will encourage you to look back and forth along the edge, wasting time.

## Beware 'Mickey Mouse' certificates no one will trust

Don't waste time and money studying for qualifications that won't enhance your career. Choose courses where the final exam is marked by external examiners. For instance, GCSEs, A levels and university degrees. Employers are familiar with these exams, and value them – because external marking guarantees quality control on grades.

But beware GNVQs. They are less well known and largely coursework-based. You may find yourself having to justify them to sceptical employers. Worst still are little-known courses with coursework and examinations set and marked by internal staff. It's a fact that some colleges adjust papers and marking criteria to ensure that large and increasing numbers continue to pass.

## Do you make these six classic mistakes in business etiquette?

In the past, conventional manners were observed both with friends and with business associates. So knowing how to act in formal situations was easier and more natural than today. Now it can be too easy to come across as over-friendly or too informal. Here are the top tips used by senior business executives to make the right impression every time.

**1. Always be polite and civil.** Treat everyone with the same consideration. Make a point of being nice to receptionists and secretaries – the gatekeepers of the business world.

**2. Show an interest in other people's lives.** Ask about holidays, children, hobbies, what they did at the weekend.

**3. Avoid getting drawn into details of personal lives though.** Unless you become friends outside of work, it might be seen as intrusive – and that's rude.

**4. Enjoy your working lunches, and make sure everyone else does too!** Now established as a way of doing business, they can be a great way to explore relationships, discuss an idea, or simply timetable your schedule for the coming week.

**5. Treating clients to a meal out?** Get there ten minutes early to confirm the reservation. Always stand up to greet your guests personally. Never pay for the meal with cash. Pay by credit card instead. Best practice is to discreetly visit the cashdesk on your way to the toilet when everyone else is drinking their coffee.

**6. Deal with awkward situations gracefully.** Spot trouble early, and you can divert any conflict in business meetings or negotiations. Watch for unexpected formality (calling you 'Mr. Jones' instead of the usual 'Jim' for instance), or avoiding direct eye contact, or raised voice. Obviously, the other person is trying to restrain his anger – so give him a chance! Say "I'm sorry you feel so strongly about this. Maybe we can meet in a few days' time when we've both had time to reflect." This will avoid a loss of face.

## Men! Why you need to keep a close eye on the women you work with...

New studies find female managers outshine their male counterparts in almost every measure. But by watching how women work, you can mimic their natural management abilities – and boost your career prospects too.

- Don't get bogged down on one project. Women juggle their workload, to make sure each task keeps heading towards completion. To mimic this successful habit, write a plan every evening of what you have to do the next day – in priority order. Cross out each task as you go along. If you have a few tasks left over, move them to the top of tomorrow's priority pile.
- Drop the stringent rules. Women are less 'rank conscious' than you. Be more relaxed within the workplace, and stop evaluating where you are in the pecking order. It doesn't matter as much as getting the job done.
- Unless you're Alex Ferguson, your employees aren't footballers. So stop rewarding only the high-fliers who score. Women are more oriented towards what's called 'intrinsic motivation' – rewarding the whole team when a task goes well.
- Talk more, listen more. Women enjoy building relationships with people, projects and work. Hence their desire to talk a lot – too much sometimes! In contrast, men like being the boss and having order. Build relationships with your staff and ask for input and ideas instead.
- Say 'thank you' more often. Politeness results in better motivation and better results.

- Admit when you're wrong. You'll improve all of your relationships and appear far more human to your staff, your boss and your family.
- Stop thinking the core unit is just 'you'. Team players take pride in any accomplishment the team achieves. Self-reliance only helps hermits.

## Warning! Why booking a holiday could end your career

If you don't know what your company's policy on internet use is, ask your line manager today. Many firms haven't developed a policy yet – but it could end badly for both of you if not.

At Focus Management Consultants, an employee was dismissed because she used a company computer to gather holiday information for personal use. A court judged her dismissal fair. You have been warned!

## How to give advice to your colleagues

Offering direct advice to work colleagues is hard to do. Typically, it sounds blunt, like when you say "It would be better if you did this". Your colleague may feel defensive, undermined and patronised. Instead, get them talking so that new ideas are generated by them. For example, asking them "How do you do that, Mike?", "What other ways can it be done?", "Have you tried those ways?".

## Do you have your verbal CV ready?

Few people take the time to prepare the answer they give when asked "So what do you do?". But having a verbal CV ready at all times could prove crucial to your career success.

A verbal CV is a summary of what makes your experience and skills unique. Everybody needs one. Best used during networking opportunities and at more formal job interviews, it can also open new doors at social events when you meet new contacts or friends of friends. Put together six to ten key phrases in your mind. Refer to three or four of the most appropriate ones as and when needed.

## Why you should never trust what your boss says

It's sad but true – a man's word is rarely his bond these days. Personal relationships may lead to easy-going 'gentleman's agreements'. But bosses can overturn them without a second thought.

Get everything in writing – in business deals, for purchase orders, and most especially, when you agree employment terms. Verbal contracts are hard to prove in a court of law. A simple letter confirming the main points of a discussion is effective and binding.

## New shoes? Don't wait until interview to discover they don't fit!

Don't wait until your interview day to try out new shoes. If your feet hurt, your mind will be on the pain rather than the interview. Plus, hobbling into the interview room will not impress.

## Looking for a pay rise? Why you should never threaten to resign

Sometimes it's hard not to believe your skills are indispensable to your employer. But these days, no one is irreplaceable. And if you use the threat of resignation to squeeze a pay rise out of your boss, you had better be willing to see it through should he/she refuse. What if they call your bluff? Staying in your job will prove embarrassing and awkward. Leaving will be plain stupid. So only threaten to resign when you're prepared to walk away and not look back. And never – ever – withdraw a resignation. If you do, your position will be undermined forever.

## How to get a raise by telling your boss what you really think of him

It can feel difficult, even intimidating, to speak up for yourself at work. But asserting your opinion will build your self-esteem, enhance your career, and could even get you that well-deserved raise.

**1. Plan what you want to say.** Don't try to challenge your manager without preparing.

**2. Then tell your boss, in a quiet moment,** "I would like to talk to you about my workload/schedule/responsibilities/colleagues/salary."

**3. Add details to deepen your statement.** Most people can start a serious discussion. But they forget to prepare details and evidence to continue it!

**4. Make your boss take you seriously.** Avoid weak words like "I'm sorry but…". This signals you don't value your own opinion. Nor will your boss.

**5. Know when you've said your piece.** Because you have prepared, you will know when you have said all you want to. Be sure to congratulate yourself. Now leave the ball in your boss's court.

# Index

## A

A levels 322

AA 101

Aborigines 40

absenteeism 319

abusive relationships 103–4

accidental damage, insurance policies 124

accommodation addresses, personal post 99

accountancy skills 320–1

ACE-inhibitors 163

Achilles tendon 26

acidophilus uses, dirty food 259–60

acne 144

addictions, over-the-counter medicines 31–2

adult education, easy money 217–18

advertisements

    business tips 290–1

    employment 307

www.adviceguide.org.uk 137

aeroplane hijackings 110

affairs 162, 246–7

age-related macular degeneration (AMD) 48

AIM-listed shares 89, 238

air fresheners 251–2, 257

Air Transport Users' Council 129

air travel

    see also holidays/overseas travel

    aeroplane hijackings 110

    airline 'bumping' tips 116–17

    cheap tickets 117–20

    complaints 129

    courier clubs 134

    crime 110–11

    health tips 63–4

    Internet bookings 120

    skin-cancer links 46

airbags, dangers 39

airports, crime 110–11

alcohol effects 9, 23, 24, 47, 59, 60–1, 142, 154, 157, 166

    blood pressure 59

    cancer links 46

    hangovers 252

    heart disease 47, 59

    impotence 49

    magnesium levels 23

    osteoporosis 60–1

    skin 142

    vitamin B 24

alert necklaces, medical conditions 36

allergies, food 42, 65

almond oil, shining hair 147

almonds 170, 253

aloe vera 244–5

alpha-androstenol 166

Alzheimer's Disease 52, 67

AMD see age-related macular degeneration

American ice hockey, betting tips 188–9

www.amnesty.org.uk 133

anaemia 24–5

angular cheilosis 23–4

ankle-stretching exercises, back pain 26

anti-depressants 35, 159, 163

antibiotics 37, 154

antihistamines 42, 43, 66

antioxidants 141–3, 152–3

    see also vitamin...

antiques, easy money 197, 220–7

Antiques Roadshow 223

antiseptic properties, honey 39, 142

aphrodisiacs 149, 170

apples 50, 259

apricots 54

arbitrage, betting tips 177–9

areca palm 264

art critics, free tickets 120

art investments 92–3, 129

arthritis 25, 28–30, 46

artichokes 48–9

Arts Council of England 129

Asian Handicaps, betting 185–6

asparagus 65

Association of Credit Unions 92

Association of Residential Letting Agents 14

asthma 206, 245, 252

www.atg-online.com 223

athlete's foot 262, 269

auctions

    easy money 220–4

    house-buying tips 10

Internet 224
tips 10, 135, 220–3
Australian sport, betting tips 189–90, 192–3
autographs, easy money 199–201
avocados 42, 147, 258–9

# B

B&Bs, easy money 206–7
babies 243–4, 254
baby oil 170
baby shampoos 54
back pain 26–7, 128, 168, 267
bacon butties 261
bacopa 52
bacterial content, food 37–8, 153–4
bad breath, dogs 272
bad debts
    see also debt problems
    business tips 285–6
baggage, travel tips 111, 119–20
baking soda 170, 255, 260–2, 265, 276
bananas
    aphrodisiacs 149
    fruit-ripening uses 258–9, 260
    high-blood pressure 33
    insomnia 49
    patent-leather shining 257
    warts 262
banks 79, 82, 84, 91–2, 98–100, 232, 281–4
    see also loans
    `6-year rule' 84
    best deals 82, 281–2
    business tips 281–4
    credit unions 91–2
    identity frauds 98–100
    overdraft charges 79
    statements 232
barbecues
    cancer dangers 46
    weathering protection 268
Bargain Hunt 220
baseball, betting tips 190–1
basil 54
bathrooms
    enhancements 9, 17, 254
    shining tiles 254
baths

beauty treatments 148
body odour 154
bubble baths 262
stubborn marks 256
www.bbc.co.uk 223
beans 42, 46, 261
beauty tips 139–70
Beckham, David 201
bee stings
    arthritis 29
    removal 65–6
Benign Prostatic Hyperplasia (BPH) 56
Benzoyl Peroxide 144
berberine 53
berries 24, 48, 50, 141 3
`best buy' reports, financial journalists 81–2
beta-blockers, sex drive 163
betaine HCL pepsin 142
www.betbrain.com 177, 179
www.betfair.com 173–4, 192–3
betting tips 171–93, 207–9
    amateur mistakes 178
    American ice hockey 188–9
    arbitrage 177–9
    Asian Handicaps 185–6
    Australian sport 189–90, 192–3
    baseball 190–1
    Big Brother 175–6
    Blackjack 202
    casinos 202, 216–17
    country cricket 182
    cricket 182, 192–3
    doubles 179, 180
    Dutching 187–8
    football league 182–7, 189–92
    fourfolds 180
    handicap betting 181
    Internet 177–9, 191–2
    `Martingale' system 217
    odds-comparison websites 178–9
    professional-punter's form guide tips 174–5, 177
    rigged games 184–5
    roulette 216–17
    Round Robins 179–80
    Rugby League 180–2
    Single-Stakes-About bets 179–80
    spot-the-ball competitions 185

stock market 207–9
tennis 177–8, 192
time-of-year tips 175
trebles 179, 180
two-year old winners 174–5
Yankee bets 176–7
`beware of the dog' signs, crime prevention 101
Biba clothes 223
Big Brother 175–6, 316
bin bags, identity frauds 98–9
Biocare, Bio-Acidophilus 38, 154
birth certificates 98–100, 231
black cohosh 68, 148
black eyes 253
black tea see tea
blackberries 143
blackcurrants 42
Blackjack, easy money 202
bleeding gums 24
blindness 48
blood stains 271
blue-chip shares 89
blueberries 53, 141–3
body language
    cats 273
    job interviews 310–11, 313, 315
    sex 165–6
body mass index 61
body odour 154, 260–1
bodyscrubs
    caster sugar 147
    salt 261
boils 155
bookmakers 173–93, 207–9
books
    dealing tips 199–200
    easy money 199–200, 211–14
    free books 134
    `price guide' books 223
    writing tips 211–14
Boots 40
bosses see employers
Bovril 254
bowel disorders 37–8, 46–9, 153–4
BPH see Benign Prostatic Hyperplasia
brainstorming techniques 295
brainwalking techniques 295

brainwriting techniques 295
brakes, cars 277
Brando, Marlon 200
breakdown recovery services 101
breasts 43–5, 67, 148, 157–8
    cancer 43–5, 67
    exercises 148
    size enhancements 148
British Medical Association 153
broad beans, anti-cancer effects 46
broccoli 24, 46, 54, 56, 65, 157
broken glass, lint rollers 256
broken veins, nose 142
brown rice 23, 37, 65, 154, 157
bruises 25, 253
Brussel sprouts 24, 48, 157
bruxism 57
bubble baths 262
bubble wrap, gardens 266
BUPA 61
burglaries 100–1, 124–5, 239–40
    see also thieves
burns 38–9, 245
burnt pans 255, 261
business tips 279–96
    see also finance
    advertisements 290–1
    bad debts 205–6
    bad news 318
    business plans 282–4
    complaints-handling techniques 293, 323
    creativity 295–6
    credit-rating checks 291
    creditors 286
    customer-mimicry benefits 292
    CV checks 291, 304–5
    directors' liabilities 286
    etiquette 322–3
    `four Ds' 294
    freelance contacts 285
    hand-shaking scenarios 291
    home-working scams 294
    intellectual property 285, 294–5
    Internet 286–9
    invoices 285
    leadership techniques 295–6, 318, 323–4

limited companies 285, 286
loans 281–4
marketing 285, 289, 291–2
meetings 292–3
motivation issues 294
National Insurance 284
networking 285, 289, 320, 323–4
pain/pleasure principles 291–2
patents 285, 294–5
radio shows 290–1
recruitment advice 291, 293, 299, 304–18
retention-of-title clauses 286
spousal employment 284
start-up capital 281–2
tax 284
telephone techniques 289, 292–3, 318
time-management issues 289–90
trade shows 289
trademarks 285, 294–5
VAT 284
vision 295–6
working lunches 322–3
written contracts 325
butter 253, 262, 271
butterbur, hay fever 43
buy-to-let investments 11–15, 232
see also rented properties
buyback bargains, shares 91
www.buy.co.uk 122
`buying crap' trap 84
buying tips, cars 273–6

# C

cabbages 50, 54, 56, 65, 157
cacti properties 264
Caine, Michael 201
calcium 54, 61, 150, 157
Calendula cream 38
camcorders, deterioration problems 241
cameras
carjacking crime 103
holidays/overseas travel 135–6
wedding photographers 218–19
camomile tea, sunburn 39
camouflage passports 105
camping trips, baking soda 262

cancers 43–7, 67, 146–7
alcohol effects 46
anti-cancer foods 45, 46–7, 55
barbecued beef 46
broad beans 46
garlic 47
Herceptin 45
milk 45
mouthwashes 46
olive oil 46–7
Candida 37, 153
cans, beans 261
capital gains 13, 76–7
capsicum 64
carbonated drinks, osteoporosis 61
cardiopulmonary resuscitation (CPR) 47
careers see employment
www.carhire4less.co.uk 117
carjacking crime 101–3
Carlton Ware 223
carotenoids 48, 66
carpets, colour enhancements 255
carrots 50, 65
carry-forward losses, tax savings 74
cars
airbags 39
boot sales 197, 223–7
brakes 277
buying tips 273–6
car-hire discounts 117–18
carjacking crime 101–3
cleaning tips 276
colour tips 273
driver fatigue 137
engine trouble 275
licence identity-frauds 98–100
maintenance tips 274–7
`one careful owner' warnings 274
personal safety 101–3, 137, 277
radios 275
road rage 101–3
rust spots 276
safe parking 105
scratches 274
speeding tips 276–7
steering mechanisms 274
thieves 101–3, 105, 276
tips 101–5, 117–18, 137, 273–7

used cars 274–6
washing-up liquid 276
wax 254
windscreens 274
`Carte Profesionelle' requirements, French properties 16
cash discounts, shopping tips 130
casinos, betting tips 202, 216–17
caster sugar, bodyscrubs 147
caterpillars 267
cats 266, 271–3
cauliflowers 56, 157
cayenne pepper 64
CCJs see County Court Judgements
CCTV car parks 105
celebrity autographs, easy money 200–1
celebrity-style spa experiences 39–40
celery 42, 50, 54, 259
Certified Accountants 77
chairs, Display Screen Equipment Regulations 1992 128
chalk, damp problems 269
chamomile tea 65
Channel Five 190
Chaplin, Charlie 200
charities, tax savings 74, 238
Chartered Accountants 77
chemotherapy 45
chewing gum, removal methods 257–8
chicken 37, 42, 154
children
        see also families
        babies 243–4, 254
        divorces 240–1
        earache 245
        easy-money books 212–13
        home education 234–5
        hospitals 243–4
        meningitis 245–6
        mothers' CVs 306
        painkiller dangers 245
        pocket money 232–3
        private education 234–6
        stakeholder pensions 234
        tax credit 75
        universities 236–7
        well-behaved children 244
chilli pepper 64

China 41, 52
Chinese restaurants 116
chocolate 65, 154
cholesterol levels 46, 49
Christie, Agatha 199
cider vinegar, heartburn 259
cinema, free tickets 120
cinnamon 54, 65, 170
Citizens Advice Bureau 80, 127, 137
www.citizensconnection.net 133
CLA see Conjugated Linoleic Acid
Clarinex 35
Clarityn 35
Cleopatra 170
clingfilm, burns 38–9
clothes, tips 125–6, 223, 257, 258, 263, 269–71, 309
Coca Cola 252, 271, 276
coconuts 169
Codeine Linctus 31
coeliac disease 36
coffee 23, 24, 29–30, 61, 157
        air fresheners 251–2
        arthritis 29–30
        decaf coffee 30
        magnesium levels 23
        osteoporosis 61
        vitamin B 24
cold-calling methods, employment 310–12
colds 50–1
collars, shirts 269–70
collectibles, easy money 197, 220–7
Collis Brown mixture 31
comfrey 38
comics, easy money 197–8
commitment benefits, employment 319
communication benefits, employment 300, 310–18, 323–4, 325–6
complaints
        business tips 293, 323
        finance 87, 127, 137
        holidays/overseas travel 129
        legal letters 136
        letters 130–1, 136–7
        local authorities 132–3
        MPs 130–2
        restaurants 126–7
        shopping tips 126–9, 137

small claims courts 127, 137
tips 87, 126–32, 137, 293
completion times, house-buying tips 5
computers
see also Internet
Display Screen Equipment
Regulations 1992 128
employee-protection rights 128
ergonomic considerations 26–7, 128
hand/wrist stresses 27, 128
identity frauds 99
passwords 106
printer cartridges 133
skills 320–1
concerts, free tickets 120
condoms 56, 149–50, 152, 158–9
conifers, snow damage 268
Conjugated Linoleic Acid (CLA) 45
conjunctivitis 53
`consent orders' 83
consolidation loans, debt problems 84
consumer consultants, easy money 203
consumer-protection laws 126–9, 137
conveyancing see house...
cookies, Internet 106
cooking oil, paint splashes 258
Cookson, Catherine 199
copper-cleaning uses, lemons 255
cornflour 260–1
cosmetic counters, free samples 121
costume jewellery, perfumes 144
councils see local authorities
country cricket, betting tips 182
county courts
County Court Judgements 80, 83, 291
divorces 240–1
courgettes 48
courier clubs 134
CPR see cardiopulmonary resuscitation
cracks
crockery 262
lips 25
mouth 23–5
cranberry juice 53
creases, trousers 270
creativity, business tips 295–6
credit cards 65–6, 81–3, 97–100, 109, 130, 288–9

better-management tips 81
cash discounts 130
crime 97–100, 107, 288–9
identity frauds 97–100, 288–9
insurance policies 81
Internet 288–9
mortgages 83
overseas travel 109
pin numbers 99
sting removal 65–6
credit ratings 5–6, 15, 80–1, 83, 98, 291
credit reference agencies 5–6, 15, 80–1, 83, 98
credit repair agencies, loan sharks 81
credit unions (CUs) 91–2
creditors
see also loans
business tips 286
cricket, betting tips 182, 192–3
crime 97–111, 124, 239–40, 276, 288–9
see also thieves
abusive relationships 103–4
burglaries 100–1, 124–5, 239–40
carjacking 101–3
cars 101–3, 105, 276
credit cards 97–100, 107, 288–9
employment 307
home security 100–1, 239–40
hotel rooms 110
identity frauds 97–100, 105
Internet 99, 105, 106, 288–9
locks 110, 124, 239, 276
monitored security systems 100
muggings 99, 104–5
Neighbourhood Watch schemes 124
personal details 97–100
road rage 101–3
stalkers 103
super-rich avoidance methods 106–7
crisps, sickness bugs 38
crow's feet, exercises 146
cucumbers 155
curcumin 30
curried foods, arthritis 30
CUs see credit unions
Customs & Excise 8, 284
cut glass, factory shops 125–6
cuts and burns 38, 245

CVs 291, 304–5, 307–12, 324
cystitis 53

# D

Daily Mail, betting tips 187–8
dairy products 29, 37, 42, 50, 65, 154
damp problems 6–7, 269
dandruff 54
dark circles, eyes 42–3, 155–6
Data Protection Act 291
date-of-birth targeting, identity frauds 97–100
dates 50
Dead Sea products 40
Debt Management Unit, government bonds 90
debt problems 5–6, 15, 80–1, 83–5, 285–6
  see also loans
    `6-year rule' 84
    bad debts 285–6
    consolidation loans 84
    creditor payments 84
    `full and final' offers 85
    tips 83–5, 285–6
decaf coffee, arthritis 30
dehumidifiers 7, 9
dehydration effects, flying 63–4
demand factors, house values 4, 11–12, 18–19
demonstrations, local-authority decisions 132–3
dental problems 27–8, 55, 57, 59
denture tablets 255, 262
deodorant marks, removal 256–7
deposits, buy-to-rent properties 15
dermatitis 24, 53
designer clothes, factory shops 125–6
desks, Display Screen Equipment Regulations 1992 128
www.desktoplawyer.co.uk 136
DHEA 148, 153
diabetcs 36
diary-keeping benefits, symptoms 32–3, 52
Dickinson, David 220
digestive system 37–8, 46–7, 48–50, 142, 153–4, 259
Dimmock, Charlie 205

Diosgenin 148
directors' liabilities, business tips 286
discounts 9–11, 222, 226–7
dismissal, employment 301–4
Display Screen Equipment Regulations 1992 128
disputes, Inland Revenue 75–6, 77–8
dividend ratios, share bargains 90–1
divorces 240–1
DIY
  homebuilders 8
  house surveys 6
  wills 247–8
dizziness, celery and honey 259
doctors
  appointment duration 23, 32, 36
  communication improvements 32–3, 61–2
  diary-keeping benefits 32–3, 52
  homeopathic supplements 35
  insurance claims 109
  interruptive propensities 32, 62
  lab-test results 36
  patient rights 36, 108–9
  personal data 107–9
  pharmaceutical companies 34–6, 68
  prescription drugs 33–4, 122
  privacy issues 108–9
  questions 33
  records 107–9
  training issues 61–2
document archives, families 231–2
www.dogpile.com 306
dogs 271–3
Doube, Dr Alan 29
double chins, exercises 145
double-glazing costs 7–8, 133–4
doubles, betting tips 179, 180
drains, baking soda 265
draught problems 264–5
dress codes, employment 309, 313, 325
dried apricots 54
dried figs 54
dried flowers 263
dripping taps, string 259
driving
  see also cars
  fatigue 137

licence identity-frauds 98–100
drugs
   see also health; prescription drugs
   addictions 31–2
   crime 97
   doctors 33–4
   dosage instructions 34
   harmful effects 34
   high-blood pressure 59
   HRT 66–9, 146
   over-the-counter medicines 31–2, 245
   painkiller dangers 245
   pharmaceutical companies 34–6, 68
   prices 35–6
   re-released drugs 35–6
   sex drive 163
   success rates 34
dry rot 6–7
dummies, earache 245
dust 50, 255–7
Dutching, betting tips 187–8

## E

E111 forms 124
earache
   chamomile tea 65
   dummies 245
earnings 4, 90, 231, 325
earnings per share (EPS) 90
easy money 195–227
   see also finance; investments
   adult education 217–18
   antique traders 197, 220–7
   auctions 220–4
   autographs 199–201
   B&Bs 206–7
   Blackjack 202
   book dealers 199–200
   book-writing tips 211–14
   car-boot sales 197, 223–7
   celebrity autographs 200–1
   children's books 212–13
   collectible traders 197, 220–7
   comics 197–8
   gardening 204–6
   hanging baskets 205
   horses 198–9

   import-export agents 201–2
   indexing services 210–11
   Internet 200, 203, 209, 221–2, 224, 227
   mystery shoppers 203–4
   plants and seedlings 204–6
   PR stories 209–10
   roulette 216–17
   stock-market betting 207–9
   tour guides 215
   TV extras 214–15
   vintage cars 198
   voiceover artists 219–20
   wedding photographers 218–19
   wines 93–4, 198
   writing tips 211–14
Easymove 5
www.ebay.co.uk 224, 288–9
eczema 24, 53
eggs 42, 48, 153, 251, 257, 261
electoral register, credit ratings 80
electricity bills see utility bills
Eli Lilly 35
emails
   see also Internet
   CVs 310
   identity frauds 99
   privacy problems 106
   spam 106
EMIS drug database 35
employers
   see also business tips
   employee relations 300, 319–20, 324–6
employment
   see also pensions
   absenteeism 319
   advertisements 307
   applications advice 291, 293, 299, 304–18
   bad news 301–4, 318
   career breaks 300–1
   cold-calling methods 310–12
   colleagues 322–4
   commitment benefits 319
   communication benefits 300, 310–18, 323–4, 325–6
   contacts 299

crime 307
CVs 291, 304–5, 307–12, 324
dismissal 301–4
Display Screen Equipment
Regulations 1992 128
dress codes 309, 313, 325
earnings 4, 231, 325
employer relations 300, 319–20, 324–6
etiquette 322–4
European comparisons 299
flexible options 300, 319
forty-plus interview tips 312–13
gap years 300–1
general specialists 319
GNVQs 322
holiday dangers 324
house-value links 4–5
Internet 306, 310, 324
interviews 306–18
learning benefits 302, 304, 319, 320–2
mothers 306
new jobs 299, 304–18
offers 316–18
panel interviews 315
part-time portfolios 300
pension contributions 74–5
reading skills 321–2
recruitment advice 291, 293, 299, 304–18
redundancies 301, 303–4
references 317–18
resignations 325
security tips 299–300
self-employment tips 284–5
skills 302, 304, 318–19, 320–2
smiling benefits 315, 318
task-analysis benefits 319–20
tips 284–5, 291, 293, 297–326
training 302, 304, 319, 320–2
unemployment figures 4–5
unfair dismissal 301–3
Value Innovation 319–20
warnings 301–2
weaknesses 311–12
written contracts 301–2, 325
young mothers 306

Employment Tribunals 301–2
encryption benefits, computer data 99
endorphins
    exercises 157
    flirting 162
energy savings 122–3, 263
    see also utility bills
engine trouble, cars 275
entertainment, free tickets 120
EPS see earnings per share
Equifax 5, 80, 98
Equitable life 73, 80
equities see shares
erections, penis 49, 149–53, 156, 158–61, 163–4, 170
ergonomic considerations, computer users 26–7, 128
escrow companies 288
Eskimos 40
www.espn.com 188, 190
estate agents 3, 8–9, 17, 18–19
`ethical' funds 88
etiquette, business tips 322–3
eucalyptus oil, sticky labels 257
European Union 116–17
    employment comparisons 299
    rented property comparisons 13–14
evening primrose oil 158
Exchange Traded Funds 87
exercises
    back pain 26–7, 168
    benefits 49, 59–61, 143–6, 157–61, 167–9
    blood pressure 59
    breasts 148
    crow's feet 146
    double chins 145
    endorphins 157
    Five Rites 167–9
    frown lines 145–6
    impotence 49
    lips 146
    neck 145, 168–9
    PC muscle 160–1
    pelvic bouncing 161
    stomach 143
    vagina 159–60
    worry lines 145

wrinkles 144–6
younger looks 144–6, 167–9
Experian 6, 98
extras on TV, easy money 214–15
eyelids
anti-wrinkle exercises 144–5
ill-health 23, 42–3, 51–2
eyes
black eyes 253
blindness 48
conjunctivitis 53
dark circles 42–3, 155–6
job interviews 310–11, 313, 315
puffiness 155
sexual body-language 165
strain 26–8, 128
tests 61, 128
tired eyes 155–6
whites 48

# F

fabric softeners 255, 257
facelifts 147
factory shops 125–6
Fame Academy, betting tips 175–6
families 75–7, 80, 95–111, 137, 229–48
see also children; marriage
babies 243–4, 254
burglaries 100–1, 124–5, 239–40
credit ratings 80
divorces 240–1
document archives 231–2
genealogical searches 242–3
gifts 232, 235, 238–9, 241–2
home education 234–5
home gifts 235, 238–9, 241–2
home security 100–1, 239–40
hospitals 243–4
inheritance tax 234, 237–9
married couple's allowances 75, 231
personal safety 95–111, 137, 239–40
premium bonds 237
record-keeping tips 75–6, 78–9, 231–2
residential care 235, 241–2
tax 75–7, 231–2, 237–9, 284
tips 75–7, 80, 95–111, 229–48

trusts 233, 239
will-writing 60, 238, 247–8
young mothers 306
Family Records Centre 242
fast lanes, car safety 102
FDA 35
felt-tip stains 263
fences 240, 271
FENSA Scheme 8
fertilisers, grass 266
fertility 150–3
see also sex
figs 54
final salary schemes 85
see also pensions
finance 71–94, 127, 195–248, 279–96
see also easy money; investments; tax
banks 79, 82, 84, 91–2, 98–100, 232, 281–4
`best buy' reports 81–2
betting tips 171–93, 207–9, 216–17
business tips 279–96
CCJs 80, 83
complaints 87, 127, 137
credit cards 65–6, 81–3, 97–100, 109, 130, 288–9
credit ratings 5–6, 15, 80–1, 83, 98, 291
debt problems 5–6, 15, 80–1, 83–5, 285–6
family tips 75–7, 80, 229–48
IFAs 86–8
www.moneyfacts.co.uk 82
mortgages 4–6, 11–15, 19, 82–3, 86
pensions 74–5, 85–6, 89–90, 234, 304
retirement 10–11, 17–18, 41, 71–94, 234, 235, 238–9, 241–2
savings 73–7, 85, 88–9, 122–3, 232–3, 237
shares 15, 76–7, 82, 87–91, 207–9
stock market 207–9
twenty-six money-making ideas 197–227
Financial Ombudsman Service 87
Financial Services Authority (FSA) 127, 137
financial statements, careful reviews 98
Financial Times 4, 5, 18, 88, 90

fingernails 25, 42, 254, 268
firelighters 253
fish oils 31, 37, 154
Five Rites, exercises 167–9
fixed-odds football betting 182–4
fixed-rate mortgages 12
flats, house comparisons 14, 16–17
flavonoids 25, 48
flax seed oil 157–8
fleas 272
flirting, endorphins 162
flooding/subsidence factors, insurance policies 124–5
flossing benefits, health 59
flowerbeds, cats 266
flu 50–1
fluorescent lighting, ill-health 27–8
fluoride 69
flying see air travel
food 23–55, 64–5, 141–2, 245, 251–3, 258–62
        see also individual foods; vitamins
        allergies 42, 65
        anti-cancer foods 45, 46–7, 55
        antioxidants 141–3, 152–3
        aphrodisiacs 149, 170
        arthritis 28–30, 46
        bacteria 37–8, 153–4
        calcium 54, 61, 150, 157
        colds and flu 50–1
        digestive system 37–8, 48–50, 142, 153–4, 259
        dirty food 259–60
        flavonoids 25, 48
        France 167
        health 23–5, 28–31, 37–40, 42, 45–55, 64–5, 141–2, 245, 251–3, 259–62
        health-food supplements 31, 38, 152
        heart disease 47–9, 55, 64
        meal sizes 167
        pets 272–3
        sex 148–63
        younger-looking skin 141–3, 166, 169–70
football league, betting tips 182–7, 189–92
footrests, Display Screen Equipment Regulations 1992 128

Foreign Office 109
fourfolds, betting tips 180
France
        house-buying tips 15–16
        meal sizes 167
        sex 164
        spa treatments 30
free books 134
free bottles of wine 121
free energy-saving appliances 123
free tickets 116–17, 120–1
freelance contacts, business tips 285
fridge-freezers 123, 125–6
Friends Reunited 305
frothiness, urine 51–2
frown lines, exercises 145–6
fruits 24–5, 33, 37–9, 48–56, 65–9, 141–3, 149, 154, 157, 166, 245
        see also individual foods
FSA see Financial Services Authority
www.fsa.gov.uk 127, 137
FSL see full-spectrum lighting
FTSE 15, 87, 208–9
`full and final' offers, debt problems 85
full-spectrum lighting (FSL), benefits 28
furniture boots, hammer marks 256

# G

G-spot 156
Galcodine Linctus 31
gambling tips see betting...
gap years, employment 300–1
garages 9, 100–1
gardening
        easy money 204–6
        tips 265–8
gargles 50
garlic 42, 47, 157, 260, 272
gas bills see utility bills
Gazetteer 118
gazumping pitfalls, house-buying tips 19
GCSEs 322
genealogical searches, families 242–3
general specialists, employment 319
www.genuki.org.uk 242–3
geranium 260–1
Germans, holidays 116

gifts 74, 232, 235, 238–9, 241–2
gilts see government bonds
ginger 29–30, 42, 149
    aphrodisiacs 149, 170
    arthritis 29–30
gingko biloba 52
ginseng 52, 68, 170
glass-topped tables, dust-free solution 257
glassware, denture tablets 262
www.globaltestmarket.com 203
globulin 157
gloves, colds and flu 51
gluthione 152
glycerin benefits, soaps 142
GNVQs 322
www.google.co.uk 125, 308
goose bumps 24
government bonds 89–90
GPs see doctors
Graffenberg, Dr Ernst 156
grants, energy bills 123
grapes 48, 50, 53, 65
grass, gardining tips 265–8
gratuities, restaurants 115
gravelled driveways, crime prevention 101, 239–40
grease stains 270, 271
`green' funds 88
green tea 55, 65, 149
Grisham, John 199
guava 24
gum disease, heart disease 59

# H

haggling benefits, holidays/overseas travel 119
hair 67, 142, 147, 272
hairspray, ink stains 258
Hallmark Cards 295
hammer marks, furniture boots 256
hand-shaking scenarios, business tips 291
handicap betting, Rugby League 181
hands
    computer stresses 27, 128
    dryness 62
    gardening tips 268
    health indicators 57–8
    sex 170
hangers, rubber bands 270
hanging baskets 205, 266
hangovers 252
hard skin 254
hardboiled eggs 261
`have-a-go-heroes', muggings 104–5
hay fever 43, 65
HCL 142
HDL enhancers 47
head lice 252
headaches 26–8, 42, 253
health 23–70, 139–70, 243–6, 251–3, 259–62, 267
    see also drugs; individual ailments; vitamins
    Alzheimer's Disease 52, 67
    arthritis 25, 28–30, 46
    asthma 206, 245, 252
    back pain 26–7, 128, 168, 267
    blood pressure 33, 48, 59
    bowel disorders 37–8, 46–9, 153–4
    burns 38–9, 245
    cancers 43–7, 55, 67, 146–7
    Candida 37, 153
    colds 50–1
    dental problems 27–8, 55, 57, 59
    digestive system 37–8, 46–7, 48–50, 142, 153–4, 259
    doctors 23, 32–6, 108–9, 122
    E111 forms 124
    earache 65, 245
    flu 50–1
    food 23–5, 28–31, 37–40, 42, 45–55, 64–5, 141–2, 245, 251–3, 259–62
    hair 67, 142, 147
    hands 27, 57–8, 62, 128
    hangovers 252
    headaches 26–8, 42, 253
    heart disease 47–9, 55, 59, 64, 67
    HRT 66–9, 146
    IBS 37, 48–9, 153
    inoculation jabs 243
    kidney disease 51–2
    looking/feeling-good tips 139–70
    medical insurance policies 61, 133
    medical-alert necklaces 36
    meningitis 245–6

menopause 66–70, 146–7
motion sickness 244
nose 142, 252
operations 62
orgasms 60, 66, 141, 150, 152–3, 156, 158–65
osteoporosis 60–1, 69, 147
private health 61, 109, 122, 133, 304
prostate problems 45, 55–6, 150
sex 60, 66, 139, 141, 149–70
skin 45–6, 65, 141–4, 147, 148, 166, 169–70, 254, 262, 269
strokes 56
tell-tale ill-health signs 23–5
ulcers 23–4, 58
weight loss 59, 142–3, 167
younger looks 141–8, 166–70
health-food supplements 31, 38, 152
hearing 53–4
heart disease 47–9, 67
see also high-blood pressure
alcohol effects 47, 59
cayenne pepper 64
CPR 47
early-morning attacks 47
garlic 47
gum disease 50
mobile phones 48
tea 55
heartburn, cider vinegar 259
heating bills 263
see also utility...
heels 254, 269
Herceptin, cancers 45
hiccups 54
high-blood pressure
see also heart disease; strokes
bananas 33
beta-blockers 163
reduction strategies 59
whites of the eyes 48
holiday-swap arrangements 118
holidays/overseas travel 109–11, 116–20
see also air travel
aeroplane hijackings 110
airline `bumping' tips 116–17
baggage 111, 119–20
career dangers 324

cheap tickets 117–20
complaints 129
courier clubs 134
Gazetteer 118
Germans 116
haggling benefits 119
holiday-swap arrangements 118
house-sitter services 118
import-export agents 201–2
insurance policies 118–19, 124
photocopying tips 109
photographs 135–6
safety checks 109–11
home education, children 234–5
home security, crime prevention 100–1, 239–40
home-gifting dangers, older people 235, 238–9, 241–2
home-working scams 294
homeopathic supplements 35
honey 39, 142, 169–70, 252, 259
Hong Kong 40
hormone replacement therapy (HRT) 66–9, 146
horn-sounding tactics, carjacking crime 102
horseradish gargles 50
horses 171–88, 198–9
hospitals, children 243–4
hot flushes 67–9
hot water bottles 49
hotel rooms, crime 110
House of Commons 130–1
house values
averages 4
demand factors 4, 11–12, 18–19
determinants 3–5, 9, 11
earnings 4
employment links 4–5
flat/house comparisons 14, 16–17
fluctuations 3–5, 11
future prospects 3–5, 11–12, 18
home improvements 9, 16–17
income links 4
increases 3–5, 9
interest rates 4, 12
London averages 4
mortgage links 4, 12
value-adding enhancements 9, 16–17

house-building tips, cost savings 8
house-buying tips 4–19
    auctions 10
    buy-to-let investments 11–15, 232
    completion times 5
    costs 3, 5–10, 17
    damp problems 6–7
    discounts 9–11
    DIY surveys 6
    estate agents 3, 8–9, 17, 18–19
    France 15–16
    gazumping pitfalls 19
    insurance 10
    prices 8, 9–11, 18–19
    property companies 18
    repairs quotes 7
    retirement fund investors 17–18
    reversion agreements 10–11
    solicitors' fees 3, 5
    surveys 6–7, 16
    ugly-home bargain-discounts 9
    up-and-coming areas 9, 16–17
    Victorian/Georgian properties 18
    viewing tips 19
house-selling tips
    estate agents 3, 8–9, 17, 18–19
    home improvements 9, 16–17
    quick sales 8–9, 11
    second properties 76
    tax 76
    value-adding enhancements 9, 16–17
    window replacements 7–8
house-sitter services 118
house/flat comparisons 14, 16–17
household tips 9, 17, 251, 254–65
HRT see hormone replacement therapy
humming benefits 38
hypertension see high-blood pressure

# I

IBS 37, 48–9, 153
ibuprofen dangers 245
ice cream, weight loss 142–3
ice cubes
    acne 144
    blood stains 271
    hanging baskets 266

    nose bleeds 252
ice hockey, betting tips 188–9
ID tags, baggage 111, 119–20
identity frauds 97–100, 105
IFAs see independent financial advisors
IHT see inheritance tax
ill-health see health
import-export agents, easy money 201–2
impotence 49, 156
incense sticks, draught problems 264
income
    see also earnings
    mortgage links 4
    rented properties 11–15
independent financial advisors (IFAs) 86–8
independent schools 234–6
indexing services 210–11
India 52, 167
Individual Savings Accounts (ISAs) 85, 88–9
Indonesia, import-export agents 201–2
inflation 4
inheritance tax (IHT) 234, 237–9
ink stains, hairspray 258
Inland Revenue 74–9, 231–3, 321
    see also tax
inoculation jabs 243
insects
    bites 253
    repellents 254
www.insolvency.gov.uk 291
insomnia 49
insurance claims, medical-information release forms 109
insurance policies
    accidental damage 124
    cost savings 123–5
    credit cards 81
    flooding/subsidence factors 124–5
    holidays/overseas travel 118–19, 124
    house-buying tips 10, 124
    IFA recommendations 86
    `in trust' arrangements 74
    medical policies 61, 133
    tax 74
    trusts 239
    voluntary excess 124
intellectual property, business tips 285,

294–5
intelligence enhancers 52, 62–3
interest rates 4, 12, 233, 285
Internet
        see also emails; individual websites
        airline flights 120
        antiques 221–2
        auctions 224
        betting tips 177–9, 191–2
        business tips 286–9
        celebrity autographs 200
        cookies 106
        credit cards 288–9
        crime 99, 105, 106, 288–9
        easy money 200, 203, 209, 221–2,
        224, 227
        employment 306, 310, 324
        genealogical searches 242–3
        hard-disc improvements 136
        medical tests 109
        mystery shoppers 203
        speedier surfing 136
        stock-market betting 209
        television-show tickets 121
        website designs 287–8
interviews
        see also employment
        employment applications 306–18
investigations, tax 77–8, 107
investment clubs, buy-to-let investments 13
investments 9, 11–15, 18, 73–94, 232–3
        see also easy money; finance; shares
        antiques 197, 220–7
        art 92–3, 129
        autographs 199–201
        buy-to-let investments 11–15
        comics 197–8
        `ethical' funds 88
        fund managers 73
        government bonds 89–90
        horses 198–9
        overseas investments 89
        Pibs 87–8
        property companies 18
        risks 88–9
        safety-first tips 88–9
        tax savings 76–7, 89
        ugly-home bargain-discounts 9

unit trusts 15
wines 93–4, 198
invoices, business tips 285
iodine 142
iron 24–5
ISAs see Individual Savings Accounts
Israel 41
Italy, import-export agents 202
itching wrists, watches 42
ivy 264

# J

Japan 47, 51, 55
Jason, David 201
`Jen-Mo' point 165
Jeremy, Ron 164–5
jet lag 64
job sharing 300
jobs see employment
jump leads, car safety 101

# K

Kegel exercises 161
kelp 23, 142
kidney beans 42
kidney disease 51–2
kidney stones 52
kissing, sex 163
kitchen foil, rust spots 276
kitchens 9, 17, 254
kiwi fruit 245
knees, gardening tips 267
Kundalini energy 161

# L

lab-test results, existing conditions 36
Ladbrokes 178
lady palm 264
lagged pipes 263
www.lastminute.com 120
Late Payment of Commercial Debts Act 285
lavender oil 63–4, 260–1
lawns, gardening tips 265–8
laws see legal issues

leadership techniques, business tips 295–6, 318, 323–4

learning benefits, employment 302, 304, 319, 320–2

leaves, gardening tips 268

leeks 50, 253

legal issues

see also crime

auction packs 136

Citizens Advice Bureau 80, 127, 137

complaints' letters 136

consumer-protection laws 126–9, 137

divorces 240–1

employee-protection rights 128

employment references 317–18

Sale of Goods Act 1979 128–9

Supply of Goods and Services Act 1982 128–9

unfair dismissal 301–3

legumes 24

lemon balm, IBS 49

lemonade, sickness bugs 38

lemons

acne 144

bathroom tiles 254

cat-scratched furniture 271

copper-cleaning uses 255

felt-tip stains 263

flu remedies 50

insect bites 253

rust stains 257

letterboxes, thieves 99

letters, complaints 130–1, 136–7

letting agents, buy-to-let investments 14

liars, identification methods 137

life assurance see insurance policies

lighting benefits, crime prevention 100, 239–40

limes 253

limescale, salt uses 256

limited companies, business tips 285, 286

Lineker, Gary 200

linoleum, nail-polish remover 254

Linos, Dr Athena 28

lint rollers, broken glass 256

lips 25, 146

lipstick stains 271

liver nutrients 24–5

loans

see also banks

'6-year rule' 84

bad debts 285–6

business tips 281–4

cheap availability 12, 82

credit reference agencies 5–6, 80–1

debt problems 5–6, 15, 80–1, 83–5, 285–6

directors' liabilities 286

lobby groups, MPs 131

local authorities

complaints 132–3

home education 234

window replacements 8

locks, crime 110, 124, 239, 276

loft conversions 9

London, house values 4

longevity tips 59–60

looking/feeling good, tips 139–70

Los Angeles Police Department 97, 111

Losec 35

losses, tax savings 74

Lotensin 163

lubricants 149–50, 164

lung cancer 55

lutein 48

# M

Mackenzie, Gordon 295

magic plants, NASA space programme 264

magnesium levels 23, 150

maintenance tips, cars 274–7

Malaysia, import-export agents 201–2

male drivers, car safety 102

management techniques 295–6, 318, 323–4

margarine 147

marketing, business tips 285, 289, 291–2

marriage 75–7, 231–2, 246–7, 284

see also families

affairs 162, 246–7

certificates 232

divorces 240–1

gifts 238

married couple's allowances 75, 231

spousal employment 284

'Martingale' system 217

massage, panic attacks 41
maternity leave 108
mayonnaise, head lice 252
meadowsweet, beauty treatments 148
medical-alert necklaces 36
medicines
    see also drugs; health
    addictions 31–2
meetings, business tips 292–3
Melittin 29
Members of Parliament (MPs), complaints 130–2
men 60, 66, 141, 149–52
    see also sex
    fertility 150–3
    impotence 49, 156
    interview clothes 309, 313, 325
    management skills 323–4
    Million Dollar Point 150
    PC muscle 160–1
    penis 49, 149–53, 156, 158–61, 163–4, 170
    premature ejaculations 158–9
meningitis, children 245–6
menopause 66–70, 146–7
menu selections, restaurants 115–16
MEPs 132
milk
    anti-cancer effects 45
    blood stains 271
    bright eyes 155
    crockery cracks 262
    insomnia 49
    storage 260
    tobacco stains 258
Million Dollar Point 150
Mills & Boon 211
MMS book 34
mobile phones
    see also phones
    car safety 101
    heart disease 48
    `pay as you go' phones 103
    stalkers 103
    surveillance dangers 103
    tariff comparisons 122
moisturisers 55, 142, 147, 254
Mondays, restaurants 116

www.moneyfacts.co.uk 82
monitored security systems, property crime 100
Monroe, Marilyn 200
mortgages 4–6, 11–15, 19, 82–3, 86
    see also loans
mothers, employment 306
mother's maiden name, identity frauds 99
motion sickness 244
motivation issues, business tips 294
mouth 23–5, 46, 146
    cancer 46
    ill-health signs 23–5
mouthwashes, cancer links 46
MPs see Members of Parliament
muggings 99, 104–5
    see also robbery
mystery shoppers, easy money 203–4

# N

nail varnish, itching wrists 42
nail-polish remover, linoleum 254
nails see fingernails
name targeting, identity frauds 97–100
NASA space programme, plants 264
National Curriculum 234
National Institute for Health Care Management (NIHCM) 35–6
National Insurance 74–5, 98–100, 284
www.nc.uk.net 234
neck exercises 145, 168–9
Nectar Ease 29
neighbourhood noise, water features 266–7
Neighbourhood Watch schemes 124
neighbours, crime prevention 100, 239–40
nephritic syndrome 51–2
net curtains, denture tablets 255
networking, business tips 285, 289, 320, 323–4
new businesses, tax savings 75
new shoes, heels 269
Nexium 35
www.ngfl.gov.uk 234
NHS
    E111 forms 124
    NHS/private contrasts, prescription drugs 122

night sweats, menopause 69–70
NIHCM see National Institute for Health
Care Management
`nil rate band discretionary trusts' 239
Norwich Union 124
nose
    bleeds 252
    broken veins 142
Nurofen Plus 31
nuts 23–4, 38, 40, 42, 154, 170, 253

# O

oats 42
obesity 167
    see also weight loss
www.oddschecker.co.uk 178
oestrogens 66–70, 146–7, 156–8
Ofex-listed shares 89, 238
offers, employment 316–18
Office of Fair Trading 275
oily fish 31, 37, 154
Old Steiff 223
older people
    see also retirement
    fifty-plus sex tips 163–4
    forty-plus job tips 312–13
    home-gifting dangers 235, 238–9,
    241–2
    property reversions 10–11
    residential care 235, 241–2
    siesta dangers 41
olive oil, benefits 28–9, 39–40, 46–7, 53–4,
147
Olympia 220
omega-3 oils 31, 40
`one careful owner' warnings, cars 274
onions 50, 65, 142, 155, 157, 253, 260, 267
operations, foods to avoid 62
orange blossom, beauty treatments 148
orange flower 166
oranges 245, 270
    asthma 245
    flu remedies 50–1
    shoe polish 270
ordinary shares see shares
orgasms, health 60, 66, 141, 150, 152–3,
156, 158–65

O'Rourke, James 296
osteoarthritis 28–30
    see also arthritis
osteoporosis 60–1, 69, 147
over-the-counter medicines, addictions 31–2,
245
overdraft charges 79
overseas investments 89
overseas travel see holidays/overseas travel
oysters 50–1

# P

pain perceptions 55
painkiller dangers, children 245
paint splashes, cooking oil 258
palm readings 57–8
palmetto berries 56
panel interviews 315
panic attacks 40–1
paper towels, wallpaper marks 255
paracetamol dangers 245
Parliament 130–1
Parliamentary Questions, MPs 131
part-furnished benefits, rented properties 12
part-time portfolios, employment 300
passports
    camouflage passports 105
    identity frauds 98–100, 105
    losses 231
    photocopying tips 109
passwords 106
pasta 24, 154, 157
patent leather, egg whites 257
www.patent.gov.uk 295
patents 285, 294–5
pay slips, document archives 231
`pay as you go' phones 103
PC muscle see pubococcygeus muscle
peaches 48
peanuts, allergies 42
pearls, perfumes 144
pears 260
peas 42
penalties, tax 74
penis 49, 149–53, 156, 158–61, 163–4, 170
pensions 74–5, 85–6, 89–90, 234, 304
    see also employment; finance;

retirement
    employer contributions 74–5
    final salary schemes 85
    IFA recommendations 86
    National Insurance 74–5
    personal pensions 85
    recommended contributions 89–90
    redundancies 304
    stakeholder pensions 85–6, 234
    state retirement pensions 75
    tax savings 74–5
peppers 24, 48, 65
    AMD 48
    arthritis 29
pepsin 142
perfumes 143–4, 166
Permanent Interest Bearing Shares (Pibs) 87–8
personal ads, women 106
personal details
    see also families
    doctors 107–9
    family documents 231–2
    identity frauds 97–100
personal pensions 85
    see also pensions
personal safety 95 111, 137, 239 40, 276 7
    see also crime
personal-injury claims 125
PEs see price-earnings ratios
Peter Rabbit moneyboxes 223
petitions, local-authority decisions 132–3
petrol cans, car safety 101
pets, tips 271–3
PGP see Pretty Good Privacy
pharmaceutical companies 34–6, 68
phones
    see also mobile...
    identity frauds 98–100
    stalkers 103
    surveillance dangers 103
    voicemail services 103
Phosphatidyl Serine (PS) 62–3
photocopying tips, overseas travel 109
photographs
    holidays/overseas travel 135–6
    wedding photographers 218–19
pianos shiners 265

Pibs see Permanent Interest Bearing Shares
pickpockets 111
piles 48
Pilkington K glass 7–8
pillowcases
    washing machines 269
    wrinkles 147
pin numbers, credit cards 99
pine nuts 150
pineapples 169
pizza smells, sex 166
plants and seedlings
    easy money 204–6
    gardening tips 265–8
    magic plants 264
    NASA space programme 264
plastic bags, vases 258
plastics, health issues 69
plums 42
pocket money, children 232–3
pomegranates 166
Pop Idol, betting tips 175–6
pornography 153, 164–5
potassium 33, 155, 253
potatoes 29, 50, 147, 155, 157, 253, 258–9, 269
Potter, Beatrix 223
PR see public relations
prawns 42
pre-menstrual cycle 156–7
preference shares see shares
pregnancy, vitamin A 25
premature ejaculations 158–9
Premier Voicemail Ltd 103
premium bonds 237
prescription drugs
    see also drugs
    charges 122
    doctors 33–4, 122
    dosage instructions 34
    NHS/private contrasts 122
    pharmaceutical companies 34–6, 68
    sex drive 163
Pretty Good Privacy (PGP) 99
Previthal centre 30
`price guide' books, antiques 223
price-earnings ratios (PEs) 91
price/research ratios (PRRs) 91

price/sales ratios (PSRs) 91
prices, house-buying tips 8, 9–11, 18–19
Prilosec 35
printer cartridges, rip-off 133
private education 234–6
private health
    checks 61, 109
    insurance policies 61, 133, 304
    prescription drugs 122
private residence tax reliefs 76
probiotic supplements 38, 154
professional advisors, tax 77
professional thieves 97
professional-punter's form guide tips, betting
tips 174–5, 177
progesterone 67–70
property 3–19, 76, 100–1, 235, 237–40,
241–2
    see also house...
    B&Bs 206–7
    home security 100–1, 239–40
    home-gifting dangers 235, 238–9,
    241–2
    inheritance tax 234, 237–9
    'nil rate band discretionary trusts' 239
    reversion agreements 10–11
    sources of information 5
    tips 3–19, 76
property companies, stock market 18
propylene glycol 55
ProShare 13
prostaglandins 156–7
prostate problems 45, 55–6, 150
Prozac 35, 159, 163
PRRs see price/research ratios
PS see Phosphatidyl Serine
psoriasis 53
PSRs see price/sales ratios
psychological profiles 108
Public Interest Research Group 97–8
public relations (PR), easy money 209–10
pubococcygeus muscle (PC muscle) 160–1
puffy eyes 155
pulses 50
pumpkin seeds 25, 48, 50, 150
puppies 273

**Q**

questions, employment applications 306–18
quick sales, house-selling tips 8–9, 11
quotations, house repairs 7

**R**

rabbits 223, 267
RAC 101
Racing Post 173–5, 179–80
www.racingpost.co.uk 173–4, 179–80
radiators 263
radio shows
    business tips 290–1
    phone-in competitors 122
radios, cars 275
reading skills 321–2
rebates, tax savings 79
receipts, shopping tips 232
record-keeping tips
    doctors 108–9
    family documents 75–6, 78–9, 231–2
    tax 75–6, 78–9, 231–2, 284
recruitment advice, employment 291, 293,
299, 304–18
red grapes 48, 53
red skin 142
red wines 47, 257
    see also wines
redundancies 301, 303–4
references, employment 317–18
refunds 8, 125–9, 137
www.registry-trust.org.uk 291
rehydration sachets 38
rejection letters, job offers 317
rented properties 11–15, 76
    see also buy-to-let investments
    classic mistakes 12–13
    costs 12–14
    deposits 15
    European comparisons 13–14
    part-furnished benefits 12
    rents 14–15, 76
    tax savings 76
    tenant selections 13, 15
    unoccupied periods 12, 13

rented rooms, tax savings 76
repairs
    quotes 7
    rented properties 13
residential care 235, 241–2
resignations, employment 325
restaurants
    complaints 126–7
    free bottles of wine 121
    free meals 120–1
    menu selections 115–16
    Mondays 116
    refunds 126–7
    reviewer privileges 120–1
    trade secrets 115–16, 120–1
retention-of-title clauses, business tips 286
retirement 10–11, 17–18, 41, 71–94, 234, 235, 238–9, 241–2
    see also finance; older people; pensions
    home-gifting dangers 235, 238–9, 241–2
    property reversions 10–11
    residential care 235, 241–2
    stakeholder pensions 85–6, 234
    tax savings 74, 77, 85–6
retirement fund investors, house-buying tips 17 10
return on capital employed (ROCE) 91
reversion agreements, house-buying tips 10–11
rheumatoid arthritis 25, 28–30, 46
    see also arthritis
rhubarb 54, 261
rice 23–4, 37, 65, 157
rigged games, betting tips 184–5
rising damp 6–7
risks, investments 88–9
road rage 101–3
robbery 99, 101–5, 106–7
    see also muggings; thieves
ROCE see return on capital employed
rocking chairs, aches and pains 57
rose water 166
rosy cheeks 142
roulette, easy money 216–17
Round Robins, betting tips 179–80
Rowling, J.K. 211

Royal Doulton 223
rubber bands, hangers 270
rubber plants 264
Rugby League, betting tips 180–2
rust stains 257, 268, 276

# S

safety advice 95–111, 137, 239–40, 276–7
    see also crime
sage
    pets 271, 272
    tea 69–70
St John's wort 68
salaries see earnings
Sale of Goods Act 1979 128–9
    see also shopping tips
salespersons, complaints 126–9
salicin 253
salmon 37, 40, 42, 154
salt 29, 30, 33, 37, 154, 157, 255–6
    arthritis 29, 30
    bodyscrubs 261
    carpet enhancements 255
    dust 255–6
    gargles 50
    high-blood pressure 33
    limescale removal 256
    rust stains 257
SARA see sexually acquired reactive arthritis
Sarafem 35
SAS 97
satin pillowcases, wrinkles 147
savings 73–7, 85, 88–9, 122–3, 232–3, 237
scars 38
scratches
    appliances 254
    cars 274
www.screentrade.co.uk 123
scurvy 24
second properties, tax savings 76
secretaries, job applications 314
security systems, property crime 100
security X-ray machines, crime 111
seedlings, easy money 204
seeds 24, 38, 42, 54, 154
selenium 56

self-employment tips 284–5
    see also business tips
self-ticketing machines, thieves 111
Sellotape 265
Seroxat 159
service providers, Supply of Goods and
Services Act 1982 128–9
sesame seeds 149
sewing tips 270
sex
    affairs 162
    aphrodisiacs 149, 170
    body language 165–6
    boredom-beating activities 162–3
    breasts 148, 157–8
    condoms 56, 149–50, 152, 158–9
    DHEA levels 148, 153
    fertility 150–3
    fifty-plus tips 163–4
    food 148–63
    France 164
    frequency recommendations 153, 164
    G-spot 156
    hands 170
    health 60, 66, 139, 141, 149–70
    impotence 49, 156
    kissing 163
    lubricants 149–50, 164
    Million Dollar Point 150
    orgasms 60, 66, 141, 150, 152–3,
    156, 158–65
    PC muscle 160–1
    pelvic bouncing 161
    penis 49, 149–53, 156, 158–61,
    163–4, 170
    pornography 153, 164–5
    premature ejaculations 158–9
    prescription drugs 163
    smells 166
    tips 60, 66, 139, 141, 149–70
    vagina 150–2, 156, 159–60
sexually acquired reactive arthritis (SARA)
152
shampoos 54, 273
    see also soaps
shares 15, 76–7, 82, 87–91, 207–9, 231
    see also investments; stock market;
    unit...
AIM-listed shares 89, 238
bargains 90–1
betting tips 207–9
buyback bargains 91
certificates 231
dividend ratios 90–1
EPS ratios 90
`ethical' funds 88
Exchange Traded Funds 87
key ratios 90–1
newspaper tips 82
Ofex-listed shares 89, 238
overseas investments 89
PEs 91
Pibs 87–8
ROCE 91
safety-first tips 88–9
tax savings 76–7, 89
tracker funds 87
shirt collars 269–70
shoelaces 270
shoes 269–71, 325
shopping tips 7–8, 116–17, 120–30, 133–4,
273–6
    antiques 197, 220–7
    auctions 10, 135, 220–4
    www.buy.co.uk 122
    car-boot sales 197, 223–7
    cars 273–6
    cash discounts 130
    complaints 126–9, 137
    consumer-protection laws 126–9, 137
    double-glazing costs 7–8, 133–4
    factory shops 125–6
    import-export agents 201–2
    mystery shoppers 203–4
    printer cartridges 133
    receipts 232
    Sale of Goods Act 1979 128–9
shredding machines, identity frauds 99
Siberian ginseng 68
sickness
    bugs 38
    flying 64
siestas 41
silence, job interviews 316
Single-Stakes-About bets 179–80
sinuses, vinegar 65

sinusitis 38, 65
sitting positions, back pain 26, 128
skills
    employment 302, 304, 318–19, 320–2
    reading skills 321–2
skin 45–6, 65, 141–4, 147–8, 166, 169–70,
254, 262, 269
    acne 144
    alcohol effects 142
    athlete's foot 262, 269
    boils 155
    bruises 25, 253
    cancer 45, 46
    crow's feet 146
    eczema 24, 53
    frown lines 145–6
    hard areas 254
    moisturisers 55, 142, 147, 254
    psoriasis 53
    red skin 142
    warts 262
    worry lines 145
    wrinkles 65, 144–5
    younger-looking skin 141–3, 148,
    166, 169–70
Sky TV 181, 190
sleep benefits 148
SLES see sodium laureth sulphate
slippery soles 269
SLS see sodium lauryl sulphate
small businesses see business tips
small claims courts 127, 137
smells, sex 166
smiling benefits
    employment 315, 318
    health 60
smoking see tobacco
sneezing 51
snoring tips 41–2
snow damage, conifers 268
soaps
    see also shampoos
    felt-tip stains 263
    glycerin benefits 142
    rabbit deterrents 267
    squash players 254
Society of Indexers 211
www.socind.demon.co.uk 211

sodium
    see also salt
    high-blood pressure 33
sodium laureth sulphate (SLES) 54
sodium lauryl sulphate (SLS) 54
solicitors
    buy-to-let investments 13
    divorce fees 240
    property fees 3, 5
Sotheby's 200
soups, colds and flu 51
soya 42, 146–8
spa treatments 30, 39–40
spam emails 106
speeding tips, cars 276–7
spider plants 264
spinach 46, 48, 54
spot-the-ball competitions 185
spouses see marriage
sprains 253
sprouts 24, 48, 157
squash players, soaps 254
The Stage 214
stakeholder pensions 85–6, 234
    see also pensions
    children 234
stalkers 103
state retirement pensions, qualifying income
levels 75
statements of correction, credit reference
agencies 5–6, 98
steering mechanisms, cars 274
stereo lids, dust-free solution 257
sticky labels, eucalyptus oil 257
stock market 15, 87, 208–9
    see also shares
    betting tips 207–9
    fluctuations 3, 17–18, 207–9
    FTSE 15, 87, 208–9
    key ratios 90–1
    property companies 18
stomach
    cinnamon 65
    exercises 143
    ulcers 58
stopping distances, car safety 102
strawberries 143, 259
stress

computer users 26
  magnesium levels 23
  teeth-grinding problems 57
  vitamins 24
string, dripping taps 259
strokes 56
  see also high-blood pressure
stuffy noses 66
Sudafed 31
suede, grease spots 270
sugar 37, 54, 69, 147, 154, 157, 253, 262
sunburn
  carotenoids 66
  suntan lotion 64
  tea bags 39
sunflower seeds 42
suntan lotion 64
super-rich people
  restaurant gratuities 115
  theft-avoidance methods 106–7
supermarket loyalty cards 107
Supply of Goods and Services Act 1982
128–9
surgical masks, colds and flu 51
surgical spirit, cats 271
surveillance dangers, phones 103
surveys 6–7, 16
sweet potatoes 65
sweetcorn 48
sweets, panic attacks 40–1
symptoms, diary-keeping benefits 32–3, 52
Syndol 31

# T

talcum powder, grease stains 271
tantric shortcuts, sexual pleasure 149, 161
taps
  dripping taps 259
  toothpaste polish 251, 256
tax
  allowances 13, 74–9, 231
  B&Bs 207
  buy-to-let allowances 13, 232
  capital gains 76–7
  disputes 75–6, 77–8
  educational courses 321
  families 75–7, 231–2, 237–9, 284

`for the attention of an inspector'
  communications 73
  gifts 74, 232, 235, 238–9, 241–2
  inheritance tax 234, 237–9
  investigations 77–8, 107
  losses 74
  marriage 75–7, 231, 284
  married couple's allowances 75, 231
  penalties 74
  professional advisors 77
  queries 73
  rebates 79
  record-keeping tips 75–6, 78–9,
  231–2, 284
  reduction tips 73–9, 234, 237–9, 284
  rented rooms 76
  retirement 74, 77, 85–6
  retirement allowances 74
  return forms 79
  second properties 76
  shares 76–7, 89
  stakeholder pensions 85–6, 234
  supermarket loyalty cards 107
  tips 73–9, 231–2, 234, 237–9, 284
  VAT 8, 75, 284
tax avoidance legislation, share transfers
76–7
Taxpayers' Charter 78
tea
  arthritis 30
  carpet enhancement 255
  chamomile tea 65
  ginger 149
  green tea 55, 65, 149
  sage tea 69–70
  sunburn 39
  tired eyes 155
  toothache 253
tea tree oil 53, 144, 269
teaspoons, Bovril 254
teeth-grinding problems 57
  see also dental problems
tele-working concepts 300
telephone techniques
  business tips 289, 292–3, 318
  job interviews 310–11, 312, 318
television screens, dust-free solution 257
television shows

Antiques Roadshow 223
audience tickets 121, 138
Bargain Hunt 220
Big Brother 175–6, 316
competitors 122, 138, 175–6
extras 214–15
phone-in competitors 122
tenant selections, buy-to-let investments 13, 15
tennis, betting tips 177–8, 192
testicular cancer 44
thalassotherapy 30
theatre, free tickets 120
thieves 97–111, 124, 239–40
see also burglaries; crime; robbery
carjacking 101–3
cars 101–3, 105, 276
credit cards 97–100, 107, 288–9
home security 100–1, 239–40
hotel rooms 110
identity frauds 97–100, 105
locks 110, 124, 239, 276
Neighbourhood Watch schemes 124
pickpockets 111
self-ticketing machines 111
super-rich avoidance methods 106–7
victim targeting 97–100, 106–7
www.thisismoney.com 233
throat cancer 46
time-management issues, business tips 289–90
time-of-year betting tips 175
timer switches, crime prevention 100
The Times 88
www.tip-ex.com 178
tired eyes 155–6
Titchmarsh, Alan 205
tits, caterpillars 267
tobacco
impotence 49
odour removal 257
osteoporosis 60–1
puckering lips 146
stain removal 258
vitamin C 24, 31
tofu 23, 68
tomatoes 29, 65, 154–5, 251, 267
arthritis 29

body odour 154
conjunctivitis 53
dog shampoos 273
whitefly 267
tongue
cancer 46
ill-health 24–5
toothache, tea 253
toothbrushes
car-cleaning tips 276
sterilisation 260
toothpaste
bath marks 256
lipstick stains 271
polish 251, 256
tour guides, easy money 215
TR Henderson 15
tracker funds, shares 87
trade secrets 113–38, 249–77
trade shows, business tips 289
trademarks, business tips 285, 294–5
Trading Standards 127
traffic lights, carjacking crime 102
training, employment 302, 304, 319, 320–2
training shoes, window-cleaning fluid 270
travel advice 109–11, 116–20
see also holidays...
travel agents
complaints 129
Gazetteer 118
trebles, betting tips 179, 180
trellised fences, crime prevention 240
trouser creases 270
trusts 15, 77, 233, 239
tuna 37, 154
Turkey, import-export agents 201–2
turmeric, arthritis 30
twitching eyelids, ill-health 23
two-year old winners, betting 174–5

## U

www.uacc.org 200
UCAS 236–7
ugly-home bargain-discounts 9
www.ukscreen.com 219
ulcers 23–4, 58
unemployment figures 4–5

see also employment
unfair dismissal, employment 301–3
uninhabited homes, crime prevention 100–1
unit trusts
    buy-to-let investments 15
    tax savings 77
unit-linked bonds, tax savings 74
Universal Autograph Collectors Club 200
universities 236–7, 322
unoccupied periods, rented properties 12, 13
up-and-coming areas, house-buying tips 9,
16–17
urine
    frothiness 51–2
    men 45, 55–6
    pets 272
    prostate problems 45, 55–6
    vinegar 272
    women 62
USA Today 188
used cars, tips 274–6
utility bills
    credit ratings 80
    grants 123
    price cuts 122–3, 263
    tariff comparisons 122

## V

vacuum cleaners 50
vagina 150–2, 156, 159–60
Value Innovation, employment 319–20
value-adding enhancements, home
improvements 9, 16–17
vanilla
    insect repellents 254
    weight loss 142–3
vases, plastic bags 258
vasodilation 49
VAT 8, 75, 284
    see also tax
    business tips 284
    homebuilding refunds 8
vegetables 24–9, 37–9, 46–8, 50–6, 62–9,
142, 154, 157, 258–9
    see also individual foods
verbal CVs 324
Victorian/Georgian properties 18

viewing tips, house buying 19
vinegar
    air fresheners 251, 257
    head lice 252
    pet urine 272
    sinuses 65
    stains 257
    sunburn 39
    wilted vegetables 259
vintage cars, easy money 198
violent crime 97
VIP lounges, airports 110
vision, business tips 295–6
vitamins
    A 24–5, 144, 260
    B 24–5, 37, 144, 147, 150, 154
    C 24, 31, 48, 50, 69, 141, 152, 157,
    245
    D 69, 147
    E 56, 66, 147, 152, 157–8
    K 25, 48
vodka
    hair loss 142
    wrinkles 65
voicemail services 103
voiceover artists, easy money 219–20
voluntary excess, insurance policies 124
voluntary reduced work time, concepts 300

## W

waiters/waitresses see restaurants
wall-leaning exercises, back pain 27
wallpaper marks, removal 255
walnuts 40
warts 262
washing machines
    moving aids 261
    pillowcases 269
    scratches 254
washing-up liquid, cars 276
wasp stings, removal 65–6
watches, itching wrists 42
water features, noise-dampening benefits
266–7
wax removal, furniture 258
weaknesses, employment applications
311–12

wealth see finance
web see Internet
weddings
see also marriage
easy-money photographers 218–19
gifts 238
weeds, grass length 265
weight loss
benefits 59
health 59, 142–3, 167
vanilla 142–3
well-behaved children 244
see also children
wet rot 6–7
wheelbarrow tips 267
Which? 82
white bread, wallpaper marks 255
white spots, fingernails 25
white vinegar, air fresheners 251
white wines 257
see also wines
whitefly, tomatoes 267
whites, eyes 48
whole wheat 23–4, 50
widow's bereavement allowance 75
wild game 40, 42
wild yam 68, 148
will-writing tips
DIY guidelines 247–8
health benefits 60
inheritance tax 238
William Hill 178
window-cleaning fluid, trainers 270
windows
opening tips 263
replacements 7–8
windscreens, cars 274
wines
investments 93–4, 198
red wines 47, 257
stains 257
white wines 257
with-profits bonds, tax savings 74
women
see also sex

abusive relationships 103–4
breasts 43–5, 67, 148, 157–8
CVs 306
G-spot 156
interview clothes 309, 313, 325
management skills 323–4
maternity leave 108
menopause 66–70, 146–7
oestrogens 66–70, 146–7, 156–8
pelvic bouncing 161
personal ads 106
pre-menstrual cycle 156–7
vagina 150–2, 156, 159–60
young mothers 306
wooden furniture, cat scratches 271
woodworm 6–7
working lunches 322–3
worry lines, exercises 145
worthless wallets, muggings 105
wrinkles 65, 144–7
exercises 144–6
satin pillowcases 147
vodka 65
wrists
computer stresses 27, 128
itching wrists 42
Writers' & Artists Yearbook 210–11, 211
writing tips, easy money 211–14
written contracts, employment 301–2, 325

# Y

Yankee bets 176–7
yeast 29, 37, 42, 154
yoghurt 65, 259–60
younger looks 141–8, 166–70

# Z

zeaxanthin 48
zero dividend preference shares, tax savings 77
zinc levels 24–5, 50–1, 144, 150, 155
deficiencies 24–5, 144, 155
food sources 25, 50–1, 144, 150

Indexed by TERRY HALLIDAY, Indexing Specialists Ltd, 202 Church Road, Hove, East Sussex, BN3 2DJ. Tel.: 01273 323309.